Computer Vision: Teaching AI to See the World

Gilbert Gutiérrez

Computer vision is revolutionizing the way machines perceive and understand the world. From facial recognition and self-driving cars to medical imaging and augmented reality, the ability to interpret visual data is one of the most exciting frontiers in artificial intelligence. But how do machines "see"? How do they recognize objects, detect motion, and understand complex scenes?

Welcome to **Computer Vision: Teaching AI to See the World**, the ninth installment in the highly acclaimed *AI from Scratch series*. This book provides a comprehensive, step-by-step guide to mastering computer vision, blending foundational theories with hands-on implementation. Whether you are a beginner looking to understand the basics or an advanced practitioner aiming to develop cutting-edge applications, this book will take you through the entire journey of building computer vision models, from classical techniques to deep learning.

Why Read This Book?

In today's AI-driven world, computer vision has become a fundamental skill for researchers, engineers, and developers. This book is designed to be an accessible yet thorough guide, covering topics ranging from image processing and feature extraction to deep learning-based object detection and segmentation. Unlike other books that focus only on theory or code, Computer Vision: Teaching AI to See the World strikes a perfect balance, ensuring you understand the "why" behind every concept while also equipping you with practical implementation skills using Python, OpenCV, TensorFlow, and PyTorch.

By the end of this book, you will have a strong grasp of computer vision fundamentals, the ability to develop real-world applications, and an understanding of where this field is headed in the future.

What's Inside the Book?

This book is divided into five key parts, each designed to build upon the last.

Part 1: Foundations of Computer Vision

Before diving into advanced topics, you need to understand how computer vision works at a fundamental level.

- Chapter 1: **Introduction to Computer Vision** – Learn the history, evolution, and key applications of computer vision, from early image processing techniques to AI-driven systems.
- Chapter 2: **Mathematical Foundations** – Master the essential math concepts behind image transformations, including linear algebra, probability, and convolution operations.
- Chapter 3: **Digital Images and Processing** – Explore how images are represented, manipulated, and enhanced using filters, edge detection, and transformations.

Part 2: Classical Computer Vision Techniques

Before deep learning dominated the field, classical techniques played a major role in computer vision. Understanding these methods provides a strong foundation.

- Chapter 4: **Feature Detection and Extraction** – Discover how keypoints and descriptors (SIFT, SURF, ORB) are used for image matching and object tracking.
- Chapter 5: **Object Detection and Recognition** – Explore traditional methods like template matching, HOG (Histogram of Oriented Gradients), and Viola-Jones face detection.
- Chapter 6: **Geometric Transformations & 3D Vision** – Learn how images can be transformed using homography, stereo vision, and structure-from-motion techniques.

Part 3: Deep Learning for Computer Vision

Deep learning has redefined what is possible in computer vision. This section introduces neural networks and their applications.

- Chapter 7: **Introduction to Convolutional Neural Networks (CNNs)** – Understand the architecture of CNNs and how they process images. Build your first CNN from scratch.
- Chapter 8: **Object Detection with Deep Learning** – Dive into cutting-edge models like YOLO (You Only Look Once), SSD, and Faster R-CNN for real-time detection.
- Chapter 9: **Image Segmentation and Semantic Understanding** – Learn about U-Net and DeepLab for segmenting objects in images, a crucial step for medical AI and autonomous systems.
- Chapter 10: **Generative Models for Computer Vision** – Explore GANs (Generative Adversarial Networks) and how they create realistic synthetic images.

Part 4: Advanced Topics and Applications

This section covers the latest research trends and real-world applications of computer vision.

- Chapter 11: **Vision Transformers (ViTs) and Self-Attention** – Learn how transformers are replacing CNNs in computer vision tasks.
- Chapter 12: **Multi-Modal AI: Combining Vision with Other Modalities** – Discover how models like CLIP understand both text and images, and how AI is used in AR/VR.
- Chapter 13: **Building Real-World Applications** – Apply computer vision to real-world projects like AI-powered security, facial recognition, and robotics.

Part 5: Practical Implementations and Future Trends

To become an expert, you must know how to deploy models and understand ethical concerns.

- Chapter 14: **Building Computer Vision Projects from Scratch** – Learn dataset collection, model training, and deployment strategies for cloud and edge devices.
- Chapter 15: **Ethics and Challenges in Computer Vision** – Understand AI bias, privacy concerns, and adversarial attacks that can trick AI models.
- Chapter 16: **The Future of Computer Vision** – Explore emerging trends like self-supervised learning, quantum computing, and next-gen applications.

Who Is This Book For?

This book is perfect for:

✓ **AI Enthusiasts & Beginners** – No prior knowledge is needed! This book explains concepts in an intuitive way before diving into code.

✓ **Developers & Data Scientists** – Learn to implement computer vision models using OpenCV, TensorFlow, and PyTorch.

✓ **Researchers & Engineers** – Stay updated with cutting-edge models, from CNNs to Vision Transformers.

✓ **Students & Educators** – A structured and hands-on approach to learning computer vision from scratch.

What You Will Gain

🎯 **Deep Understanding of Computer Vision** – Master everything from classical techniques to state-of-the-art AI models.

🎯 **Hands-On Coding Experience** – Build practical projects using Python and open-source libraries.

🎯 **Real-World Applications** – Work on case studies in healthcare, security, retail, and autonomous systems.

🎯 **Insights into AI Ethics & Future Trends** – Understand responsible AI development and where the field is headed.

This book is not just about theory—it's about application. By the end, you will have built and deployed real-world computer vision solutions, gaining the expertise needed to advance your AI career.

Final Thoughts

Computer vision is changing the way we interact with technology. From unlocking your smartphone with face recognition to self-driving cars navigating the roads, AI-powered vision systems are transforming industries worldwide. But the journey to mastering computer vision requires both theoretical knowledge and practical implementation.

With Computer Vision: Teaching AI to See the World, you'll gain a clear, structured, and hands-on learning experience, making complex concepts accessible while diving deep into real-world AI applications.

Are you ready to teach AI how to see? Let's embark on this exciting journey together! 🚀

1. Introduction to Computer Vision

Computer vision is a field of artificial intelligence that enables machines to interpret and understand the visual world. From early image processing techniques to modern deep learning-driven vision systems, this technology has evolved to power applications like facial recognition, autonomous vehicles, and medical imaging. In this chapter, we will explore the history, key concepts, and real-world applications of computer vision, laying the foundation for building intelligent systems that can analyze and process images and videos with human-like perception. Whether you're new to the field or looking to deepen your understanding, this chapter will provide a strong starting point for mastering computer vision.

1.1 What is Computer Vision?

Computer Vision is a field of Artificial Intelligence (AI) that enables machines to interpret and understand visual data, much like humans do. It allows computers to analyze images and videos, extract meaningful information, and make decisions based on that information. From facial recognition and autonomous vehicles to medical imaging and industrial automation, computer vision is transforming numerous industries. But what exactly is computer vision, how does it work, and why is it so crucial in AI development?

In this section, we will explore the fundamentals of computer vision, its key concepts, real-world applications, and its evolution from traditional image processing to modern deep learning-based techniques.

Understanding Computer Vision

At its core, computer vision seeks to answer one fundamental question: "How can machines gain a high-level understanding of images and videos?" Humans can effortlessly recognize objects, identify faces, and interpret scenes, but for computers, this task is far more complex. Unlike humans, machines do not "see" images in the way we do. Instead, they process images as arrays of numerical values (pixels), and through advanced algorithms, they attempt to extract patterns and meaningful insights.

Computer vision is closely related to fields like image processing, pattern recognition, and machine learning. It involves multiple sub-tasks, such as:

- **Image Classification**: Determining the category of an object in an image (e.g., recognizing cats vs. dogs).
- **Object Detection**: Identifying and locating multiple objects within an image.
- **Image Segmentation**: Dividing an image into different regions for precise analysis (e.g., medical imaging).
- **Facial Recognition**: Identifying or verifying a person based on facial features.
- **Optical Character Recognition (OCR):** Extracting text from images or scanned documents.
- **Scene Understanding**: Analyzing and interpreting the context of an entire image or video.

The Evolution of Computer Vision

Early Image Processing (1960s - 1990s)

The origins of computer vision date back to the 1960s when researchers began developing algorithms for basic image processing. Early systems used mathematical techniques to manipulate pixel values and extract edges, shapes, and patterns. Techniques like edge detection (Sobel, Canny), histogram equalization, and filtering were used to enhance and analyze images.

During the 1980s and 1990s, feature-based methods like Scale-Invariant Feature Transform (SIFT) and Histogram of Oriented Gradients (HOG) were developed. These techniques allowed computers to detect and recognize objects based on predefined features.

Machine Learning & Classical Vision (1990s - 2010s)

With the rise of machine learning, computer vision systems improved significantly. Instead of manually designing features, researchers started training models to learn patterns from data. Support Vector Machines (SVMs) and decision trees were used for tasks like facial recognition and object classification.

A major breakthrough came with the introduction of Haar cascades for face detection, which became widely used in security and photography applications. During this period, OpenCV (Open-Source Computer Vision Library) emerged as a powerful tool for implementing classical vision techniques.

Deep Learning Revolution (2010s - Present)

The biggest leap in computer vision came with the rise of deep learning, particularly Convolutional Neural Networks (CNNs). CNNs revolutionized image analysis by automatically learning hierarchical features from images, eliminating the need for manual feature extraction. Key milestones include:

- **AlexNet (2012):** Demonstrated the power of CNNs in image classification, winning the ImageNet competition.
- **VGGNet, ResNet (2014-2015):** Improved architectures that enhanced accuracy and efficiency.
- **YOLO (You Only Look Once) & SSD (Single Shot Detector):** Enabled real-time object detection.
- **Generative Adversarial Networks (GANs):** Opened new possibilities for AI-generated images and deepfakes.
- **Vision Transformers (ViTs):** Introduced self-attention mechanisms to outperform CNNs in some vision tasks.

Today, computer vision is driven by large datasets, high-performance GPUs, and state-of-the-art deep learning models, enabling applications once thought impossible.

Key Components of Computer Vision

To understand how computer vision works, it's important to break it down into its core components:

1. Image Acquisition

- The first step in computer vision is obtaining visual data. This can come from cameras, sensors, drones, medical imaging devices, or satellite imagery.
- Images are represented as pixel matrices, with color channels (RGB) or grayscale values.

2. Image Preprocessing

Before analysis, images often require preprocessing to enhance quality and remove noise. Common techniques include:

- **Resizing & Normalization**: Standardizing image size and pixel values.
- **Denoising**: Removing unwanted noise using filters.
- **Edge Detection**: Extracting boundaries using Canny or Sobel filters.
- **Histogram Equalization**: Improving contrast in low-light images.

3. Feature Extraction

- Features are key points or patterns within an image that help identify objects or textures.
- Classical methods include HOG, SIFT, and ORB, while deep learning models learn features automatically.

4. Object Recognition & Classification

- Machine learning or deep learning models analyze extracted features to classify objects or recognize patterns.
- CNNs and Transformer-based models like ViTs are commonly used for high-accuracy predictions.

5. Post-Processing & Decision Making

- Once objects are detected, AI models make decisions based on the extracted information.
- This step is used in applications like autonomous driving (detecting pedestrians), medical imaging (detecting tumors), and retail (identifying products for checkout).

Real-World Applications of Computer Vision

Computer vision is powering some of the most exciting innovations in AI today. Here are a few real-world applications:

✅ **Autonomous Vehicles**: Self-driving cars use vision systems to detect lanes, traffic signs, pedestrians, and other vehicles.

✅ **Healthcare & Medical Imaging**: AI-powered diagnostic tools analyze X-rays, MRIs, and CT scans to detect diseases.

✅ **Facial Recognition**: Used in security systems, smartphones, and social media for authentication and tagging.

✅ **Retail & E-commerce**: Automated checkout systems recognize products, while recommendation engines suggest visually similar items.

✅ **Agriculture**: AI-powered drones and vision systems monitor crop health, detect pests, and optimize farming techniques.

✅ **Surveillance & Security**: Smart cameras detect suspicious activities and improve public safety.

☑ **Augmented Reality (AR) & Virtual Reality (VR):** Enhancing user experiences in gaming, shopping, and education.

Computer vision is one of the most transformative fields in AI, enabling machines to "see" and interpret the world around them. From traditional image processing techniques to deep learning-powered vision models, this field has rapidly evolved, unlocking new possibilities across industries. As research continues, advancements in self-supervised learning, 3D vision, and multi-modal AI will push the boundaries even further.

By mastering the fundamentals of computer vision, you are stepping into a future where AI-powered vision systems will continue to redefine technology, automation, and human-machine interaction.

1.2 Evolution of Computer Vision: From Pixels to AI

Computer vision has come a long way from simple pixel-based image processing to advanced AI-driven vision systems capable of understanding complex scenes. In the early days, researchers relied on mathematical techniques to manipulate images, extract edges, and identify patterns. Over time, machine learning algorithms improved accuracy, but it was the deep learning revolution that truly transformed the field. Today, AI-powered models can recognize objects, analyze medical images, power self-driving cars, and even generate realistic images.

In this section, we will explore the evolution of computer vision, covering its historical milestones, key breakthroughs, and how deep learning has reshaped the way machines interpret visual data.

1. The Early Days: Basic Image Processing (1960s - 1980s)

The foundations of computer vision were laid in the 1960s, when researchers started developing algorithms to process digital images. At this stage, computers could only perform basic pixel manipulations, such as adjusting brightness and contrast. The goal was to enhance images for better analysis, rather than understanding their content.

Key Developments:

- **1963**: Larry Roberts, considered one of the pioneers of computer vision, proposed that 3D objects could be reconstructed from 2D images using edge detection and shape analysis.
- **Edge Detection Algorithms**: The development of techniques like the Sobel Operator and Canny Edge Detector allowed machines to identify object boundaries in images.
- **Binary Image Processing**: Early image segmentation techniques helped in distinguishing objects from backgrounds using thresholding methods.

At this stage, computer vision was still in its infancy, with limited real-world applications. However, it laid the groundwork for more sophisticated techniques that would emerge in the following decades.

2. Feature-Based Methods & Machine Learning (1990s - 2010s)

As computational power improved, researchers moved beyond pixel-level analysis to feature-based methods, where key points and patterns in an image were identified to help recognize objects.

Key Developments:

- **Feature Extraction Algorithms**: Techniques like Scale-Invariant Feature Transform (SIFT) and Histogram of Oriented Gradients (HOG) enabled more robust object recognition, allowing machines to detect objects regardless of their scale, rotation, or lighting conditions.
- **Haar Cascades for Face Detection**: The famous Viola-Jones algorithm (2001) introduced a fast and reliable method for detecting human faces in images, leading to widespread adoption in security and photography.
- **Machine Learning Models**: Support Vector Machines (SVMs) and Random Forests were used to classify objects based on extracted features.

At this stage, computer vision was beginning to see real-world adoption in applications like facial recognition, medical imaging, and industrial automation. However, these methods still required manual feature engineering, meaning experts had to design the features the model would use for recognition. This approach was effective but limited in its ability to scale.

3. The Deep Learning Revolution (2012 - Present)

The real breakthrough in computer vision came with deep learning, particularly with the introduction of Convolutional Neural Networks (CNNs). Unlike traditional machine learning methods that relied on hand-crafted features, CNNs could automatically learn the best features from data, significantly improving accuracy.

Key Milestones:

2012: AlexNet Wins ImageNet Challenge

AlexNet, a deep CNN model developed by Geoffrey Hinton and his team, outperformed all previous computer vision models, reducing image classification errors by nearly 50%. This marked the beginning of deep learning's dominance in computer vision.

2014-2015: VGGNet & ResNet Improve Accuracy

VGGNet introduced deeper architectures, and ResNet solved the problem of vanishing gradients, enabling networks with over 100 layers. These advancements led to even higher accuracy in object recognition.

2015-Present: Object Detection & Real-Time Vision

Models like YOLO (You Only Look Once) and SSD (Single Shot MultiBox Detector) allowed real-time object detection, enabling applications in autonomous driving, security surveillance, and robotics.

With deep learning, computer vision systems became more accurate than humans in many tasks, such as identifying objects in images, diagnosing diseases from medical scans, and detecting fraud in financial transactions.

4. The Rise of Generative Models & Vision Transformers (2020s - Future)

While CNNs have been dominant in computer vision, new advancements are pushing the field even further. Generative AI and Vision Transformers (ViTs) are two key trends shaping the next phase of computer vision.

Generative Models (GANs & VAEs):

- Generative Adversarial Networks (GANs) allow AI to generate realistic images, create deepfakes, and even restore damaged photos.

- Variational Autoencoders (VAEs) help in tasks like image denoising and super-resolution.
- AI models like DALL·E and Stable Diffusion can generate photorealistic images from textual descriptions.

Vision Transformers (ViTs):

- Unlike CNNs, Vision Transformers (ViTs) use self-attention mechanisms to analyze images more holistically.
- Models like Swin Transformer and DEiT (Data-Efficient Image Transformers) have achieved state-of-the-art results in tasks like object classification, surpassing CNNs in some cases.
- ViTs are expected to power future applications in autonomous robots, AI-powered medical imaging, and smart surveillance systems.

5. The Future of Computer Vision

The next decade of computer vision is expected to be driven by multi-modal AI, self-supervised learning, and real-time edge computing. Some exciting possibilities include:

✅ **Self-Supervised Learning**: AI models will learn from unstructured visual data without the need for labeled datasets, making them more scalable and cost-effective.

✅ **Neuromorphic Vision**: Inspired by the human brain, neuromorphic computing will enable energy-efficient AI vision systems for real-time processing in edge devices like drones and wearables.

✅ **AI-Powered Augmented Reality (AR) & Virtual Reality (VR):** Computer vision will enhance AR/VR experiences, revolutionizing fields like education, gaming, and remote collaboration.

✅ **Ethical & Explainable AI**: As AI becomes more powerful, ensuring fairness, transparency, and ethical use of computer vision technology will be a major focus.

The evolution of computer vision from simple pixel-based analysis to powerful AI-driven systems has been extraordinary. From early edge detection methods to deep learning-powered models and generative AI, the field has transformed how machines perceive and interact with the world.

Today, computer vision is no longer just an academic concept—it is revolutionizing industries like healthcare, automotive, retail, security, and entertainment. With the rise of Vision Transformers, self-supervised learning, and generative AI, the future of computer vision holds limitless possibilities.

By understanding its evolution, we gain insight into where the field is headed and how we can leverage these advancements to build intelligent, real-world applications. 🚀

1.3 Key Applications: Healthcare, Autonomous Vehicles, and More

Computer vision is transforming industries by enabling machines to interpret and analyze visual data with incredible accuracy. From diagnosing diseases in healthcare to powering self-driving cars, this technology is revolutionizing the way businesses operate and how humans interact with machines. In this section, we will explore some of the most impactful applications of computer vision, focusing on healthcare, autonomous vehicles, retail, agriculture, security, and entertainment.

1. Healthcare: AI-Powered Medical Imaging and Diagnosis

Healthcare is one of the most significant beneficiaries of computer vision. AI-driven image analysis has enhanced the accuracy, speed, and efficiency of medical diagnosis, leading to early detection and improved patient outcomes.

Key Applications in Healthcare:

✅ Medical Image Analysis

- AI models analyze X-rays, MRIs, CT scans, and ultrasound images to detect diseases like cancer, tumors, and fractures.
- Deep learning algorithms, such as CNNs (Convolutional Neural Networks), U-Net, and ResNet, help in precise medical image segmentation and classification.

✅ Disease Detection and Diagnosis

- AI-powered systems can detect pneumonia, tuberculosis, diabetic retinopathy, and even COVID-19 from chest X-rays with high accuracy.

- Skin cancer detection using dermoscopy images has achieved dermatologist-level precision through deep learning.

✅ Pathology and Microscopic Analysis

- AI assists pathologists in analyzing blood samples, biopsy slides, and tissue scans, automating time-consuming tasks.
- Computer vision enables automated cell counting, bacteria detection, and cancerous cell identification in pathology labs.

✅ Surgical Assistance & Robotics

- AI-powered robotic surgery systems use real-time image recognition to guide surgeons in delicate procedures.
- Endoscopic and laparoscopic surgeries benefit from AI-assisted vision, improving precision and reducing human error.

✅ Patient Monitoring & Wearable Devices

- AI-driven vital sign monitoring from facial expressions or skin color changes helps detect stroke, heart failure, or respiratory distress.
- Wearable health devices use computer vision for fall detection, movement tracking, and anomaly detection in elderly patients.

Impact on Healthcare

AI-powered computer vision has made medical diagnostics faster, more accurate, and widely accessible, even in remote areas. By reducing human errors and assisting doctors, it is saving lives and revolutionizing patient care.

2. Autonomous Vehicles: Computer Vision for Self-Driving Cars

Self-driving cars rely heavily on computer vision to navigate roads, detect obstacles, and make real-time driving decisions. AI-powered vision systems help these vehicles interpret their surroundings, ensuring safety and efficiency.

Key Applications in Autonomous Vehicles:

✅ Lane Detection & Road Understanding

- Computer vision helps identify lanes, road markings, and traffic signs using deep learning models like CNNs and Vision Transformers.
- Algorithms like Canny edge detection and Hough transform assist in lane tracking and road boundary recognition.

✅ Object Detection & Pedestrian Recognition

- AI models detect cars, pedestrians, cyclists, and other obstacles to avoid collisions.
- Advanced techniques like YOLO (You Only Look Once), SSD (Single Shot Detector), and Faster R-CNN enable real-time object detection.

✅ Traffic Sign & Signal Recognition

- AI-powered vision systems interpret stop signs, speed limits, and traffic lights, ensuring vehicles obey road rules.
- Optical Character Recognition (OCR) extracts text from traffic signs to improve navigation.

✅ Driver Monitoring & Safety Systems

- AI detects driver fatigue, distraction, and drowsiness using facial analysis to prevent accidents.
- Vision-based gesture recognition allows for touch-free control inside vehicles.

✅ SLAM (Simultaneous Localization and Mapping)

- AI-powered 3D mapping and LiDAR vision help vehicles understand their environment and plan routes.
- Self-driving cars use stereo vision, depth estimation, and sensor fusion for accurate path planning.

Impact on Transportation

Autonomous driving technology is reshaping the future of transportation by making vehicles safer, smarter, and more efficient. It aims to reduce traffic accidents, optimize fuel efficiency, and improve urban mobility.

3. Retail: AI-Driven Shopping & Smart Stores

Retailers are leveraging computer vision to enhance customer experiences, automate inventory management, and optimize store operations. AI-powered vision systems are transforming how people shop.

Key Applications in Retail:

✅ Automated Checkout & Cashierless Stores

- AI-powered self-checkout systems recognize products in a shopping cart and automatically charge customers.
- Amazon Go stores use computer vision for frictionless shopping, where customers walk out without standing in checkout lines.

✅ Shelf & Inventory Management

- AI monitors shelves in supermarkets to ensure products are always stocked.
- Vision-based tracking prevents out-of-stock issues and optimizes restocking.

✅ Visual Search & Recommendation Engines

- E-commerce sites use AI to allow customers to search for products using images instead of text.
- AI-driven recommendation engines suggest similar products based on images.

Impact on Retail

Computer vision is revolutionizing shopping experiences by reducing checkout times, improving inventory management, and enhancing product recommendations, leading to higher sales and customer satisfaction.

4. Agriculture: AI for Smart Farming

Computer vision is helping farmers improve crop yields, detect diseases, and automate labor-intensive tasks through precision agriculture.

Key Applications in Agriculture:

✅ **Crop Health Monitoring**

AI-powered drones scan fields and detect crop diseases, pest infestations, and soil health issues using hyperspectral imaging.

✅ **Automated Harvesting**

AI-driven robots use vision-based detection to pick ripe fruits and vegetables, reducing labor costs.

✅ **Weed & Pest Detection**

AI identifies weeds and optimizes pesticide use, reducing chemical waste and improving sustainability.

Impact on Agriculture

AI-powered vision systems help farmers increase productivity, reduce waste, and ensure food security by making agriculture more efficient and data-driven.

5. Security & Surveillance: AI-Powered Threat Detection

AI-powered vision systems are improving security in public places, workplaces, and homes by detecting threats, identifying individuals, and preventing crimes.

Key Applications in Security:

✅ **Facial Recognition for Identity Verification**

AI-based facial recognition is used for access control, border security, and crime prevention.

✅ **Smart Surveillance Systems**

AI-powered CCTV cameras can detect suspicious activities, unauthorized access, and perimeter breaches in real time.

✅ Anomaly Detection & Crowd Monitoring

AI identifies unusual behavior in crowded areas to prevent theft, riots, or terrorist attacks.

Impact on Security

Computer vision enhances safety and crime prevention by enabling real-time monitoring and proactive threat detection.

6. Entertainment: AI in Gaming, AR & VR

AI-powered vision is transforming gaming, virtual reality (VR), and augmented reality (AR) experiences.

Key Applications in Entertainment:

✅ Facial Animation & Deepfake Technology

- AI animates facial expressions for movies, video games, and virtual avatars.
- Deepfake technology allows realistic AI-generated videos.

✅ Augmented Reality (AR) & Virtual Reality (VR)

- Computer vision enables real-time AR effects, such as Snapchat filters and Instagram effects.
- AI-powered gesture recognition allows users to interact with virtual environments.
- Impact on Entertainment
- AI-driven vision enhances user engagement, content creation, and immersive experiences in gaming, film, and social media.

Computer vision is transforming industries, improving efficiency, safety, and automation across multiple domains. From healthcare and autonomous vehicles to retail, agriculture, security, and entertainment, AI-powered vision is revolutionizing how machines interact with the world. As technology advances, we can expect even more innovative applications that will further enhance our daily lives. 🚀

1.4 Challenges and Limitations of Current Systems

Despite the impressive advancements in computer vision, the technology still faces significant challenges and limitations. While AI-powered vision systems can detect objects, recognize faces, and even understand complex visual scenes, they are not flawless. Issues such as data bias, computational costs, real-world unpredictability, and ethical concerns continue to hinder the widespread adoption of computer vision across industries. In this section, we will explore the key challenges affecting computer vision today and discuss potential solutions to overcome these limitations.

1. Data Challenges: Quality, Quantity, and Bias

A. Data Dependency & Large Dataset Requirements

Computer vision models, especially deep learning-based ones, require massive amounts of high-quality labeled data to function effectively. Unlike humans, who can recognize objects with very little prior exposure, AI models need thousands or even millions of labeled images to generalize well.

Challenges:

- **Data scarcity**: For certain industries (e.g., medical imaging), collecting and annotating large datasets is expensive and time-consuming.
- **Class imbalance**: Some objects or classes may appear more frequently than others, leading to biased predictions.
- **Privacy concerns**: Collecting personal images (e.g., for facial recognition) raises serious privacy and legal issues.

B. Bias in AI Models

If training datasets are biased, the resulting AI models will inherit and amplify those biases. For example, a facial recognition system trained mostly on lighter-skinned individuals may struggle with accurate identification of darker-skinned individuals, leading to unfair and potentially harmful outcomes.

Real-World Consequences:

- AI misidentifications in law enforcement leading to wrongful arrests.

- Healthcare AI failing to diagnose diseases in underrepresented demographics.
- E-commerce recommendation engines favoring certain products or categories over others.

Potential Solutions:

✅ **Diverse and inclusive datasets**: Ensuring datasets are well-balanced across different demographics and scenarios.

✅ **Bias detection algorithms**: Developing AI models that can actively detect and mitigate bias.

✅ **Synthetic data generation**: Using AI to create artificial but realistic training data when real-world examples are scarce.

2. Computational Costs and Hardware Limitations

A. High Computational Power Requirements

Deep learning models, especially Convolutional Neural Networks (CNNs) and Vision Transformers (ViTs), require massive amounts of computational resources to train and run effectively. This makes real-time processing and deployment on edge devices challenging.

Challenges:

- **Training deep learning models is expensive**: Training large-scale models like GPT-4 Vision or ViTs requires specialized hardware (GPUs, TPUs) and significant energy consumption.
- **Real-time performance limitations**: Running complex models on low-power devices (e.g., smartphones, IoT sensors, embedded systems) is difficult.

B. Storage and Memory Constraints

Handling high-resolution images and video streams requires vast amounts of memory and storage space, making it impractical for some applications.

Potential Solutions:

✅ **Model optimization techniques** (e.g., quantization, pruning, knowledge distillation) to reduce computational load.

✅ **Edge AI**: Deploying smaller, optimized models directly on devices rather than relying on cloud computing.

✅ **Federated learning**: Decentralized AI training without sharing raw data, improving both privacy and efficiency.

3. Real-World Variability and Environmental Factors

A. Handling Complex and Unpredictable Scenarios

Unlike controlled lab conditions, real-world environments are highly unpredictable. Computer vision models often struggle in low-light conditions, extreme weather, or occluded views.

Challenges:

- Object recognition in cluttered or noisy environments (e.g., security cameras in crowded spaces).
- Motion blur, occlusion, and partial object visibility affecting detection accuracy.
- Poor performance under changing lighting conditions (e.g., self-driving cars at night).

B. Generalization Across Domains

A model trained on a specific dataset may fail when exposed to a different environment or dataset. For example, an AI trained on Western road signs may struggle when deployed in Asia, where signs have different languages and shapes.

Potential Solutions:

✅ **Domain adaptation**: Training models to generalize across diverse datasets.

✅ **Few-shot learning**: Teaching AI to recognize new objects with minimal examples.

✅ **Continuous learning**: Updating models dynamically to adapt to new environments.

4. Ethical and Privacy Concerns

A. Facial Recognition and Privacy Violations

Computer vision is widely used in surveillance, social media, and security, but its ability to track individuals raises serious privacy concerns. Many governments and advocacy groups are calling for stricter regulations on facial recognition technology.

Ethical Issues:

- Mass surveillance leading to privacy invasion.
- Deepfakes and misinformation spreading fake videos and images.
- Unethical AI usage in workplace monitoring (e.g., tracking employees without consent).

B. AI Decision Transparency and Explainability

Most computer vision models, especially deep neural networks, function as black boxes, meaning their decision-making processes are not always interpretable. This lack of transparency makes it difficult to trust AI predictions in critical applications like healthcare and law enforcement.

Potential Solutions:

✓ **Explainable AI (XAI):** Developing models that can justify their predictions.
✓ **Regulatory frameworks**: Implementing ethical guidelines for AI deployment.
✓ **User control over data privacy**: Allowing individuals to opt out of AI-based tracking.

5. Security Risks and Adversarial Attacks

A. Vulnerability to Adversarial Attacks

Computer vision systems can be fooled by carefully designed adversarial attacks—small modifications to an image that are imperceptible to humans but cause AI models to misclassify objects.

Example Attacks:

- **Perturbed images**: Slightly modified images that AI misinterprets (e.g., a stop sign altered with stickers that an AI mistakes for a speed limit sign).
- **AI fooling techniques**: Attackers can create images that cause misclassification in facial recognition or object detection systems.

B. Data Security and Hacking Risks

Since computer vision relies heavily on cloud computing, there is a risk of data breaches where sensitive images (e.g., medical records or security footage) can be exposed.

Potential Solutions:

✅ **Adversarial training**: Training AI models to detect and resist adversarial attacks.

✅ **Secure AI pipelines**: Encrypting and anonymizing data in cloud-based computer vision applications.

✅ **Multi-factor authentication**: Preventing unauthorized access to sensitive AI systems.

While computer vision has made remarkable progress, it still faces significant challenges that prevent it from achieving human-level perception. Data biases, high computational costs, real-world variability, ethical concerns, and security risks continue to pose obstacles. However, ongoing research in areas like model optimization, ethical AI, adversarial defense, and edge computing is steadily improving the robustness and reliability of computer vision systems.

By addressing these challenges, we can move closer to a future where AI-powered vision systems are more accurate, trustworthy, and accessible, enabling breakthroughs in healthcare, transportation, security, and beyond. 🚀

2. Mathematical Foundations

At the core of computer vision lies a strong mathematical foundation that enables machines to process and analyze visual data effectively. This chapter covers essential mathematical concepts, including linear algebra, calculus, probability, and optimization, which form the backbone of image transformations, convolution operations, and deep learning models. You'll learn how matrices and vectors are used to manipulate images, how probability theory helps in object detection, and how optimization techniques improve model performance. By mastering these fundamental principles, you'll gain the mathematical intuition needed to develop and refine powerful computer vision algorithms.

2.1 Linear Algebra for Image Representation

Linear algebra is the mathematical foundation of computer vision, enabling machines to process and manipulate images efficiently. Since images are fundamentally matrices of pixel values, understanding linear algebra is crucial for tasks like image transformations, filtering, compression, and feature extraction. This section explores how images are represented as matrices, key operations like vector spaces, matrix transformations, eigenvalues, and singular value decomposition (SVD), and their role in image processing and deep learning models.

1. Images as Matrices: The Core Representation

In computer vision, an image is essentially a grid of pixels arranged in a matrix format. Each pixel has an intensity value, which can be represented numerically.

A. Grayscale Image Representation

A grayscale image is a 2D matrix, where each element represents a pixel's intensity, usually on a scale from 0 (black) to 255 (white) in an 8-bit image.

For example, a simple 3×3 grayscale image might look like this:

$$I = \begin{bmatrix} 34 & 200 & 150 \\ 90 & 255 & 180 \\ 75 & 120 & 60 \end{bmatrix}$$

Here, each number corresponds to a pixel's brightness, with higher values indicating lighter regions.

B. RGB Image Representation (3D Tensor)

A color image consists of three matrices (channels): Red, Green, and Blue (RGB). Each channel has its own intensity matrix, creating a 3D tensor representation:

$$I_{RGB} = \begin{bmatrix} R \\ G \\ B \end{bmatrix}$$

For example, an RGB pixel (150, 75, 200) means:

- 150 in the Red channel,
- 75 in the Green channel,
- 200 in the Blue channel.

This representation allows us to manipulate colors separately and apply transformations efficiently.

2. Vector Spaces and Basis Functions in Images

A. Image as a Vector in High-Dimensional Space

A grayscale image with N × M pixels can be reshaped into a long vector of size (N × M) × 1. This allows image processing techniques to be performed in high-dimensional vector spaces, similar to how machine learning handles structured data.

For example, a 4×4 image:

$$\begin{bmatrix} 100 & 120 & 130 & 140 \\ 90 & 100 & 110 & 120 \\ 80 & 90 & 100 & 110 \\ 70 & 80 & 90 & 100 \end{bmatrix}$$

can be reshaped into a 16×1 vector:

$$[100, 120, 130, 140, 90, 100, 110, 120, 80, 90, 100, 110, 70, 80, 90, 100]^T$$

This vectorized form enables operations like dot products, norms, and projections, which are fundamental in deep learning.

B. Basis Functions and Image Decomposition

Any image can be decomposed into a combination of basis functions, similar to how a function can be expressed using sine and cosine waves in Fourier analysis.

Example: Eigenfaces for Facial Recognition

- A face can be represented as a weighted sum of basis faces (Eigenfaces).
- These basis images (eigenvectors) form a lower-dimensional representation of faces, reducing the complexity of facial recognition models.

3. Matrix Operations for Image Transformations

Linear algebra enables powerful image transformations, such as scaling, rotation, shearing, and reflection. These transformations are performed using matrix multiplications.

A. Image Scaling (Resizing)

Scaling an image involves multiplying its coordinate matrix by a **scaling matrix**:

$$S = \begin{bmatrix} s_x & 0 \\ 0 & s_y \end{bmatrix}$$

where s_x and s_y are scaling factors.

Example: Scaling an image by 2x in both dimensions:

$$\begin{bmatrix} 2 & 0 \\ 0 & 2 \end{bmatrix}$$

results in a **zoomed-in effect**.

B. Image Rotation

To rotate an image by an angle θ, we multiply pixel coordinates by a rotation matrix:

$$R = \begin{bmatrix} \cos\theta & -\sin\theta \\ \sin\theta & \cos\theta \end{bmatrix}$$

Example: Rotating an image by 90 degrees:

$$\begin{bmatrix} 0 & -1 \\ 1 & 0 \end{bmatrix}$$

C. Image Shearing (Skewing)

Shearing tilts an image by applying a shear matrix:

$$H = \begin{bmatrix} 1 & sh_x \\ sh_y & 1 \end{bmatrix}$$

where **sh_x** and **sh_y** control horizontal and vertical shearing, respectively.

These transformations are widely used in data augmentation for deep learning models to improve generalization.

4. Eigenvalues, Eigenvectors, and PCA for Image Compression

A. Eigenvalues and Eigenvectors in Image Compression

Eigenvalues and eigenvectors are used in Principal Component Analysis (PCA) to reduce the dimensionality of images while preserving essential features.

Steps in PCA for Images:

- Convert the image into a high-dimensional vector.
- Compute the covariance matrix of pixel values.
- Extract eigenvectors (principal components) of the covariance matrix.
- Project the original data onto the top K eigenvectors to create a compressed representation.

B. Singular Value Decomposition (SVD) for Image Compression

SVD decomposes an image matrix I into three matrices:

$$I = U\Sigma V^T$$

where:

- U and V are orthogonal matrices containing eigenvectors,
- Σ is a diagonal matrix with singular values.

By keeping only the largest singular values, we can compress images with minimal loss in quality.

Example: JPEG Compression

JPEG format uses DCT (Discrete Cosine Transform) and SVD to remove less significant components, reducing file size without noticeable loss.

5. Convolution Operations and Image Filters

A. Convolution in Image Processing

Convolution is a fundamental operation in image processing and CNNs (Convolutional Neural Networks). It involves sliding a kernel (filter) over an image and computing a weighted sum of pixel values.

$$(I * K)(x, y) = \sum \sum I(m, n)K(x - m, y - n)$$

where I is the image matrix and K is the kernel matrix.

Common kernels:

- **Edge detection**: Sobel, Prewitt, Canny filters.
- **Blurring**: Gaussian filter.
- **Sharpening**: Laplacian filter.

B. Convolution in Neural Networks

- CNNs apply multiple convolution layers to extract features like edges, textures, and patterns.
- Pooling layers (Max Pooling, Average Pooling) reduce dimensionality while preserving important information.

Linear algebra is the foundation of image representation and processing in computer vision. Matrix operations, eigenvalues, SVD, convolutions, and vector spaces allow AI systems to manipulate images, extract features, compress data, and perform transformations efficiently. As we move further, these principles will be applied to deep learning techniques like CNNs, object detection, and image segmentation, forming the backbone of modern AI-driven vision systems. 🚀

2.2 Probability and Statistics in Vision Tasks

Probability and statistics play a crucial role in computer vision, helping AI systems handle uncertainty, noise, and variability in visual data. Since real-world images are often imperfect due to lighting, occlusions, motion blur, or sensor noise, probability helps in modeling uncertainty, while statistics aids in data analysis and feature extraction. From Bayesian inference and probability distributions to Markov models, expectation maximization, and statistical learning, this section explores how these mathematical concepts power modern vision tasks, including object detection, segmentation, and deep learning-based applications.

1. Probability Distributions in Image Processing

A. Understanding Probability Distributions

Probability distributions help in modeling pixel intensities, object locations, and noise patterns in images. In computer vision, we often encounter discrete and continuous probability distributions:

Discrete Distributions (for categorical data like object classes)

- **Bernoulli Distribution** (e.g., Is there an object in the image? Yes/No)
- **Binomial Distribution** (e.g., Counting the number of detected faces in an image)
- **Multinomial Distribution** (e.g., Probability of an image belonging to multiple classes in classification)

Continuous Distributions (for continuous-valued image data like pixel intensities)

- **Gaussian** (Normal) Distribution (e.g., Modeling pixel noise in grayscale images)
- **Exponential Distribution** (e.g., Modeling time gaps between image frames in video processing)
- **Poisson Distribution** (e.g., Estimating the frequency of object occurrences in an image)

B. Gaussian Distribution in Image Processing

The Gaussian distribution (Normal distribution) is one of the most widely used probability models in computer vision. Many natural images have pixel intensity values that follow a Gaussian distribution, making it useful for denoising, feature extraction, and segmentation.

Example: Gaussian Noise in Images

In real-world scenarios, images captured by cameras often contain Gaussian noise, caused by sensor imperfections or environmental factors. This noise is modeled as:

$$p(x) = \frac{1}{\sqrt{2\pi\sigma^2}} e^{-\frac{(x-\mu)^2}{2\sigma^2}}$$

where:

- x is the pixel intensity,
- μ is the mean intensity,
- σ² is the variance (spread of noise).

Gaussian filters are commonly used in smoothing operations to reduce noise in images before applying edge detection or segmentation algorithms.

2. Bayesian Inference in Computer Vision

A. Bayes' Theorem in Vision Tasks

Bayes' theorem is widely used in image classification, object detection, and uncertainty estimation. It provides a way to update prior knowledge when new evidence is observed.

$$P(H|E) = \frac{P(E|H)P(H)}{P(E)}$$

where:

- **P(H|E)** = Probability of hypothesis H given evidence E (posterior probability)
- **P(E|H)** = Probability of evidence E given hypothesis H (likelihood)
- **P(H)** = Prior probability of hypothesis H (before seeing data)
- **P(E)** = Total probability of the evidence

Example: Naïve Bayes for Image Classification

A Naïve Bayes classifier is used in image classification tasks where each pixel or feature is treated independently. Given an input image X, we compute the probability of it belonging to class C as:

$$P(C|X) = \frac{P(X|C)P(C)}{P(X)}$$

This method is simple but effective in face recognition, handwriting detection, and spam image classification.

3. Markov Models and Probabilistic Graphical Models

A. Markov Chains in Image Processing

Markov models are used to model sequences of observations, such as motion tracking, object tracking in videos, and texture synthesis.

In a Markov Chain, the future state depends only on the present state, not the past states.

$$P(X_{t+1}|X_t, X_{t-1}, ..., X_1) = P(X_{t+1}|X_t)$$

Example: Hidden Markov Models (HMM) in Gesture Recognition

HMMs are widely used for gesture recognition in computer vision. When recognizing hand movements, each frame of a video represents a hidden state, and the observations are the detected hand positions.

B. Conditional Random Fields (CRFs) for Image Segmentation

CRFs are probabilistic graphical models that model contextual dependencies between pixels in an image. They are used for semantic segmentation, object recognition, and scene understanding. Unlike Naïve Bayes, CRFs consider relationships between neighboring pixels, leading to better segmentation accuracy.

4. Expectation-Maximization (EM) Algorithm in Vision Tasks

The Expectation-Maximization (EM) algorithm is a statistical method used in clustering and unsupervised learning in computer vision. It iteratively estimates missing data and maximizes the likelihood function to improve model parameters.

A. Gaussian Mixture Models (GMM) for Image Clustering

GMM is a probabilistic model used in image segmentation, background subtraction, and object tracking. It represents data as a mixture of multiple Gaussian distributions.

$$P(X) = \sum_{i=1}^{k} w_i \mathcal{N}(X|\mu_i, \Sigma_i)$$

where:

- **w_i** = Weight of each Gaussian component
- **μ_i** = Mean of each Gaussian
- **Σ_i** = Covariance matrix

Example: Foreground-Background Segmentation

GMMs are used to separate foreground objects from background pixels in video streams. This is commonly applied in security surveillance to detect moving objects.

5. Statistical Learning in Deep Vision Models

A. Maximum Likelihood Estimation (MLE) in CNNs

In deep learning models like Convolutional Neural Networks (CNNs), probability plays a role in estimating parameters. The softmax function in the final layer of a classifier predicts class probabilities:

$$P(y_i) = \frac{e^{z_i}}{\sum_j e^{z_j}}$$

where z_i are the class scores. The loss function is based on cross-entropy, which is derived from Maximum Likelihood Estimation (MLE).

B. Probabilistic Neural Networks (PNNs)

PNNs use probability density functions to classify images, improving robustness against noise and occlusions.

Example: Bayesian Neural Networks (BNNs)

BNNs introduce uncertainty into deep learning models by treating weights as probability distributions instead of fixed values. This helps in uncertainty-aware decision-making in tasks like medical imaging and autonomous driving.

Probability and statistics are essential in computer vision for handling uncertainty, modeling variability, and improving decision-making in AI systems. Techniques like Gaussian distributions, Bayesian inference, Markov models, and probabilistic neural networks are widely used in tasks such as image classification, object detection, motion tracking, and segmentation. As AI progresses, integrating probabilistic methods with deep learning will enable more reliable, interpretable, and robust vision systems in real-world applications. 🚀

2.3 Convolutions and Filters: The Backbone of Vision Systems

Convolutions and filters are fundamental operations in computer vision, enabling AI to process images, detect patterns, and extract meaningful features. At the heart of modern vision systems, including Convolutional Neural Networks (CNNs), convolutions help in tasks such as edge detection, object recognition, and image enhancement. This chapter explores the mathematics of convolution, types of filters, and their real-world applications, providing a strong foundation for understanding how AI "sees" the world.

1. Understanding Convolution in Image Processing

A. What is Convolution?

Convolution is a mathematical operation that combines two functions (or matrices) to produce a third function. In computer vision, convolution between an image and a filter (or kernel) extracts specific features like edges, textures, and patterns.

Mathematically, convolution is defined as:

$$(I * K)(x, y) = \sum_m \sum_n I(m, n) K(x - m, y - n)$$

where:

- I(x, y) is the input image (a matrix of pixel values),
- K(m, n) is the filter (a small matrix with predefined values),
- The summation slides the filter over the image, computing weighted sums of pixel intensities.

B. Example: 3×3 Convolution Operation

Consider an image patch and a simple edge-detection filter:

Image Patch (3×3)

$$\begin{bmatrix} 10 & 20 & 30 \\ 40 & 50 & 60 \\ 70 & 80 & 90 \end{bmatrix}$$

Edge Detection Kernel (Sobel Filter)

$$\begin{bmatrix} -1 & 0 & 1 \\ -2 & 0 & 2 \\ -1 & 0 & 1 \end{bmatrix}$$

The convolution result for the center pixel is calculated as:

$$(-1 \times 10) + (0 \times 20) + (1 \times 30) + (-2 \times 40) + (0 \times 50) + (2 \times 60) + (-1 \times 70) + (0 \times 80) + (1 \times 90) = 0$$

This operation is repeated across the entire image to highlight vertical edges.

2. Types of Filters in Computer Vision

A. Edge Detection Filters

Edge detection helps in identifying object boundaries in images. Common filters include:

- **Sobel Filter**: Detects horizontal or vertical edges.
- **Prewitt Filter**: Similar to Sobel but with slightly different weights.
- **Laplacian Filter**: Captures all-directional edges.

B. Smoothing and Blurring Filters

These filters reduce noise and smooth out unwanted variations in images.

- **Gaussian Blur**: Uses a Gaussian function to reduce high-frequency noise.

- **Average Filter**: Computes the mean value of neighboring pixels.
- **Median Filter**: Replaces each pixel with the median of surrounding pixels, effective for salt-and-pepper noise.

C. Sharpening Filters

Sharpening enhances image details by amplifying differences between neighboring pixels.

- **Unsharp Masking**: Subtracts a blurred version of the image from the original.
- **Laplacian Filter**: Enhances edges while maintaining fine details.

D. Embossing and Texture Detection Filters

- **Emboss Filters**: Highlight edges and create a 3D effect.
- **Gabor Filters**: Detect texture and spatial frequency patterns, used in fingerprint recognition.

E. Custom Filters for Specific Applications

Researchers design task-specific filters for facial recognition, object tracking, and feature extraction.

3. Stride, Padding, and Dilated Convolutions

A. Stride in Convolution

Stride determines how far the filter moves across the image.

- **Stride = 1 (default):** The filter moves one pixel at a time, preserving spatial resolution.
- **Stride = 2 or more**: Reduces the size of the output feature map, making processing faster.

B. Padding: Preserving Image Size

Since convolution reduces image size, padding is used to maintain dimensions.

- **Valid Padding**: No padding, reducing the output size.
- **Same Padding**: Adds zeros around the image to preserve size.

C. Dilated Convolutions: Expanding the Receptive Field

Dilated convolutions introduce gaps in the filter to capture larger contextual information without increasing kernel size. They are commonly used in semantic segmentation and medical imaging.

4. Convolutions in Deep Learning: CNNs

A. Convolutional Layers in CNNs

CNNs use multiple convolutional layers to extract hierarchical features from images.

- Early layers detect edges and textures.
- Mid-level layers detect shapes and structures.
- High-level layers detect complex objects like faces, cars, or animals.

B. Pooling Layers: Downsampling Features

Pooling layers reduce feature map size while retaining essential features.

- **Max Pooling**: Selects the highest value in each region.
- **Average Pooling**: Computes the average value.

Pooling makes models more robust to minor shifts, rotations, and distortions in input images.

C. Depthwise and Pointwise Convolutions

Modern architectures like MobileNet use depthwise separable convolutions to improve efficiency.

- **Depthwise Convolution**: Applies separate filters to each input channel.
- **Pointwise Convolution (1×1 Convolution):** Combines information from all channels, reducing computation costs.

5. Real-World Applications of Convolutions

A. Face Detection and Recognition

- Convolution filters extract facial features, such as eyes, nose, and mouth.
- CNN-based models like FaceNet and DeepFace use hierarchical feature extraction for high accuracy.

B. Object Detection (YOLO, Faster R-CNN)

- Convolutional layers detect key features of objects.
- Algorithms like YOLO (You Only Look Once) use convolutional filters to detect multiple objects in real time.

C. Medical Image Analysis

- MRI and X-ray analysis use convolution filters to detect anomalies.
- Deep learning models apply convolutions for tumor detection and early disease diagnosis.

D. Image Super-Resolution and Restoration

- Convolutions help in enhancing low-resolution images using techniques like SRCNN (Super-Resolution CNN).

E. Autonomous Vehicles and Robotics

- Convolutions process camera feeds to detect lanes, pedestrians, and obstacles.
- Used in self-driving cars, drones, and robotic vision systems.

Convolutions and filters are the building blocks of modern computer vision, enabling machines to detect patterns, recognize objects, and process complex visual information. From edge detection and smoothing to CNN-based deep learning models, these operations form the foundation of AI-driven vision systems. Understanding how convolution works is essential for building advanced applications in healthcare, security, autonomous systems, and more. 🚀

2.4 Fourier Transforms and Frequency Analysis

In computer vision, images are typically analyzed in the spatial domain, where pixel values define shapes and patterns. However, an equally powerful approach is to study images in the frequency domain using Fourier transforms. Fourier analysis helps extract essential features by decomposing an image into its frequency components. This is especially useful for denoising, compression, texture analysis, and edge detection.

This chapter explores the mathematical foundation of Fourier transforms, types of frequency analysis, and their applications in modern computer vision systems.

1. Understanding Fourier Transform in Image Processing

A. What is Fourier Transform?

The Fourier Transform (FT) converts a function (or signal) from the time/spatial domain into the frequency domain. In image processing, it decomposes an image into its frequency components, helping to analyze patterns that are not easily visible in the spatial domain.

For a function $f(x)$, the **Continuous Fourier Transform (CFT)** is given by:

$$F(u) = \int_{-\infty}^{\infty} f(x)e^{-j2\pi ux}dx$$

where:

- $F(u)$ represents the transformed function in the frequency domain.

- $e^{-j2\pi ux}$ is the complex exponential function that encodes frequency information.

- u is the frequency variable.

However, since digital images are discrete, we use the Discrete Fourier Transform (DFT) instead.

B. Discrete Fourier Transform (DFT) for Digital Images

The **DFT** transforms an image $f(x, y)$ of size $M \times N$ into the frequency domain:

$$F(u, v) = \sum_{x=0}^{M-1} \sum_{y=0}^{N-1} f(x, y) e^{-j2\pi\left(\frac{ux}{M} + \frac{vy}{N}\right)}$$

where:

- (x, y) are spatial coordinates in the image.

- (u, v) represent frequency components.

- The result $F(u, v)$ is the frequency representation of the image.

C. Inverse Discrete Fourier Transform (IDFT)

To convert back from the frequency domain to the spatial domain, we use the Inverse DFT (IDFT):

$$f(x, y) = \frac{1}{MN} \sum_{u=0}^{M-1} \sum_{v=0}^{N-1} F(u, v) e^{j2\pi\left(\frac{ux}{M} + \frac{vy}{N}\right)}$$

This allows us to reconstruct the original image after processing in the frequency domain.

D. Fast Fourier Transform (FFT) for Efficient Computation

DFT calculations can be slow, especially for large images. The Fast Fourier Transform (FFT) is an optimized version that reduces computational complexity from O(N²) to O(N log N), making it the preferred method for practical applications.

2. Frequency Representation of Images

- A. Low-Frequency vs. High-Frequency Components
- An image consists of low-frequency and high-frequency components:

Low-Frequency Components

- Represent smooth variations (e.g., background, large structures).
- Important for image compression and smoothing.

High-Frequency Components

- Represent sharp edges, textures, and fine details.
- Crucial for edge detection, sharpening, and feature extraction.

B. Visualizing the Frequency Domain

After applying the Fourier Transform, we get a frequency spectrum where:

- The center contains low-frequency components (smooth areas).
- The edges contain high-frequency components (sharp transitions and edges).

By applying a log transformation, we can better visualize frequency details in the transformed image.

3. Applications of Fourier Transform in Computer Vision

A. Image Filtering in the Frequency Domain

Fourier Transform allows us to apply filters directly in the frequency domain, making image processing more efficient.

1. Low-Pass Filtering (LPF) – Image Smoothing

- Removes high-frequency details (edges, noise).
- Useful for blurring, denoising, and compression.
- **Example**: Gaussian Low-Pass Filter (GLPF).

2. High-Pass Filtering (HPF) – Edge Detection

- Retains high-frequency details (edges, textures).
- Used in sharpening, edge enhancement, and feature extraction.
- **Example**: Laplacian High-Pass Filter.

3. Band-Pass Filtering – Feature Extraction

- Extracts specific frequency ranges.
- Used for texture analysis and fingerprint recognition.
- **Example**: Gabor filters.

B. Image Compression (JPEG Encoding)

Fourier Transform is used in JPEG image compression, where:

- The image is transformed into the frequency domain using the Discrete Cosine Transform (DCT) (a variant of FT).
- High-frequency components (less important details) are removed to reduce file size.
- The remaining components are stored efficiently.
- This technique reduces image storage size while maintaining perceptual quality.

C. Motion Detection and Video Processing

- The Fourier Transform is applied in motion estimation and video compression (e.g., MPEG encoding).
- Moving objects cause shifts in the frequency domain, which can be detected and analyzed.

D. Pattern and Texture Analysis

- Fourier analysis helps in fingerprint recognition, texture classification, and material analysis.
- Gabor filters (based on Fourier principles) detect oriented textures and repetitive patterns in images.

E. Medical Imaging (MRI, CT, Ultrasound)

- Fourier Transform is widely used in Magnetic Resonance Imaging (MRI) to reconstruct high-resolution medical images from frequency data.
- It also aids in X-ray enhancement and ultrasound image filtering.

4. Practical Implementation: Fourier Transform in Python

Using Python and OpenCV, we can apply Fourier Transform to an image:

```
import cv2
import numpy as np
import matplotlib.pyplot as plt
```

```
# Load the image in grayscale
image = cv2.imread('image.jpg', 0)

# Compute the 2D Fourier Transform
f_transform = np.fft.fft2(image)
f_shift = np.fft.fftshift(f_transform)  # Shift the DC component to the center

# Compute the magnitude spectrum for visualization
magnitude_spectrum = 20 * np.log(np.abs(f_shift))

# Display the image and its frequency representation
plt.figure(figsize=(10,5))
plt.subplot(1,2,1), plt.imshow(image, cmap='gray'), plt.title('Original Image')
plt.subplot(1,2,2), plt.imshow(magnitude_spectrum, cmap='gray'), plt.title('Magnitude
Spectrum')
plt.show()
```

This code:

- Reads an image in grayscale.
- Computes the 2D Fourier Transform.
- Shifts the frequency spectrum for better visualization.
- Displays the original image and its frequency representation.

Fourier Transforms are essential in image processing, denoising, compression, and feature extraction. By converting an image into the frequency domain, we can analyze patterns, remove noise, detect edges, and perform texture classification efficiently. With applications in computer vision, medical imaging, and multimedia compression, Fourier analysis continues to be a powerful tool for building AI-driven vision systems.

3. Digital Images and Processing

Understanding how images are represented and manipulated is fundamental to computer vision. This chapter explores the structure of digital images, including pixels, color spaces, and image formats, as well as essential processing techniques such as filtering, edge detection, thresholding, and histogram equalization. You'll learn how images are stored and modified, how to enhance image quality, and how preprocessing techniques improve the performance of vision models. By the end of this chapter, you will have a solid grasp of image processing fundamentals, enabling you to prepare and refine visual data for AI applications.

3.1 Understanding Pixels and Color Models (RGB, CMYK, HSV)

At the core of every digital image lies the pixel—the smallest unit of a picture, storing color and brightness information. Pixels form the foundation of image processing, computer vision, and deep learning-based visual analysis. To interpret, manipulate, or extract insights from images, understanding how color is represented, stored, and processed is crucial.

This chapter explores the structure of pixels, different color models (RGB, CMYK, HSV), and their role in computer vision applications such as object detection, medical imaging, and artistic rendering.

1. What is a Pixel?

A. Definition of a Pixel

A pixel (picture element) is the smallest controllable unit of an image. Each pixel carries color information in the form of intensity values across different channels (e.g., red, green, blue).

In a grayscale image, each pixel holds a single intensity value between 0 (black) and 255 (white). In a color image, a pixel typically consists of three values representing Red, Green, and Blue (RGB) intensities.

B. Image Resolution and Pixel Density

- **Resolution**: Defined as width × height (e.g., 1920 × 1080 pixels for Full HD images).
- **Pixel Density (PPI/DPI):** Measured in pixels per inch (PPI) or dots per inch (DPI), impacting image clarity and print quality.
- **Higher resolution** → More pixels → Sharper images but larger file sizes.

2. Color Models in Computer Vision

A color model defines how colors are represented in an image. Different color models serve specific purposes in digital displays, printing, and vision-based applications.

2.1 RGB (Red, Green, Blue) – The Digital Standard

A. Understanding RGB Representation

RGB is the most common color model for digital screens, cameras, and computer vision systems. Each pixel consists of three values:

$$(R, G, B)$$

where each component ranges from 0 to 255 in an 8-bit image.

- B. How RGB Colors Are Created
- (255, 0, 0) → Pure Red
- (0, 255, 0) → Pure Green
- (0, 0, 255) → Pure Blue
- (255, 255, 255) → White (maximum intensity of all channels)
- (0, 0, 0) → Black (absence of light)

C. RGB Applications

- Computer screens and digital images (PNG, JPEG, BMP).
- Deep learning and neural networks, as most vision models process RGB input.
- Color-based object tracking and segmentation in vision systems.

2.2 CMYK (Cyan, Magenta, Yellow, Black) – The Printing Standard

A. Understanding CMYK Representation

Unlike RGB (which is additive), CMYK is a subtractive color model used in printing. Colors are created by subtracting light from a white background using four ink components:

$$(C, M, Y, K)$$

where:

- Cyan absorbs red light,
- Magenta absorbs green light,
- Yellow absorbs blue light,
- Black (K) adds contrast and depth.

B. Why CMYK is Used in Printing

RGB works for screens that emit light, while printers need CMYK to reflect light from paper. RGB colors must be converted to CMYK before printing to ensure accuracy.

C. CMYK Applications

- Offset and digital printing (magazines, brochures, books).
- Color correction for print media.
- High-quality photographic prints.

2.3 HSV (Hue, Saturation, Value) – The Perceptual Model

A. Understanding HSV Representation

Unlike RGB (which is hardware-oriented), HSV is a perceptual color model designed to match human vision better. It separates color information into:

- **Hue** (H): The type of color (e.g., red, blue, green), ranging from 0° to 360°.
- **Saturation** (S): Intensity or purity of the color (0 = grayscale, 100 = vivid color).
- **Value** (V): Brightness (0 = black, 100 = full brightness).

B. Why HSV is Useful in Computer Vision

The separation of color and intensity makes it robust to lighting variations.

- Easier color-based segmentation (e.g., identifying traffic signals, detecting objects).
- More intuitive color adjustments than in RGB.

C. HSV Applications

- Object detection and tracking (e.g., detecting skin tones, traffic lights).
- Image enhancement (adjusting brightness and contrast separately).
- Augmented reality (AR) applications that require adaptive color filtering.

3. Converting Between Color Models

Computer vision applications often require switching between color models. OpenCV provides easy functions for conversion:

A. Converting RGB to Grayscale

```
import cv2

image = cv2.imread('image.jpg')
gray_image = cv2.cvtColor(image, cv2.COLOR_BGR2GRAY)
cv2.imwrite('gray_image.jpg', gray_image)
```

B. Converting RGB to HSV

```
hsv_image = cv2.cvtColor(image, cv2.COLOR_BGR2HSV)
cv2.imwrite('hsv_image.jpg', hsv_image)
```

C. Converting RGB to CMYK (Approximation)

OpenCV does not natively support CMYK, but we can approximate it using NumPy:

```
import numpy as np

rgb_image = cv2.imread('image.jpg') / 255.0
K = 1 - np.max(rgb_image, axis=2)
C = (1 - rgb_image[..., 0] - K) / (1 - K + 1e-8)
```

$M = (1 - rgb\_image[..., 1] - K) / (1 - K + 1e\text{-}8)$
$Y = (1 - rgb\_image[..., 2] - K) / (1 - K + 1e\text{-}8)$

$cmyk\_image = (np.dstack([C, M, Y, K]) * 255).astype(np.uint8)$

4. Choosing the Right Color Model for Vision Tasks

Color Model	Best For	Limitations
RGB	Digital screens, deep learning	Sensitive to lighting changes
CMYK	Printing, high-quality photographs	Not suitable for screen-based applications
HSV	Object detection, segmentation	Needs conversion from RGB
Grayscale	Feature detection, edge detection	Loses color information

When to Use Each Model in Computer Vision

- Use RGB for deep learning models and digital display processing.
- Use HSV for color-based segmentation, filtering, and tracking.
- Use Grayscale for edge detection, object recognition, and noise reduction.
- Use CMYK for image preparation in printing applications.

Understanding pixels and color models is fundamental in computer vision, as images are represented in different formats depending on the application. The RGB model is dominant in digital displays, CMYK is essential for printing, and HSV is powerful for color-based segmentation and tracking. Choosing the right color model ensures efficient image analysis, processing, and AI-driven decision-making.

3.2 Image Resizing, Cropping, and Normalization

In computer vision, images come in various sizes, resolutions, and formats. However, machine learning models and image processing tasks often require images to be in a consistent format. Image resizing, cropping, and normalization are essential preprocessing techniques that ensure uniformity, improve model efficiency, and enhance feature extraction.

This chapter explores how resizing, cropping, and normalization work, their mathematical foundations, and how to implement them in Python using OpenCV and NumPy.

1. Image Resizing

A. What is Image Resizing?

Resizing involves changing an image's dimensions (width and height) while maintaining its visual integrity. It is commonly used in:

- Deep learning models (e.g., resizing all images to 224×224 for CNNs).
- Reducing storage space by compressing large images.
- Standardizing dataset images for better training stability.

B. Common Image Resizing Methods

There are several interpolation techniques used in resizing:

Method	Description	Use Case
Nearest Neighbor	Assigns the nearest pixel value to new pixels.	Fast but may create blocky images.
Bilinear Interpolation	Takes the weighted average of the four nearest pixels.	Smooth results, commonly used in deep learning preprocessing.
Bicubic Interpolation	Uses 16 nearest pixels for smoother resizing.	Produces high-quality resized images.
Lanczos Interpolation	Uses sinc function to compute pixel values.	Best for high-quality downsizing.

C. Implementing Image Resizing in OpenCV

In Python, OpenCV provides the cv2.resize() function for resizing images.

Example: Resizing an Image to 256×256

```
import cv2

# Load image
image = cv2.imread('image.jpg')

# Resize image to 256x256
resized_image = cv2.resize(image, (256, 256), interpolation=cv2.INTER_AREA)
```

```
# Save and display
cv2.imwrite('resized_image.jpg', resized_image)
cv2.imshow('Resized Image', resized_image)
cv2.waitKey(0)
cv2.destroyAllWindows()
```

D. Aspect Ratio and Maintaining Proportions

When resizing, it is important to maintain the aspect ratio to prevent distortion. The aspect ratio is given by:

$$\text{Aspect Ratio} = \frac{\text{Original Width}}{\text{Original Height}}$$

If we want to resize an image to a fixed width while maintaining the aspect ratio:

```
new_width = 256
aspect_ratio = image.shape[1] / image.shape[0]
new_height = int(new_width / aspect_ratio)

resized_image = cv2.resize(image, (new_width, new_height),
interpolation=cv2.INTER_AREA)
```

2. Image Cropping

A. What is Image Cropping?

Cropping removes unwanted parts of an image by selecting a specific region of interest (ROI). It is useful for:

- Focusing on relevant objects in an image.
- Data augmentation for training machine learning models.
- Improving composition in photography and design.

B. Implementing Image Cropping in OpenCV

To crop an image, we specify the pixel range for the region of interest:

Example: Cropping the Center of an Image

```
import numpy as np

# Load image
image = cv2.imread('image.jpg')

# Get dimensions
height, width = image.shape[:2]

# Define cropping area (center 200x200 pixels)
start_x = width // 2 - 100
start_y = height // 2 - 100
end_x = start_x + 200
end_y = start_y + 200

cropped_image = image[start_y:end_y, start_x:end_x]

# Save and display
cv2.imwrite('cropped_image.jpg', cropped_image)
cv2.imshow('Cropped Image', cropped_image)
cv2.waitKey(0)
cv2.destroyAllWindows()
```

C. Automatic Cropping for Object Detection

In some applications, cropping is automated using object detection models. For example, in face recognition, a face detector first identifies the bounding box, and then cropping is applied to extract only the face.

3. Image Normalization

A. What is Image Normalization?

Normalization scales pixel values to a standardized range (e.g., 0 to 1 or -1 to 1). This process is essential for:

- Improving neural network performance by ensuring consistent input values.
- Reducing computation time by preventing large pixel intensity differences.

- Enhancing contrast and removing lighting variations.

B. Common Normalization Methods

Normalization Type	Formula	Typical Range
Min-Max Scaling	$X' = \frac{X - X_{min}}{X_{max} - X_{min}}$	0 to 1
Mean Normalization	$X' = \frac{X - \mu}{\sigma}$	-1 to 1
Division by 255	$X' = \frac{X}{255}$	0 to 1

C. Implementing Normalization in OpenCV & NumPy

1. Min-Max Normalization (Scaling Pixel Values Between 0 and 1)

```
import numpy as np

# Load image
image = cv2.imread('image.jpg', cv2.IMREAD_GRAYSCALE)

# Convert pixel values to 0-1 range
normalized_image = image.astype(np.float32) / 255.0

# Display
cv2.imshow('Normalized Image', normalized_image)
cv2.waitKey(0)
cv2.destroyAllWindows()
```

2. Mean Normalization (-1 to 1 Scaling for Neural Networks)

```
# Convert to float and normalize between -1 and 1
normalized_image = (image.astype(np.float32) - 127.5) / 127.5
```

D. When to Use Normalization?

- **For deep learning**: Normalization is required before feeding images into CNNs.
- **For image enhancement**: Scaling helps balance brightness and contrast.
- **For real-time applications**: Normalization reduces computational cost.

4. Combining Resizing, Cropping, and Normalization in a Pipeline

In real-world applications, we often apply resizing, cropping, and normalization together in an image preprocessing pipeline.

Example: Preprocessing for a Deep Learning Model (ResNet, VGG, etc.)

```
def preprocess_image(image_path, target_size=(224, 224)):
    # Load the image
    image = cv2.imread(image_path)

    # Resize while keeping aspect ratio
    resized_image = cv2.resize(image, target_size, interpolation=cv2.INTER_AREA)

    # Convert to float and normalize
    normalized_image = resized_image.astype(np.float32) / 255.0

    return normalized_image

# Preprocess an image
processed_image = preprocess_image('image.jpg')
```

Image resizing, cropping, and normalization are fundamental preprocessing techniques in computer vision. Resizing standardizes image dimensions, cropping focuses on relevant regions, and normalization improves model efficiency. These operations form the backbone of deep learning pipelines, ensuring consistent and optimized input data.

3.3 Edge Detection: Sobel, Canny, and Laplacian Filters

Edges are fundamental features in images, representing object boundaries, texture variations, and structural details. Edge detection is a crucial step in computer vision, helping in object recognition, image segmentation, and motion tracking. Various mathematical techniques, such as Sobel, Canny, and Laplacian filters, allow us to identify edges by detecting intensity changes in an image.

In this chapter, we explore the principles of edge detection, key algorithms, and their implementation in OpenCV.

1. What is Edge Detection?

A. Definition of Edges in an Image

An edge is a significant change in pixel intensity, typically occurring at object boundaries. It represents a transition between different regions in an image.

Mathematically, an edge is where the gradient (rate of intensity change) is high. The gradient of an image is computed using partial derivatives:

$$G_x = \frac{\partial I}{\partial x}, \quad G_y = \frac{\partial I}{\partial y}$$

where:

- G_x detects horizontal changes.
- G_y detects vertical changes.

The magnitude of the gradient determines edge strength:

$$G = \sqrt{G_x^2 + G_y^2}$$

B. Applications of Edge Detection

- **Object detection and tracking** (e.g., detecting lane markings in self-driving cars).
- **Medical image analysis** (e.g., identifying tumors in MRI scans).
- **Image compression** (e.g., preserving key structures while reducing file size).

2. Sobel Edge Detection

A. What is the Sobel Filter?

The Sobel operator is a simple and efficient edge detection method that uses a pair of 3×3 convolution kernels to compute the gradient in both horizontal and vertical directions.

B. Sobel Kernels for Edge Detection

Sobel X (detects vertical edges):

$$G_x = \begin{bmatrix} -1 & 0 & 1 \\ -2 & 0 & 2 \\ -1 & 0 & 1 \end{bmatrix}$$

Sobel Y (detects horizontal edges):

$$G_y = \begin{bmatrix} -1 & -2 & -1 \\ 0 & 0 & 0 \\ 1 & 2 & 1 \end{bmatrix}$$

C. Implementing Sobel Edge Detection in OpenCV

```
import cv2
import numpy as np

# Load image in grayscale
image = cv2.imread('image.jpg', cv2.IMREAD_GRAYSCALE)

# Apply Sobel filter
sobel_x = cv2.Sobel(image, cv2.CV_64F, 1, 0, ksize=3)
sobel_y = cv2.Sobel(image, cv2.CV_64F, 0, 1, ksize=3)

# Compute gradient magnitude
sobel_edges = cv2.magnitude(sobel_x, sobel_y)

# Convert to 8-bit image
sobel_edges = np.uint8(sobel_edges)

# Display results
cv2.imshow('Sobel Edges', sobel_edges)
cv2.waitKey(0)
cv2.destroyAllWindows()
```

D. Advantages & Limitations of Sobel Operator

✅ Advantages

- Fast and simple to implement.
- Good for detecting edges in noise-free images.

✖ Limitations

- Sensitive to noise.
- Cannot detect edges with varying thickness.

3. Canny Edge Detection

A. What is the Canny Algorithm?

The Canny Edge Detector is a multi-step edge detection technique that improves accuracy and noise resistance. It consists of the following steps:

- **Gaussian Blur** → Smooths the image to remove noise.
- **Compute Gradient** → Uses Sobel filters to detect intensity changes.
- **Non-Maximum Suppression** → Removes weak edges that are not part of a continuous boundary.
- **Hysteresis Thresholding** → Defines strong and weak edges based on two thresholds.

B. Implementing Canny Edge Detection in OpenCV

```
# Apply Canny Edge Detector
canny_edges = cv2.Canny(image, 50, 150)

# Display results
cv2.imshow('Canny Edges', canny_edges)
cv2.waitKey(0)
cv2.destroyAllWindows()
```

The two parameters (50, 150) are the low and high thresholds. Adjusting these values helps in detecting more or fewer edges.

C. Advantages & Limitations of Canny Edge Detection

✔ Advantages

- Produces sharp and clean edges.
- Less sensitive to noise due to Gaussian smoothing.
- Uses double thresholding to reduce false edges.

✘ Limitations

- Computationally expensive.
- Requires fine-tuning of parameters.

4. Laplacian Edge Detection

A. What is the Laplacian Operator?

The Laplacian operator detects edges by computing the second-order derivative of the image intensity:

$$\nabla^2 I = \frac{\partial^2 I}{\partial x^2} + \frac{\partial^2 I}{\partial y^2}$$

Since the Laplacian uses second derivatives, it highlights edges regardless of direction but is more sensitive to noise.

B. Laplacian Kernel

$$\begin{bmatrix} 0 & -1 & 0 \\ -1 & 4 & -1 \\ 0 & -1 & 0 \end{bmatrix}$$

C. Implementing Laplacian Edge Detection in OpenCV

```
# Apply Laplacian filter
laplacian_edges = cv2.Laplacian(image, cv2.CV_64F, ksize=3)
```

```
# Convert to 8-bit image
laplacian_edges = np.uint8(np.absolute(laplacian_edges))

# Display results
cv2.imshow('Laplacian Edges', laplacian_edges)
cv2.waitKey(0)
cv2.destroyAllWindows()
```

D. Advantages & Limitations of Laplacian Operator

✓ Advantages

- Detects edges regardless of orientation.
- Works well for texture analysis.

✗ Limitations

- Very sensitive to noise.
- Can produce double edges.

5. Choosing the Right Edge Detection Method

Method	Best For	Limitations
Sobel	Simple edge detection, fast computations	Sensitive to noise
Canny	Accurate, noise-resistant edge detection	Computationally expensive
Laplacian	Detecting all-directional edges	May highlight noise too strongly

When to Use Each Method?

- Use Sobel for simple, fast edge detection in clean images.
- Use Canny when noise is a concern and sharp edges are needed.
- Use Laplacian for texture analysis and detecting fine details.

Edge detection is a foundational step in computer vision that helps in feature extraction, object recognition, and segmentation. The Sobel operator computes gradients for basic edge detection, Canny filtering provides a more refined and noise-resistant method, and the Laplacian filter highlights high-frequency regions effectively.

3.4 Image Thresholding and Contour Detection

Image thresholding and contour detection are essential techniques in computer vision used for object segmentation, shape analysis, and pattern recognition. Thresholding simplifies an image by converting it into a binary format, making it easier to detect objects, while contour detection extracts the outlines of objects. These methods are widely used in applications like optical character recognition (OCR), medical imaging, and object tracking.

In this chapter, we explore different thresholding techniques, contour detection methods, and their practical implementation using OpenCV in Python.

1. Image Thresholding

A. What is Image Thresholding?

Thresholding converts an image into a binary (black and white) format by setting a threshold intensity value.

Mathematically, thresholding is defined as:

$$I'(x, y) = \begin{cases} 255, & I(x, y) > T \\ 0, & I(x, y) \leq T \end{cases}$$

where:

- $I(x, y)$ is the original pixel intensity.

- $I'(x, y)$ is the thresholded pixel intensity.

- T is the threshold value.

B. Types of Image Thresholding

Type	Description	Best For
Simple Thresholding	Converts pixels to either 0 or 255 based on a fixed threshold.	High-contrast images.
Adaptive Thresholding	Computes different thresholds for different image regions.	Images with varying lighting.
Otsu's Thresholding	Automatically determines the best threshold value.	Automatic segmentation.

2. Simple Thresholding

A. How Simple Thresholding Works

- If a pixel intensity is above the threshold, it becomes white (255).
- If it is below the threshold, it becomes black (0).

B. Implementing Simple Thresholding in OpenCV

```
import cv2

# Load image in grayscale
image = cv2.imread('image.jpg', cv2.IMREAD_GRAYSCALE)

# Apply simple thresholding
_, binary_image = cv2.threshold(image, 127, 255, cv2.THRESH_BINARY)

# Display results
cv2.imshow('Binary Threshold', binary_image)
cv2.waitKey(0)
cv2.destroyAllWindows()
```

Here, 127 is the threshold value, and 255 is the maximum pixel intensity.

3. Adaptive Thresholding

A. Why Use Adaptive Thresholding?

In images with uneven lighting, a fixed threshold does not work well. Adaptive thresholding dynamically determines the threshold for different regions of an image.

B. Implementing Adaptive Thresholding in OpenCV

```
# Apply adaptive thresholding
adaptive_thresh = cv2.adaptiveThreshold(image, 255,
cv2.ADAPTIVE_THRESH_GAUSSIAN_C,
                        cv2.THRESH_BINARY, 11, 2)

# Display results
cv2.imshow('Adaptive Threshold', adaptive_thresh)
cv2.waitKey(0)
cv2.destroyAllWindows()
```

The 11 represents the block size (region size), and 2 is a constant subtracted from the mean threshold.

4. Otsu's Thresholding

A. What is Otsu's Method?

Otsu's thresholding automatically calculates the best threshold value by analyzing the image histogram and maximizing the variance between foreground and background pixels.

B. Implementing Otsu's Thresholding in OpenCV

```
# Apply Otsu's thresholding
_, otsu_thresh = cv2.threshold(image, 0, 255, cv2.THRESH_BINARY +
cv2.THRESH_OTSU)

# Display results
cv2.imshow('Otsu Thresholding', otsu_thresh)
cv2.waitKey(0)
cv2.destroyAllWindows()
```

This method is useful when the image has multiple peaks in its histogram.

5. Contour Detection

A. What are Contours?

A contour is a curve that connects all continuous points along the boundary of an object with the same color or intensity.

Contours are useful for:

- Shape analysis (e.g., detecting circular or rectangular objects).
- Object detection and recognition.
- Measuring object properties (e.g., area, perimeter).

B. How Contour Detection Works?

- Convert the image to grayscale.
- Apply thresholding or edge detection to create a binary image.
- Use the cv2.findContours() function to extract object boundaries.

C. Implementing Contour Detection in OpenCV

```
# Convert image to grayscale
gray = cv2.cvtColor(image, cv2.COLOR_BGR2GRAY)

# Apply binary thresholding
_, binary = cv2.threshold(gray, 127, 255, cv2.THRESH_BINARY)

# Find contours
contours, _ = cv2.findContours(binary, cv2.RETR_EXTERNAL,
cv2.CHAIN_APPROX_SIMPLE)

# Draw contours on the original image
image_with_contours = cv2.drawContours(image.copy(), contours, -1, (0, 255, 0), 2)

# Display results
cv2.imshow('Contours', image_with_contours)
cv2.waitKey(0)
cv2.destroyAllWindows()
```

Here:

- cv2.RETR_EXTERNAL retrieves only outer contours.
- cv2.CHAIN_APPROX_SIMPLE removes unnecessary points for efficiency.

6. Contour Properties and Applications

A. Measuring Contour Properties

Property	Formula	Use Case
Contour Area	`cv2.contourArea(contour)`	Measuring object size.
Perimeter	`cv2.arcLength(contour, True)`	Detecting object boundaries.
Bounding Box	`cv2.boundingRect(contour)`	Object detection and tracking.
Centroid	$C_x = \frac{\sum x}{N}, C_y = \frac{\sum y}{N}$	Locating object center.

Example: Computing Contour Area and Centroid

```
for contour in contours:
    area = cv2.contourArea(contour)
    M = cv2.moments(contour)
    cx = int(M["m10"] / (M["m00"] + 1e-5))
    cy = int(M["m01"] / (M["m00"] + 1e-5))

    print(f"Contour Area: {area}, Centroid: ({cx}, {cy})")
```

B. Contour Approximation (Polygonal Shapes)

To approximate contours into simpler shapes:

```
epsilon = 0.02 * cv2.arcLength(contour, True)
approx = cv2.approxPolyDP(contour, epsilon, True)
cv2.drawContours(image, [approx], -1, (255, 0, 0), 2)
```

This technique is used for detecting triangles, rectangles, and circles.

7. Choosing the Right Thresholding and Contour Method

Method	Best For	Limitations
Simple Thresholding	High-contrast images	Fixed threshold is not adaptive
Adaptive Thresholding	Uneven lighting	Slower than simple thresholding
Otsu's Thresholding	Automatic segmentation	Assumes bimodal histogram
Contour Detection	Shape analysis	Requires a binary image

When to Use Each Method?

- Use Simple Thresholding for high-contrast images.
- Use Adaptive Thresholding for images with varying lighting.
- Use Otsu's Thresholding when an automatic threshold is needed.
- Use Contours for detecting and analyzing object shapes.

Image thresholding and contour detection are powerful techniques for image segmentation, object recognition, and shape analysis. Thresholding simplifies images into binary format, while contour detection extracts object boundaries. These methods form the foundation of computer vision applications like OCR, medical imaging, and autonomous navigation.

4. Feature Detection and Extraction

In computer vision, identifying key features in an image is crucial for tasks like object recognition, tracking, and scene reconstruction. This chapter delves into feature detection techniques such as edge detection, corner detection (Harris, FAST), and blob detection (DoG, MSER). You'll also explore feature extraction methods like SIFT, SURF, and ORB, which enable machines to recognize objects regardless of scale, rotation, or lighting changes. By the end of this chapter, you will understand how to detect and extract meaningful features from images, laying the groundwork for advanced applications like image matching and object tracking.

4.1 What Are Features? Understanding Keypoints and Descriptors

In computer vision, "features" play a crucial role in understanding and analyzing images. They help in object detection, image matching, and scene recognition by identifying unique patterns within an image. Features can be simple elements like edges and corners or complex structures like textures and shapes.

Two critical components of feature-based image analysis are:

- **Keypoints** – Distinctive points in an image that remain unchanged under different transformations.
- **Descriptors** – Mathematical representations of the region around a keypoint, used for matching and recognition.

In this chapter, we dive deep into keypoints, descriptors, and their importance in modern computer vision applications.

1. What Are Features in Computer Vision?

A. Definition of Features

A feature is a measurable pattern or structure in an image that helps distinguish objects or scenes. Features should be:

✓ **Unique** – Different from other points in the image.

✓ **Invariant** – Unchanged under transformations like rotation, scaling, and lighting variations.

✓ **Repeatable** – Detected consistently across different images of the same object.

B. Types of Features

- **Low-level features** – Edges, corners, and textures.
- **High-level features** – Object shapes and regions.

Feature Type	Description	Examples
Edges	Sharp changes in intensity	Sobel, Canny filters
Corners	Points where two edges meet	Harris corner detector
Blobs	Regions with distinct intensity patterns	Difference of Gaussians
Descriptors	Numeric representations of features	SIFT, SURF, ORB

2. Keypoints: Detecting Important Image Points

A. What Are Keypoints?

Keypoints are distinctive locations in an image that are stable under different transformations. Good keypoints remain visible even if the image is rotated, scaled, or partially occluded.

B. Common Keypoint Detection Algorithms

Algorithm	Detects	Transformation Invariance
Harris Corner Detector	Corners	Rotation
SIFT (Scale-Invariant Feature Transform)	Blobs & corners	Scale, rotation
SURF (Speeded-Up Robust Features)	Blobs	Scale, rotation
FAST (Features from Accelerated Segment Test)	Corners	Rotation
ORB (Oriented FAST and Rotated BRIEF)	Corners	Rotation, scale

C. Detecting Keypoints in OpenCV (SIFT Example)

```
import cv2
import matplotlib.pyplot as plt
```

```
# Load image
image = cv2.imread('image.jpg', cv2.IMREAD_GRAYSCALE)

# Detect keypoints using SIFT
sift = cv2.SIFT_create()
keypoints = sift.detect(image, None)

# Draw keypoints on the image
image_with_keypoints = cv2.drawKeypoints(image, keypoints, None)

# Display results
plt.imshow(image_with_keypoints, cmap='gray')
plt.show()
```

Here, SIFT detects stable keypoints in the image, making them useful for tasks like object recognition and tracking.

3. Feature Descriptors: Representing Keypoints

A. What Are Feature Descriptors?

A feature descriptor is a numerical representation of a keypoint's surrounding area. Descriptors allow us to match features across different images, enabling applications like image stitching and object detection.

B. Properties of Good Descriptors

✅ **Distinctive** – Clearly differentiates one feature from another.
✅ **Robust** – Resistant to changes in lighting, rotation, and scale.
✅ **Compact** – Efficiently stored and computed.

C. Common Feature Descriptors

Algorithm	Descriptor Type	Advantages
SIFT	128-dimensional vector	Scale & rotation invariant
SURF	64-dimensional vector	Faster than SIFT
BRIEF	Binary vector	Fast but not scale-invariant
ORB	Binary vector (rotation-invariant)	Efficient & fast

D. Extracting Descriptors in OpenCV

```
# Compute keypoints and descriptors using SIFT
keypoints, descriptors = sift.compute(image, keypoints)

# Print descriptor shape
print("Descriptor Shape:", descriptors.shape)
```

Each descriptor is a numeric representation of a detected keypoint.

4. Matching Features Between Images

A. Why Match Features?

Feature matching helps in:

- **Object recognition** – Identifying an object in different images.
- **Image stitching** – Combining multiple images into a panorama.
- **Augmented reality** – Detecting real-world objects for overlaying digital content.

B. Feature Matching Algorithms

Algorithm	Description
Brute Force (BF) Matcher	Compares every descriptor from one image with all descriptors in another image.
FLANN (Fast Library for Approximate Nearest Neighbors)	Faster than BF for large datasets.
Ratio Test (Lowe's Test)	Filters matches by comparing distances between nearest and second-nearest neighbors.

C. Implementing Feature Matching in OpenCV

```
# Load two images
image1 = cv2.imread('image1.jpg', cv2.IMREAD_GRAYSCALE)
image2 = cv2.imread('image2.jpg', cv2.IMREAD_GRAYSCALE)

# Detect keypoints and descriptors
kp1, des1 = sift.detectAndCompute(image1, None)
kp2, des2 = sift.detectAndCompute(image2, None)

# Match features using BFMatcher
bf = cv2.BFMatcher()
matches = bf.knnMatch(des1, des2, k=2)

# Apply Lowe's ratio test
good_matches = [m for m, n in matches if m.distance < 0.75 * n.distance]

# Draw matches
image_matches = cv2.drawMatchesKnn(image1, kp1, image2, kp2, [good_matches],
None, flags=cv2.DrawMatchesFlags_NOT_DRAW_SINGLE_POINTS)

# Display results
plt.imshow(image_matches)
plt.show()
```

This process helps match similar features between two images.

5. Choosing the Right Feature Detection Method

Method	Best For	Limitations
SIFT	Object recognition, scene matching	Computationally expensive
SURF	Fast object detection	Patent restrictions (not free)
ORB	Real-time applications, tracking	Less accurate than SIFT/SURF
Harris Corner	Simple shape detection	Not scale-invariant

When to Use Each Method?

- Use SIFT for accurate but slower feature matching.
- Use ORB for real-time applications like mobile vision.

- Use Harris Corner for simple feature detection.

Feature detection and description are fundamental in computer vision. Keypoints highlight important image regions, while descriptors enable matching across images. Advanced methods like SIFT, ORB, and BRIEF provide robust solutions for real-world applications like object tracking, face recognition, and augmented reality.

4.2 Harris Corner Detection and Shi-Tomasi Method

Corners are one of the most important features in an image because they are stable and highly distinguishable. They provide key information for various computer vision tasks, including object tracking, image stitching, and 3D reconstruction. Two widely used corner detection algorithms are:

- **Harris Corner Detector** – A mathematical approach to detecting corners using image gradients.
- **Shi-Tomasi Corner Detector** – An improvement over Harris that selects the most stable corners for tracking.

In this chapter, we will explore the theory behind these methods, their implementation, and their practical applications.

1. What Are Corners in an Image?

A corner is a point in an image where two edges meet, meaning there is a significant change in intensity in multiple directions.

◆ **Example**: The corner of a table or the intersection of two walls in an image.

A. How Do We Detect Corners?

To identify corners, we analyze changes in pixel intensity. If the intensity variation is high in multiple directions, it is classified as a corner.

B. Corner vs. Edge vs. Flat Region

Region Type	Intensity Change	Example
Flat Region	No significant change in any direction	Sky, plain background
Edge	High change in one direction	Object boundaries
Corner	High change in multiple directions	Intersection of edges

2. Harris Corner Detector

A. Overview

The Harris Corner Detector was introduced in 1988 and is one of the earliest methods for detecting corners in images. It is based on computing image gradients and analyzing how intensity varies in different directions.

B. Mathematical Explanation

The Harris corner response function is given by:

$$R = \det(M) - k \cdot (\operatorname{trace}(M))^2$$

where:

- M is the **structure tensor** calculated from gradients.
- k is a sensitivity factor (typically 0.04 – 0.06).
- **det(M)** represents the determinant of the matrix, indicating intensity variations.
- **trace(M)** represents the sum of eigenvalues, determining the structure type.

C. Interpreting the Harris Response (R Value)

R Value	Interpretation
R < 0	Edge
R ≈ 0	Flat region
R > 0	Corner detected

3. Implementing Harris Corner Detection in OpenCV

A. Steps for Corner Detection

- Convert the image to grayscale.
- Compute image gradients using Sobel filters.
- Compute the Harris response matrix.
- Apply thresholding to identify strong corners.

B. Code Implementation

```python
import cv2
import numpy as np

# Load image
image = cv2.imread('image.jpg')
gray = cv2.cvtColor(image, cv2.COLOR_BGR2GRAY)

# Harris Corner Detection
harris_response = cv2.cornerHarris(gray, blockSize=2, ksize=3, k=0.04)

# Dilate result to mark the corners
harris_response = cv2.dilate(harris_response, None)

# Set threshold and mark corners in red
image[harris_response > 0.01 * harris_response.max()] = [0, 0, 255]

# Display result
cv2.imshow('Harris Corners', image)
cv2.waitKey(0)
cv2.destroyAllWindows()
```

◆ **Explanation of Parameters:**

- **blockSize=2** → Size of the neighborhood for computing gradients.

- **ksize=3** → Aperture parameter for the Sobel operator.

- **k=0.04** → Empirical constant for corner sensitivity.

◆ **Results:**

- The detected corners are marked in red on the image.

4. Shi-Tomasi Corner Detection

A. Why Use Shi-Tomasi Instead of Harris?

While the Harris Detector is effective, it does not rank corners based on their strength. The Shi-Tomasi method improves upon Harris by selecting only the strongest and most reliable corners, making it ideal for applications like object tracking.

B. Mathematical Explanation

Instead of using the Harris response function R, Shi-Tomasi selects corners based on **eigenvalues of the structure matrix** M:

$$\lambda_{\min} > T$$

where:

- $\lambda_{\min}$ is the smaller eigenvalue.
- T is a threshold value.

If the smaller eigenvalue is above a threshold, the point is classified as a corner.

C. Benefits of Shi-Tomasi Over Harris

✓ Selects only the strongest corners, reducing noise.

✓ More stable for tracking in motion-based applications.

✓ Used in the Good Features to Track algorithm.

5. Implementing Shi-Tomasi Corner Detection in OpenCV

A. Code Implementation

```
# Load image
image = cv2.imread('image.jpg')
gray = cv2.cvtColor(image, cv2.COLOR_BGR2GRAY)
```

```
# Detect corners using Shi-Tomasi
corners = cv2.goodFeaturesToTrack(gray, maxCorners=100, qualityLevel=0.01,
minDistance=10)

# Convert corners to integer values
corners = np.int0(corners)

# Draw detected corners on image
for corner in corners:
    x, y = corner.ravel()
    cv2.circle(image, (x, y), 5, (0, 255, 0), -1)

# Display result
cv2.imshow('Shi-Tomasi Corners', image)
cv2.waitKey(0)
cv2.destroyAllWindows()
```

◆ **Explanation of Parameters:**

- **maxCorners=100** → Maximum number of corners to detect.

- **qualityLevel=0.01** → Minimum quality threshold for corner selection.

- **minDistance=10** → Minimum distance between detected corners.

◆ **Results:**

- The detected corners are marked in green.
- Only the most stable corners are selected.

6. Comparing Harris and Shi-Tomasi Corner Detectors

Feature	Harris Corner Detector	Shi-Tomasi Corner Detector
Corner Selection	Detects all corners	Selects only the strongest corners
Sensitivity to Noise	Sensitive to noise	More robust to noise
Performance	Computationally heavier	Faster and more efficient
Use Case	Edge detection, image stitching	Feature tracking, object tracking

When to Use Each Method?

- Use Harris if you need all possible corners for shape analysis.
- Use Shi-Tomasi for tracking applications like optical flow.

7. Real-World Applications of Corner Detection

✅ **Object Tracking**: Shi-Tomasi is used in Lucas-Kanade Optical Flow to track objects across frames.

✅ **Image Stitching**: Harris corners help align images for panorama generation.

✅ **Face Detection**: Used as a preprocessing step in detecting facial landmarks.

✅ **Augmented Reality**: Feature-based corner detection is used in marker-based AR applications.

Corner detection is a fundamental step in many computer vision applications. The Harris Corner Detector effectively identifies corner points, while the Shi-Tomasi method improves corner selection for motion tracking and real-time applications.

4.3 SIFT, SURF, and ORB: Feature Matching Explained

Feature matching is a fundamental task in computer vision, enabling applications like object recognition, image stitching, and 3D reconstruction. Three of the most widely used feature detection and description techniques are:

- **SIFT** (Scale-Invariant Feature Transform) – A robust but computationally expensive method.
- **SURF** (Speeded-Up Robust Features) – Faster than SIFT but with patent restrictions.
- **ORB** (Oriented FAST and Rotated BRIEF) – A free, efficient alternative suitable for real-time applications.

This chapter explores how these methods detect and describe features, their advantages, and how they compare for various applications.

1. Understanding Feature Matching in Computer Vision

A. What is Feature Matching?

Feature matching finds corresponding points between two images by detecting keypoints and describing them mathematically. These matches help:

✓ Recognize objects in different images.

✓ Stitch images together (panoramas).

✓ Enable augmented reality applications.

B. Key Components of Feature Matching

- **Feature Detection** – Identify important keypoints (corners, edges, blobs).
- **Feature Description** – Convert keypoints into numerical vectors for comparison.
- **Feature Matching** – Find similar descriptors between two images.

Now, let's explore SIFT, SURF, and ORB, three powerful methods for feature detection and description.

2. Scale-Invariant Feature Transform (SIFT)

A. Overview

SIFT was introduced by David Lowe in 1999 and is one of the most powerful feature detection techniques. It is designed to be scale-invariant and rotation-invariant, making it highly effective for matching features across images with different sizes and orientations.

B. How SIFT Works

- **Scale-Space Construction** – Images are blurred using a Gaussian filter to detect features at multiple scales.
- **Keypoint Localization** – Detect stable points using Difference of Gaussians (DoG).
- **Orientation Assignment** – Assign a dominant gradient direction to each keypoint.
- **Descriptor Computation** – Create a 128-dimensional vector based on local gradients.

C. Advantages of SIFT

✓ Highly accurate feature detection.

✓ Scale and rotation invariant, making it robust in different conditions.

✓ Works well in low-light and noisy images.

D. Implementing SIFT in OpenCV

```
import cv2
import matplotlib.pyplot as plt

# Load the image
image = cv2.imread('image.jpg', cv2.IMREAD_GRAYSCALE)

# Create SIFT detector
sift = cv2.SIFT_create()

# Detect keypoints and compute descriptors
keypoints, descriptors = sift.detectAndCompute(image, None)

# Draw keypoints on the image
image_with_keypoints = cv2.drawKeypoints(image, keypoints, None)

# Display the result
plt.imshow(image_with_keypoints, cmap='gray')
plt.show()
```

⬧ **Output**: Detected SIFT keypoints are displayed as circles.

◆ **Limitations of SIFT**

⊘ **Computationally expensive** – Not ideal for real-time applications.
⊘ **Patent restrictions** – SIFT was previously patented, making it unavailable in some libraries.

3. Speeded-Up Robust Features (SURF)

A. Overview

SURF was introduced in 2006 as a faster alternative to SIFT. It improves speed by approximating Laplacian of Gaussian (LoG) and using integral images for rapid computation.

B. How SURF Works

- **Hessian Matrix-Based Keypoint Detection** – Uses second-order derivatives for blob detection.
- **Orientation Assignment** – Determines a dominant direction for each keypoint.
- **Feature Descriptor Calculation** – Uses a 64-dimensional vector, making it faster than SIFT.

C. Advantages of SURF

✅ Faster than SIFT due to integral image computations.

✅ Robust to scale and rotation changes.

✅ Works well for real-time applications like object tracking.

D. Implementing SURF in OpenCV

(Note: OpenCV does not include SURF by default due to patent issues.)

```
import cv2

# Load image
image = cv2.imread('image.jpg', cv2.IMREAD_GRAYSCALE)

# Create SURF detector (requires OpenCV contrib module)
surf = cv2.xfeatures2d.SURF_create()

# Detect keypoints and compute descriptors
keypoints, descriptors = surf.detectAndCompute(image, None)

# Draw keypoints
image_with_keypoints = cv2.drawKeypoints(image, keypoints, None)

# Display image
cv2.imshow('SURF Keypoints', image_with_keypoints)
cv2.waitKey(0)
cv2.destroyAllWindows()
```

◆ **Limitations of SURF**

⊘ Still computationally heavy, though faster than SIFT.

⊘ Patented, restricting commercial use.

4. Oriented FAST and Rotated BRIEF (ORB)

A. Overview

ORB was introduced by Ethan Rublee in 2011 as an open-source alternative to SIFT and SURF. It is designed to be fast, efficient, and free of patent restrictions, making it ideal for real-time applications.

B. How ORB Works

- **Uses FAST for Keypoint Detection** – Detects corners quickly.
- **Applies BRIEF for Feature Description** – Converts keypoints into binary descriptors for efficient matching.
- **Adds Orientation Compensation** – Improves rotation invariance.

C. Advantages of ORB

✓ Fastest method, ideal for real-time applications.

✓ Open-source and free to use (no patents).

✓ Computationally efficient while maintaining good accuracy.

D. Implementing ORB in OpenCV

```
# Load image
image = cv2.imread('image.jpg', cv2.IMREAD_GRAYSCALE)

# Create ORB detector
orb = cv2.ORB_create()

# Detect keypoints and compute descriptors
keypoints, descriptors = orb.detectAndCompute(image, None)

# Draw keypoints
image_with_keypoints = cv2.drawKeypoints(image, keypoints, None)

# Display image
```

```
cv2.imshow('ORB Keypoints', image_with_keypoints)
cv2.waitKey(0)
cv2.destroyAllWindows()
```

◆ Limitations of ORB

⊘ Less accurate than SIFT/SURF for complex images.
⊘ Not fully scale-invariant (works best at fixed scales).

5. Comparing SIFT, SURF, and ORB

Feature	SIFT	SURF	ORB
Speed	Slow	Faster than SIFT	Fastest
Accuracy	High	Moderate	Lower than SIFT/SURF
Scale Invariance	Yes	Yes	Limited
Rotation Invariance	Yes	Yes	Yes
Computational Cost	High	Moderate	Low
Patented?	Previously patented	Yes (restricted)	No (free to use)
Best For	Object recognition, complex images	Fast detection, tracking	Real-time applications

When to Use Each Method?

- Use SIFT for high accuracy applications like medical imaging and object recognition.
- Use SURF for fast, robust feature detection in videos.
- Use ORB for real-time applications like mobile vision and AR.

SIFT, SURF, and ORB are essential feature detection techniques in computer vision. While SIFT and SURF provide superior accuracy, ORB is the best choice for real-time applications due to its speed and efficiency. Choosing the right method depends on the balance between accuracy, speed, and computational cost for your specific application.

4.4 Practical Applications of Feature Matching

Feature matching is a fundamental technique in computer vision that allows computers to identify, track, and compare objects across different images or video frames. By detecting and describing key features, algorithms like SIFT, SURF, and ORB can be used for various real-world applications, including image stitching, object recognition, augmented reality, and robotics.

In this chapter, we will explore some of the most impactful practical applications of feature matching and how they are used in real-world scenarios.

1. Image Stitching (Panorama Creation)

A. What is Image Stitching?

Image stitching is the process of combining multiple overlapping images to create a single wide-angle view, such as a panoramic photo.

B. How Feature Matching Helps

- Detect key features in each image using SIFT, SURF, or ORB.
- Match corresponding features across images.
- Align and blend the images to create a seamless panorama.

C. Example: Implementing Image Stitching in OpenCV

```
import cv2
import numpy as np

# Load images
image1 = cv2.imread('image1.jpg')
image2 = cv2.imread('image2.jpg')

# Convert to grayscale
gray1 = cv2.cvtColor(image1, cv2.COLOR_BGR2GRAY)
gray2 = cv2.cvtColor(image2, cv2.COLOR_BGR2GRAY)

# Use ORB to detect features
orb = cv2.ORB_create()
keypoints1, descriptors1 = orb.detectAndCompute(gray1, None)
keypoints2, descriptors2 = orb.detectAndCompute(gray2, None)
```

```
# Match features using Brute Force Matcher
bf = cv2.BFMatcher(cv2.NORM_HAMMING, crossCheck=True)
matches = bf.match(descriptors1, descriptors2)

# Sort matches based on distance
matches = sorted(matches, key=lambda x: x.distance)

# Draw matches
result = cv2.drawMatches(image1, keypoints1, image2, keypoints2, matches[:50],
None)

cv2.imshow('Feature Matching', result)
cv2.waitKey(0)
cv2.destroyAllWindows()
```

⬧ **Applications**: Used in Google Street View, drone mapping, and medical imaging.

2. Object Recognition and Classification

A. What is Object Recognition?

Object recognition involves identifying and classifying objects within an image using feature descriptors and machine learning models.

B. How Feature Matching Helps

- Extract key features from known objects in a database.
- Compare and match these features with objects in new images.
- Use feature similarity scores to classify the object.

C. Example: Recognizing a Logo in an Image

Feature matching is commonly used to recognize brand logos, signs, or specific objects in images.

```
# Load images
logo_template = cv2.imread('logo.jpg', 0)
scene_image = cv2.imread('scene.jpg', 0)

# Detect features using SIFT
```

```
sift = cv2.SIFT_create()
keypoints1, descriptors1 = sift.detectAndCompute(logo_template, None)
keypoints2, descriptors2 = sift.detectAndCompute(scene_image, None)

# Use FLANN-based matcher
flann = cv2.FlannBasedMatcher({'algorithm': 1, 'trees': 5}, {'checks': 50})
matches = flann.knnMatch(descriptors1, descriptors2, k=2)

# Apply ratio test
good_matches = []
for m, n in matches:
    if m.distance < 0.75 * n.distance:
        good_matches.append(m)

# Draw matches
result = cv2.drawMatches(logo_template, keypoints1, scene_image, keypoints2,
good_matches, None)

cv2.imshow('Object Recognition', result)
cv2.waitKey(0)
cv2.destroyAllWindows()
```

◆ **Applications**: Used in product recognition, industrial automation, and visual search engines.

3. Augmented Reality (AR) and Virtual Reality (VR)

A. What is Augmented Reality?

Augmented Reality (AR) overlays digital objects onto real-world environments, enhancing user experiences in gaming, retail, and education.

B. How Feature Matching Helps in AR

- Detect keypoints in the real-world scene.
- Match these keypoints with pre-stored models.
- Overlay 3D objects or animations onto detected keypoints.

C. Example: AR in Mobile Apps

Popular AR applications like Snapchat filters and Pokémon GO use feature matching to track facial features or surfaces to overlay animations.

◆ **Applications**: Used in AR navigation, real-time translation (Google Lens), and medical simulations.

4. Face Recognition and Biometrics

A. What is Face Recognition?

Face recognition systems identify individuals by comparing facial features with a stored database.

B. How Feature Matching Helps

- Detect key facial features (eyes, nose, mouth) using feature extractors.
- Compare detected features with stored face descriptors.
- Identify the person based on feature similarity.

C. Example: Implementing Face Recognition with ORB

```
import face_recognition
import cv2

# Load images
known_image = face_recognition.load_image_file("person1.jpg")
unknown_image = face_recognition.load_image_file("test_image.jpg")

# Encode faces
known_encoding = face_recognition.face_encodings(known_image)[0]
unknown_encoding = face_recognition.face_encodings(unknown_image)[0]

# Compare faces
results = face_recognition.compare_faces([known_encoding], unknown_encoding)

print("Match Found!" if results[0] else "No Match Found")
```

◆ **Applications**: Used in airport security, smartphone unlocking (Face ID), and surveillance systems.

5. Autonomous Vehicles and Robotics

A. How Feature Matching Helps Self-Driving Cars

- **Lane Detection** – Identify road lanes and boundaries.
- **Object Detection** – Recognize pedestrians, signs, and obstacles.
- **Navigation** – Match real-time camera input with pre-mapped features.

◆ **Example**: Tesla Autopilot and Google Waymo use feature matching for real-time decision-making.

◆ **Applications**: Used in robotic vision, drone navigation, and smart city traffic monitoring.

6. Medical Imaging and Diagnostics

A. How Feature Matching is Used in Healthcare

- **Tumor Detection** – Identify anomalies in MRI and CT scans.
- **X-ray Image Analysis** – Compare features of healthy and diseased tissues.
- **Surgical Assistance** – Track surgical instruments during robotic surgeries.

◆ **Example**: Feature matching helps detect Alzheimer's disease by comparing brain scans over time.

◆ **Applications**: Used in cancer detection, ophthalmology, and automated disease diagnosis.

7. Security and Forensics

A. How Feature Matching Helps in Criminal Investigations

- **Fingerprint Recognition** – Match fingerprints in forensic databases.
- **Forensic Image Analysis** – Compare crime scene photos to existing data.
- **License Plate Recognition (LPR)** – Identify vehicles from surveillance footage.

◆ **Example**: Interpol and FBI use feature matching for criminal identification and surveillance.

Feature matching is a powerful technique that extends far beyond basic image processing. From self-driving cars and augmented reality to medical imaging and forensics, feature matching enables intelligent systems to perceive and interact with the world.

5. Object Detection and Recognition

Object detection and recognition are at the heart of many computer vision applications, from facial recognition to autonomous driving. This chapter explores traditional object detection methods, including template matching, Haar cascades, and HOG (Histogram of Oriented Gradients), as well as feature-based recognition techniques. You'll learn how to identify and classify objects in images using machine learning-based approaches and understand the challenges of detecting objects in varying lighting, orientations, and occlusions. By mastering these techniques, you'll be equipped to build intelligent systems that can accurately detect and recognize objects in real-world scenarios.

5.1 Template Matching: Simple but Effective

Template matching is one of the simplest and most intuitive methods for object detection in images. It works by sliding a small reference image (template) over a larger target image to find regions that closely resemble the template. While template matching lacks the robustness of deep learning-based object detection techniques, it remains useful for industrial automation, quality control, and real-time tracking when dealing with fixed objects under controlled conditions.

In this chapter, we will explore how template matching works, its advantages and limitations, and practical applications with OpenCV.

1. How Template Matching Works

A. Basic Concept

Template matching follows these basic steps:

- **Select a Template** – Choose a smaller reference image (e.g., a company logo, a face, or a specific object).
- **Slide the Template Over the Target Image** – Compare the template against different regions in the larger image.
- **Compute Similarity Scores** – Measure how well the template matches different parts of the target image using similarity metrics.
- **Find the Best Match** – Identify the region where the similarity score is highest.

B. Common Similarity Metrics

There are several ways to measure the similarity between the template and different regions of the target image:

Method	Description	Best For
cv2.TM_CCOEFF	Measures correlation	General-purpose matching
cv2.TM_CCOEFF_NORMED	Normalized correlation coefficient	Scale-invariant matching
cv2.TM_CCORR	Measures raw correlation	Brightness-invariant matching
cv2.TM_CCORR_NORMED	Normalized correlation	Faster computations
cv2.TM_SQDIFF	Measures squared differences (lower is better)	Detecting exact matches
cv2.TM_SQDIFF_NORMED	Normalized squared difference	More robust comparisons

2. Implementing Template Matching in OpenCV

A. Basic Example

Let's implement a simple template matching algorithm using OpenCV in Python.

```
import cv2
import numpy as np

# Load target image and template
target_img = cv2.imread('target.jpg', cv2.IMREAD_GRAYSCALE)
template = cv2.imread('template.jpg', cv2.IMREAD_GRAYSCALE)

# Get template dimensions
w, h = template.shape[::-1]

# Perform template matching
result = cv2.matchTemplate(target_img, template, cv2.TM_CCOEFF_NORMED)

# Get the best match position
min_val, max_val, min_loc, max_loc = cv2.minMaxLoc(result)

# Draw a rectangle around the detected template
top_left = max_loc
bottom_right = (top_left[0] + w, top_left[1] + h)
cv2.rectangle(target_img, top_left, bottom_right, 255, 2)
```

```
# Display result
cv2.imshow('Template Matching', target_img)
cv2.waitKey(0)
cv2.destroyAllWindows()
```

◆ How It Works:

- The cv2.matchTemplate() function slides the template over the target image and computes similarity scores.
- The cv2.minMaxLoc() function finds the position of the highest similarity.
- A rectangle is drawn around the detected object.

3. Applications of Template Matching

A. Industrial Quality Control

- Defect detection in manufacturing (e.g., missing components in electronics).
- Verifying printed labels and barcodes in packaging.
- Checking product consistency in assembly lines.

◆ **Example**: A factory uses template matching to detect if a component is missing in an assembled circuit board.

B. Object Tracking in Robotics

- Identifying fixed-position objects in robotic vision.
- Detecting predefined parts for robotic arms in factories.

◆ **Example**: A robot arm identifies and picks up a specific type of screw or nut from a conveyor belt.

C. Document Scanning and Optical Character Recognition (OCR)

- Detecting specific words, signatures, or stamps in scanned documents.
- Locating form fields in automated data entry systems.

◆ **Example**: A bank scans checks and automatically identifies the signature area for verification.

D. Augmented Reality (AR) and Heads-Up Displays

- Identifying fixed icons in digital screens for AR applications.
- Overlaying information onto detected objects in smart glasses.

◆ **Example**: A car's heads-up display (HUD) recognizes speed limit signs and displays alerts.

E. Sports Analytics and Motion Tracking

- Detecting player positions in football or basketball.
- Tracking ball movement in tennis or table tennis.

◆ **Example**: A tennis replay system uses template matching to detect where the ball landed.

4. Strengths and Limitations of Template Matching

A. Advantages

✓ **Simple and Efficient** – Easy to implement with minimal computation.
✓ **Works Well for Fixed Objects** – Ideal for controlled environments.
✓ **Real-Time Capable** – Can run on low-power devices (e.g., Raspberry Pi, mobile phones).

B. Limitations

⊘ **Not Scale-Invariant** – Fails if the object size differs from the template.
⊘ **Rotation-Sensitive** – Can't detect rotated versions of the template.
⊘ **Lighting and Background Issues** – Fails under poor lighting or cluttered backgrounds.

5. Overcoming Limitations: Advanced Variants of Template Matching

Since traditional template matching struggles with scale, rotation, and lighting variations, several improved techniques have been developed:

A. Multi-Scale Template Matching

- Resize the template and match at multiple scales.
- Useful when the object can appear closer or farther in an image.

◆ **Example:**

```
for scale in np.linspace(0.5, 1.5, 10):  # Scale from 50% to 150%
    resized_template = cv2.resize(template, (0, 0), fx=scale, fy=scale)
    result = cv2.matchTemplate(target_img, resized_template,
cv2.TM_CCOEFF_NORMED)
```

B. Feature-Based Template Matching (SIFT/SURF/ORB)

- Instead of raw pixel comparison, extract key features and match them.
- Works even if the object is rotated or distorted.

◆ **Example**: Using ORB instead of traditional template matching:

```
orb = cv2.ORB_create()
keypoints1, descriptors1 = orb.detectAndCompute(template, None)
keypoints2, descriptors2 = orb.detectAndCompute(target_img, None)
```

C. Deep Learning-Based Template Matching (CNNs)

- Use a pre-trained Convolutional Neural Network (CNN) for feature extraction.
- More robust against lighting changes, distortions, and occlusions.

◆ **Example**: Use a deep learning model to detect a logo, instead of template matching.

```
from tensorflow.keras.models import load_model
model = load_model('object_detector.h5')
prediction = model.predict(target_img)
```

Template matching remains a powerful yet simple tool for object detection, particularly in industrial automation, robotics, and document scanning. While it is not as robust as deep learning-based techniques, it is fast, easy to implement, and works well for fixed objects under controlled conditions.

5.2 Histogram of Oriented Gradients (HOG) for Object Detection

Histogram of Oriented Gradients (HOG) is a widely used feature descriptor for object detection in computer vision. It extracts essential shape and structure information from an image by capturing the distribution of gradient orientations. HOG is particularly effective in detecting objects with well-defined edges, such as pedestrians, vehicles, and handwritten digits.

Unlike template matching, which relies on pixel-by-pixel comparison, HOG focuses on the gradient patterns in localized regions, making it robust to variations in lighting, scale, and minor deformations. In this chapter, we will explore how HOG works, its applications, and implement object detection using HOG and Support Vector Machines (SVMs).

1. How Histogram of Oriented Gradients (HOG) Works

A. Key Concept

HOG represents an image by computing the distribution of gradient orientations in localized regions, called cells. Instead of using raw pixel values, HOG captures the shape information of objects based on edge directions.

B. Steps in HOG Feature Extraction

- **Preprocessing the Image** – Convert the image to grayscale and normalize contrast.
- **Compute Image Gradients** – Apply the Sobel operator to compute the gradients (intensity changes) in both horizontal (x) and vertical (y) directions.
- **Divide Image into Cells** – The image is split into small regions (e.g., 8×8 pixel cells).
- **Compute Gradient Histograms** – Each cell generates a histogram of gradient orientations (e.g., 9 bins for 0° to 180°).
- **Block Normalization** – Combine multiple adjacent cells into a larger block (e.g., 2×2 cells) and normalize the gradient values to improve robustness against lighting changes.
- **Feature Vector Formation** – The final HOG descriptor is a concatenated vector of all block histograms, which can be used for object detection.

2. Implementing HOG in OpenCV

A. Computing HOG Descriptors in Python

```python
import cv2
import numpy as np
import matplotlib.pyplot as plt

# Load the image and convert to grayscale
image = cv2.imread('person.jpg', cv2.IMREAD_GRAYSCALE)

# Initialize HOG descriptor
hog = cv2.HOGDescriptor()

# Compute HOG features
hog_features = hog.compute(image)

# Display the original image
plt.imshow(image, cmap='gray')
plt.title("Original Image")
plt.axis("off")
plt.show()

print(f"HOG Descriptor Shape: {hog_features.shape}")
```

◆ **Explanation:**

- The cv2.HOGDescriptor() function initializes the HOG feature extractor.
- The hog.compute(image) function extracts the HOG feature vector from the image.
- The final output is a long feature vector that represents the object's shape.

3. Object Detection with HOG and SVM

A common approach for object detection is to use HOG as a feature extractor and then train a Support Vector Machine (SVM) to classify objects. The combination of HOG + SVM has been widely used for pedestrian detection, vehicle tracking, and face recognition.

A. HOG + SVM for Pedestrian Detection

```python
import cv2
```

```
# Initialize HOG descriptor and SVM-based pedestrian detector
hog = cv2.HOGDescriptor()
hog.setSVMDetector(cv2.HOGDescriptor_getDefaultPeopleDetector())

# Load the image
image = cv2.imread('pedestrians.jpg')

# Detect people in the image
rects, _ = hog.detectMultiScale(image, winStride=(4, 4), padding=(8, 8), scale=1.05)

# Draw rectangles around detected people
for (x, y, w, h) in rects:
    cv2.rectangle(image, (x, y), (x + w, y + h), (0, 255, 0), 2)

# Show the output
cv2.imshow("Pedestrian Detection", image)
cv2.waitKey(0)
cv2.destroyAllWindows()
```

◆ How It Works:

- The cv2.HOGDescriptor_getDefaultPeopleDetector() function loads a pre-trained SVM model for pedestrian detection.
- The hog.detectMultiScale() function scans the image at multiple scales and detects potential human figures.
- A bounding box is drawn around detected people.

4. Applications of HOG in Object Detection

A. Pedestrian Detection

- Used in self-driving cars, surveillance cameras, and traffic monitoring.
- Detects pedestrians in real-time to prevent accidents.

◆ **Example**: Tesla's Autopilot system uses HOG-based pedestrian detection as part of its vision pipeline.

B. Vehicle Detection

- Used in automated toll booths, parking management, and road safety systems.
- Identifies cars, trucks, and license plates.

◈ **Example**: HOG is used in traffic enforcement cameras to detect speeding vehicles.

C. Face Detection and Recognition

- Used in biometric authentication, emotion recognition, and security systems.
- HOG-based face descriptors help identify people in images.

◈ **Example**: Facebook's face recognition system once used HOG for feature extraction before switching to deep learning.

D. Handwritten Digit Recognition

- HOG features are widely used in Optical Character Recognition (OCR).
- Used to recognize digits in bank checks, invoices, and street signs.

◈ **Example**: The MNIST handwritten digit dataset is often classified using HOG + SVM.

5. Strengths and Limitations of HOG

A. Advantages

✓ **Rotation and Illumination Invariant** – Works well under different lighting conditions.
✓ **Good for Fixed Object Detection** – Performs well for detecting pedestrians, faces, and vehicles.
✓ **Less Data Required for Training** – Unlike deep learning models, HOG + SVM requires less training data.

B. Limitations

⊘ **Not Good for Complex Objects** – Struggles with objects that have high intra-class variations (e.g., animals).
⊘ **Slow Compared to Deep Learning** – HOG-based detection is slower than CNN-based methods like YOLO or Faster R-CNN.
⊘ **Does Not Handle Occlusions Well** – If a person is partially blocked, detection accuracy drops.

6. HOG vs. Deep Learning for Object Detection

Feature	HOG + SVM	Deep Learning (CNNs, YOLO, Faster R-CNN)
Accuracy	Good for simple objects	High for complex objects
Speed	Slower than CNNs	Faster (real-time detection)
Training Data Needed	Small datasets	Requires large labeled datasets
Robustness to Rotation & Occlusion	Limited	Handles complex variations well
Best Used For	Pedestrian detection, simple objects	Any object detection task

♦ **Future of Object Detection** – While HOG + SVM is still used in some real-world applications, most modern object detection systems are shifting towards deep learning-based approaches like YOLO, SSD, and Faster R-CNN for superior accuracy and efficiency.

Histogram of Oriented Gradients (HOG) is a powerful yet simple technique for object detection, particularly in pedestrian tracking, face recognition, and OCR. Although deep learning has surpassed HOG in accuracy and speed, HOG remains relevant for low-power devices and real-time applications where computational efficiency is important.

5.3 Viola-Jones Algorithm for Face Detection

The Viola-Jones Algorithm is one of the most well-known and historically significant methods for real-time face detection. Developed by Paul Viola and Michael Jones in 2001, it was the first framework capable of detecting faces in images and videos quickly and accurately, making it a foundation for modern facial recognition systems.

Unlike deep learning-based approaches, the Viola-Jones method does not require large datasets or GPUs, making it ideal for embedded systems and low-power devices. In this chapter, we will explore how the Viola-Jones algorithm works, its advantages and limitations, and how to implement it in OpenCV.

1. How the Viola-Jones Algorithm Works

The Viola-Jones face detection framework consists of four key steps:

- A. Haar-Like Features for Feature Extraction
- Instead of using raw pixels, Viola-Jones relies on Haar-like features, which are patterns of dark and light regions that resemble human facial structures.
- These features are computed using a box filter that sums pixel intensities in different regions and subtracts them to detect contrasts.

Common Haar-like features:

- **Edge Features** – Detects contrasts between bright and dark regions (e.g., eyes vs. cheeks).
- **Line Features** – Identifies horizontal and vertical patterns (e.g., nose bridge).
- **Four-Rectangle Features** – Detects complex patterns like eye pairs and eyebrows.

B. Integral Image for Fast Computation

- Computing Haar-like features using standard pixel summation is computationally expensive.
- To speed up the process, Viola-Jones introduces the Integral Image, which allows for rapid computation of rectangular region sums in constant time ($O(1)$ complexity).

C. AdaBoost for Feature Selection and Classification

- AdaBoost (Adaptive Boosting) is a machine learning technique used to select the most important features and build a strong classifier from weak ones.
- The system initially assigns equal weights to all Haar-like features and increases the weight of misclassified regions over multiple iterations to improve accuracy.
- The final classifier consists of a set of weak classifiers that work together to make accurate decisions.

D. Cascade Classifier for Fast Detection

- Instead of evaluating all features on every region of the image, Viola-Jones uses a cascade structure where simpler classifiers quickly discard non-face regions, and more complex classifiers analyze only promising candidates.
- This significantly speeds up detection since most non-face regions are eliminated in early stages.

2. Implementing Viola-Jones Face Detection in OpenCV

OpenCV provides a pre-trained Viola-Jones face detector that can be used to detect faces in images and real-time video feeds.

A. Face Detection in Images

```python
import cv2

# Load pre-trained Haar cascade classifier for face detection
face_cascade = cv2.CascadeClassifier(cv2.data.haarcascades +
'haarcascade_frontalface_default.xml')

# Read the image
image = cv2.imread('face.jpg')
gray = cv2.cvtColor(image, cv2.COLOR_BGR2GRAY)  # Convert to grayscale

# Detect faces in the image
faces = face_cascade.detectMultiScale(gray, scaleFactor=1.1, minNeighbors=5,
minSize=(30, 30))

# Draw rectangles around detected faces
for (x, y, w, h) in faces:
    cv2.rectangle(image, (x, y), (x + w, y + h), (0, 255, 0), 2)

# Display the result
cv2.imshow("Face Detection", image)
cv2.waitKey(0)
cv2.destroyAllWindows()
```

◆ **Explanation:**

- The cv2.CascadeClassifier() function loads a pre-trained face detector.
- The detectMultiScale() method scans the image at multiple scales to find faces.
- A bounding box is drawn around each detected face.

B. Real-Time Face Detection with Webcam

```python
import cv2
```

```
# Load pre-trained Haar cascade
face_cascade = cv2.CascadeClassifier(cv2.data.haarcascades +
'haarcascade_frontalface_default.xml')

# Start webcam
cap = cv2.VideoCapture(0)

while True:
    ret, frame = cap.read()
    gray = cv2.cvtColor(frame, cv2.COLOR_BGR2GRAY)

    # Detect faces
    faces = face_cascade.detectMultiScale(gray, scaleFactor=1.1, minNeighbors=5,
minSize=(30, 30))

    # Draw rectangles around faces
    for (x, y, w, h) in faces:
        cv2.rectangle(frame, (x, y), (x + w, y + h), (0, 255, 0), 2)

    cv2.imshow("Real-Time Face Detection", frame)

    # Press 'q' to exit
    if cv2.waitKey(1) & 0xFF == ord('q'):
        break

cap.release()
cv2.destroyAllWindows()
```

◆ How It Works:

- The program continuously captures frames from the webcam.
- Each frame is converted to grayscale and passed through the face detector.
- A green rectangle is drawn around detected faces.
- Press 'q' to stop the program.

3. Applications of Viola-Jones Face Detection

A. Security and Surveillance

- Used in CCTV cameras to detect faces in real-time.
- Helps identify intruders in restricted areas.

◆ **Example**: Airport security uses face detection for passport verification.

B. Biometric Authentication

- Used in face recognition-based login systems (e.g., smartphones, laptops).
- Provides contactless authentication in banking and ATMs.

◆ **Example**: Apple's Face ID uses advanced deep learning, but early versions relied on Viola-Jones.

C. Human-Computer Interaction

- Used in gesture recognition and eye tracking applications.
- Helps track user engagement in marketing analytics.

◆ **Example**: Social media apps apply face filters after detecting facial landmarks.

D. Emotion Detection and Healthcare

- Used to analyze facial expressions for mental health assessment.
- Helps detect drowsiness in drivers for accident prevention.

◆ **Example**: AI-based emotion recognition detects stress levels in video interviews.

4. Strengths and Limitations of Viola-Jones Algorithm

A. Advantages

✅ **Fast and Efficient** – Runs in real-time with minimal computational power.
✅ **Works on Low-Power Devices** – Suitable for embedded systems, mobile phones, and webcams.
✅ **Good for Fixed-Position Faces** – Effective for frontal face detection under controlled conditions.

B. Limitations

⊘ **Sensitive to Pose Variations** – Fails if the face is tilted, turned, or partially occluded.

⊘ **Not Robust to Lighting Changes** – Performance drops in poor lighting conditions.

⊘ **Struggles with Small Faces** – Cannot detect distant or low-resolution faces well.

⊘ **Limited to Face Detection, Not Recognition** – Cannot identify a person, only detect a face.

5. Viola-Jones vs. Deep Learning-Based Face Detection

Feature	Viola-Jones	Deep Learning (CNNs, YOLO, MTCNN)
Speed	Fast (real-time)	Slightly slower but real-time capable
Pose Sensitivity	Struggles with rotations	Handles different angles well
Lighting Robustness	Poor in low light	Performs well in various conditions
Accuracy	Moderate	High
Best Used For	Quick face detection in controlled settings	Complex face detection and recognition

◆ **Future of Face Detection**: Viola-Jones remains relevant for simple applications but is gradually being replaced by deep learning-based methods like YOLO, Faster R-CNN, and MTCNN, which offer better accuracy and robustness.

The Viola-Jones Algorithm revolutionized face detection by introducing a fast and efficient approach using Haar-like features, integral images, and a cascade classifier. While it has limitations, it remains a lightweight solution for real-time applications on embedded systems and mobile devices.

5.4 Combining Classical Methods with Deep Learning

The evolution of computer vision has seen a significant shift from classical techniques like HOG, SIFT, and Viola-Jones to powerful deep learning-based models such as CNNs, YOLO, and Vision Transformers (ViTs). However, while deep learning offers superior accuracy and flexibility, classical methods still play a crucial role in preprocessing, feature engineering, and improving model efficiency.

Instead of replacing classical techniques entirely, a hybrid approach that combines traditional methods with deep learning can lead to more robust, efficient, and interpretable computer vision systems. In this chapter, we will explore why and how classical methods can complement deep learning models, discuss real-world applications, and implement a hybrid face recognition system using OpenCV and deep learning.

1. Why Combine Classical Methods with Deep Learning?

Deep learning models are data-driven and require large labeled datasets to perform well. Classical methods, on the other hand, are rule-based and can extract meaningful features even from limited data. Combining the two approaches provides several advantages:

A. Improved Efficiency

- Classical methods like HOG, SIFT, and Edge Detection can be used to pre-process images, reducing the input size and complexity for deep learning models.
- This speeds up computation and reduces memory usage, making it useful for edge devices and embedded systems.

B. Enhanced Interpretability

- Deep learning models are often considered black boxes, making it difficult to understand their decision-making process.
- Classical feature extraction (e.g., HOG descriptors, keypoints from SIFT) can be visualized, helping to interpret deep learning outputs.

C. Handling Low-Data Scenarios

- When training data is scarce, classical methods can generate meaningful features that deep learning can learn from.
- Transfer learning combined with traditional techniques can improve performance in low-data environments.

D. Improved Generalization

- Classical techniques are often more robust to variations in lighting, rotation, and scale.
- Integrating classical pre-processing with deep learning improves generalization in real-world applications.

2. Real-World Applications of Hybrid Approaches

A. Face Detection and Recognition

Viola-Jones or HOG can be used for initial face detection, reducing the search space for deep learning-based face recognition models like FaceNet or DeepFace.

◆ **Example**: Facebook's early face recognition system used Viola-Jones for detection and deep learning for recognition.

B. License Plate Recognition (LPR)

Edge detection and morphological operations can enhance license plate segmentation before using a deep learning-based OCR (Optical Character Recognition) model.

◆ **Example**: Automated traffic cameras use HOG for plate localization and CNNs for character recognition.

C. Medical Image Analysis

Classical methods like histogram equalization enhance contrast in X-rays and MRI scans, improving deep learning model accuracy.

◆ **Example**: Cancer detection in radiology benefits from classical image pre-processing techniques before CNN-based classification.

D. Object Tracking in Videos

Feature-based tracking (e.g., SIFT, ORB) can be used to track objects between frames, reducing computational load for deep learning-based trackers.

◆ **Example**: Autonomous vehicles use a combination of optical flow, Kalman filters, and deep learning-based object detection to track moving objects.

3. Implementing a Hybrid Face Recognition System

We will now implement a hybrid approach for face recognition that uses:

- Viola-Jones (Haar cascades) for face detection
- Deep Learning (OpenCV DNN module) for face recognition

Step 1: Install Required Libraries

```
pip install opencv-python numpy
```

Step 2: Load Pre-Trained Models for Detection & Recognition

```python
import cv2
import numpy as np

# Load pre-trained Haar cascade for face detection
face_cascade = cv2.CascadeClassifier(cv2.data.haarcascades +
'haarcascade_frontalface_default.xml')

# Load deep learning-based face recognition model
recognition_model = cv2.dnn.readNetFromTorch('openface_nn4.small2.v1.t7')

# Load a sample image
image = cv2.imread('person.jpg')
gray = cv2.cvtColor(image, cv2.COLOR_BGR2GRAY)

# Detect faces using Haar cascade
faces = face_cascade.detectMultiScale(gray, scaleFactor=1.1, minNeighbors=5,
minSize=(30, 30))

for (x, y, w, h) in faces:
    # Extract face ROI
    face = image[y:y+h, x:x+w]

    # Preprocess for deep learning model
    blob = cv2.dnn.blobFromImage(face, scalefactor=1.0/255, size=(96, 96), mean=(0, 0,
0), swapRB=True, crop=False)
    recognition_model.setInput(blob)

    # Get face embedding (128-d feature vector)
    face_embedding = recognition_model.forward()

    # Draw rectangle around detected face
    cv2.rectangle(image, (x, y), (x + w, y + h), (0, 255, 0), 2)

# Display results
cv2.imshow("Hybrid Face Recognition", image)
cv2.waitKey(0)
```

cv2.destroyAllWindows()

◆ How It Works:

- Viola-Jones detects faces, reducing search space for the deep learning model.
- The face is cropped and preprocessed for the deep learning model.
- The model extracts face embeddings, which can be used for recognition.

4. Classical vs. Deep Learning: When to Use What?

Feature	Classical Methods (HOG, SIFT, Viola-Jones)	Deep Learning (CNNs, YOLO, Transformers)
Speed	Faster on low-power devices	Slower but optimized with GPUs
Data Requirement	Works well with small datasets	Needs large labeled datasets
Robustness	Sensitive to noise and lighting	More robust to variations
Feature Engineering	Hand-crafted features	Automatically learns features
Best For	Edge devices, quick detection	High-accuracy recognition tasks

When to Use Hybrid Methods?

✅ **Low-Power Devices** – Use classical methods for pre-processing before passing to a CNN.

✅ **Small Datasets** – Use feature descriptors (HOG, SIFT) before training a deep model.

✅ **Real-Time Applications** – Use cascade classifiers to filter non-relevant regions before deep learning inference.

Instead of viewing classical methods and deep learning as competing approaches, the best results are often achieved by combining them. Hybrid systems leverage the speed, interpretability, and efficiency of classical methods with the accuracy, scalability, and robustness of deep learning.

6. Geometric Transformations & 3D Vision

Computer vision isn't just about recognizing objects in 2D images—it also involves understanding spatial relationships and depth. This chapter explores geometric transformations, such as scaling, rotation, translation, and perspective warping, which are essential for image alignment and manipulation. You'll also dive into the fundamentals of 3D vision, including stereo vision, depth estimation, structure from motion (SfM), and camera calibration, which allow machines to perceive depth and reconstruct 3D scenes from 2D images. By the end of this chapter, you'll have a strong grasp of how geometric transformations and depth perception enable AI to interpret the world in three dimensions.

6.1 Homography: Understanding Perspective Transformation

In computer vision, homography plays a crucial role in understanding how different views of the same scene relate to each other. Homography is a mathematical transformation that describes how a 2D plane in one image can be mapped to another 2D plane in a different image, even when viewed from different perspectives. This transformation is widely used in applications such as image stitching, augmented reality (AR), robotics, and 3D reconstruction.

In this chapter, we will explore the concept of homography, how it is mathematically formulated, and how we can apply it to transform images and align different perspectives. Finally, we will implement homography in OpenCV to warp an image from one perspective to another.

1. What is Homography?

Homography is a transformation matrix (H) that establishes a relationship between two images of the same planar surface taken from different viewpoints. This transformation allows us to correct distortions caused by perspective changes.

A. When is Homography Used?

Homography is applicable when:

✅ The transformation occurs within the same planar surface (e.g., a painting on a wall, a book cover).

☑ The camera undergoes rotation, translation, or viewpoint change, but the object remains flat.

☑ We need to align, warp, or rectify an image from one perspective to another.

◆ Example Applications:

- **Image stitching (Panoramas)** – Aligning overlapping images to create a single wide image.
- **Augmented Reality (AR)** – Overlaying virtual objects onto real-world scenes.
- **Rectifying Images** – Correcting perspective distortions (e.g., making a tilted document appear upright).
- **Object Tracking** – Recognizing objects despite changes in viewpoint.

2. Mathematical Formulation of Homography

The homography matrix (H) is a 3×3 transformation matrix that maps points from one image to another using the equation:

$$\begin{bmatrix} x' \\ y' \\ w' \end{bmatrix} = H \cdot \begin{bmatrix} x \\ y \\ w \end{bmatrix}$$

where:

- (x, y) are the original coordinates.

- (x', y') are the transformed coordinates.

- H is the **homography matrix** of size 3×3.

- The extra term w is for **homogeneous coordinates**, which allow affine and perspective transformations.

A. The Homography Matrix

The **homography matrix** is defined as:

$$H = \begin{bmatrix} h_{11} & h_{12} & h_{13} \\ h_{21} & h_{22} & h_{23} \\ h_{31} & h_{32} & h_{33} \end{bmatrix}$$

The matrix contains eight unknown parameters (since it is defined up to a scale factor). These values are computed using at least four corresponding points between two images.

B. How Homography Works

To compute the homography matrix:

1. **Select at least four pairs of corresponding points** between two images.

2. **Solve for the unknown parameters** of H using a **system of linear equations**.

3. **Apply the transformation** to warp one image into the perspective of the other.

3. Computing Homography in OpenCV

A. Manually Selecting Corresponding Points

Let's take an image of a book and warp it to appear as if it is viewed from the front.

```
import cv2
import numpy as np

# Load the image
image = cv2.imread("book.jpg")

# Define four points in the original image (clockwise from top-left)
pts_src = np.array([[120, 40], [500, 60], [510, 380], [80, 420]])

# Define the corresponding points in the rectified (top-down) view
pts_dst = np.array([[0, 0], [400, 0], [400, 300], [0, 300]])

# Compute the homography matrix
```

```
H, status = cv2.findHomography(pts_src, pts_dst)

# Warp the perspective
warped_image = cv2.warpPerspective(image, H, (400, 300))

# Display results
cv2.imshow("Original Image", image)
cv2.imshow("Warped Image", warped_image)
cv2.waitKey(0)
cv2.destroyAllWindows()
```

◆ **Explanation:**

- We define four points on the book in the original image.
- We define their corresponding points in a rectified view.
- OpenCV's findHomography() computes the H matrix.
- warpPerspective() applies the transformation.

B. Automatic Homography with Feature Matching

Instead of manually selecting points, we can use SIFT (Scale-Invariant Feature Transform) to automatically detect and match key points between two images.

```
import cv2
import numpy as np

# Load images
img1 = cv2.imread("image1.jpg", 0)  # Reference image
img2 = cv2.imread("image2.jpg", 0)  # Target image

# Use SIFT to find keypoints and descriptors
sift = cv2.SIFT_create()
keypoints1, descriptors1 = sift.detectAndCompute(img1, None)
keypoints2, descriptors2 = sift.detectAndCompute(img2, None)

# Match features using FLANN-based matcher
index_params = dict(algorithm=1, trees=5)
search_params = dict(checks=50)
flann = cv2.FlannBasedMatcher(index_params, search_params)
matches = flann.knnMatch(descriptors1, descriptors2, k=2)
```

```
# Apply ratio test
good_matches = []
for m, n in matches:
    if m.distance < 0.75 * n.distance:
        good_matches.append(m)

# Extract matched points
src_pts = np.float32([keypoints1[m.queryIdx].pt for m in good_matches]).reshape(-1, 1, 2)
dst_pts = np.float32([keypoints2[m.trainIdx].pt for m in good_matches]).reshape(-1, 1, 2)

# Compute homography
H, mask = cv2.findHomography(src_pts, dst_pts, cv2.RANSAC, 5.0)

# Warp image
height, width = img1.shape
aligned_image = cv2.warpPerspective(img2, H, (width, height))

# Display results
cv2.imshow("Aligned Image", aligned_image)
cv2.waitKey(0)
cv2.destroyAllWindows()
```

◆ **How It Works:**

- SIFT detects keypoints in both images.
- Feature matching finds corresponding points.
- Homography is computed using RANSAC to remove incorrect matches.
- The second image is warped to align with the first.

4. Applications of Homography in Computer Vision

A. Image Stitching (Panoramas)

- Align overlapping images to create seamless panoramic views.
- Used in Google Street View, drone mapping, and 360° photography.

B. Augmented Reality (AR)

- Overlay digital objects onto real-world surfaces.
- Used in apps like Pokémon GO, Snapchat filters, and virtual try-ons.

C. Camera Calibration & Rectification

- Correct camera distortions by warping images into standard perspectives.
- Essential for robotics, medical imaging, and forensic analysis.

D. Document Scanning & OCR

- Convert tilted photos of documents into flat, readable images.
- Used in mobile scanner apps (e.g., CamScanner, Adobe Scan).

Homography is a powerful transformation that allows us to correct perspective distortions, align images, and enable AR applications. By leveraging manual point selection, feature matching, and OpenCV functions, we can apply homography to real-world problems like image stitching, face alignment, and object tracking.

6.2 Stereo Vision: Depth Perception with Multiple Cameras

Human vision allows us to perceive depth using our two eyes, which capture slightly different views of the world. This phenomenon, known as stereopsis, is the basis of stereo vision in computer vision. By using two or more cameras placed at different positions, we can reconstruct 3D depth information from 2D images. This capability is crucial in applications such as autonomous vehicles, robotics, augmented reality (AR), and medical imaging.

In this chapter, we will explore how stereo vision works, the mathematics behind depth estimation, and how to implement stereo vision using OpenCV. By the end, you will understand how to extract depth maps and reconstruct 3D scenes from stereo image pairs.

1. What is Stereo Vision?

Stereo vision is a technique for estimating depth by analyzing the differences between two images taken from slightly different viewpoints. These two images, captured by left and right cameras, simulate human binocular vision. By comparing corresponding points in both images, we can compute the disparity (shift between the points), which helps determine depth.

◆ **Example Applications:**

✅ **Autonomous Vehicles**: Detect obstacles and estimate distances.
✅ **Robotics**: Help robots navigate and interact with objects.
✅ **3D Reconstruction**: Convert 2D images into 3D models.
✅ **Augmented Reality (AR):** Place virtual objects in a real-world 3D space.

2. How Does Stereo Vision Work?

A. Disparity and Depth Estimation

Disparity is the horizontal shift between corresponding points in the left and right images. The relationship between disparity and depth is given by the equation:

$$Z = \frac{fB}{d}$$

Where:

- Z = Depth of the object (distance from the camera)

- f = Focal length of the camera

- B = Baseline (distance between the two cameras)

- d = Disparity (difference in pixel coordinates between the left and right images)

B. Stereo Camera Setup

For stereo vision, two cameras are positioned side by side, separated by a fixed baseline (B). Each camera captures a slightly different image.

◆ **Key Steps in Stereo Vision:**

- **Camera Calibration** – Ensure cameras are aligned and undistorted.
- **Stereo Rectification** – Align images so corresponding points lie on the same scanline.

- **Feature Matching** – Find corresponding points in both images.
- **Disparity Map Computation** – Calculate pixel shifts between the images.
- **Depth Estimation** – Convert disparity values to depth information.

3. Implementing Stereo Vision in OpenCV

A. Stereo Camera Calibration

Before computing depth, we must calibrate the cameras to remove lens distortions and align them correctly.

```
import cv2
import numpy as np

# Load images from stereo cameras
img_left = cv2.imread("left.jpg", 0)  # Left camera image
img_right = cv2.imread("right.jpg", 0)  # Right camera image

# Define chessboard size for calibration
chessboard_size = (9, 6)  # 9x6 grid of squares

# Prepare object points
obj_points = []
img_points_left = []
img_points_right = []

objp = np.zeros((chessboard_size[0] * chessboard_size[1], 3), np.float32)
objp[:, :2] = np.mgrid[0:chessboard_size[0], 0:chessboard_size[1]].T.reshape(-1, 2)

# Detect chessboard corners
ret_left, corners_left = cv2.findChessboardCorners(img_left, chessboard_size, None)
ret_right, corners_right = cv2.findChessboardCorners(img_right, chessboard_size, None)

if ret_left and ret_right:
    img_points_left.append(corners_left)
    img_points_right.append(corners_right)
    obj_points.append(objp)

# Calibrate both cameras
```

```
ret, mtxL, distL, _, _ = cv2.calibrateCamera(obj_points, img_points_left,
img_left.shape[::-1], None, None)
ret, mtxR, distR, _, _ = cv2.calibrateCamera(obj_points, img_points_right,
img_right.shape[::-1], None, None)

# Stereo calibration
criteria = (cv2.TERM_CRITERIA_EPS + cv2.TERM_CRITERIA_MAX_ITER, 30, 0.001)
_, _, _, _, _, R, T, _, _ = cv2.stereoCalibrate(
    obj_points, img_points_left, img_points_right, mtxL, distL, mtxR, distR,
img_left.shape[::-1],
    criteria=criteria
)

# Stereo rectification
R1, R2, P1, P2, Q, _, _ = cv2.stereoRectify(mtxL, distL, mtxR, distR, img_left.shape[::-1], R, T)

print("Stereo Calibration Complete!")
```

◆ What This Does:

- Detects a chessboard to find corresponding points.
- Calibrates both cameras to remove distortion.
- Computes the rotation (R) and translation (T) matrices.

B. Computing the Disparity Map

Once the cameras are calibrated, we can compute the disparity map, which shows how much each pixel shifts between the left and right images.

```
# Load stereo images
imgL = cv2.imread("left.jpg", 0)  # Left camera image
imgR = cv2.imread("right.jpg", 0)  # Right camera image

# Create Stereo Block Matcher
stereo = cv2.StereoBM_create(numDisparities=64, blockSize=15)

# Compute disparity map
disparity_map = stereo.compute(imgL, imgR)
```

```
# Normalize for visualization
disparity_map = cv2.normalize(disparity_map, None, alpha=0, beta=255,
norm_type=cv2.NORM_MINMAX)
disparity_map = np.uint8(disparity_map)

# Display results
cv2.imshow("Disparity Map", disparity_map)
cv2.waitKey(0)
cv2.destroyAllWindows()
```

◆ Explanation:

- StereoBM_create() initializes block matching, a method to find pixel correspondences.
- The disparity map highlights objects at different depths.
- Brighter regions are closer, darker regions are farther away.

C. Converting Disparity Map to Depth Map

To convert disparity into actual depth (Z), we use the equation:

```
# Compute depth map
focal_length = 700  # Camera-specific value
baseline = 0.1  # Distance between cameras (in meters)

depth_map = (focal_length * baseline) / (disparity_map + 1e-6)  # Avoid division by zero

cv2.imshow("Depth Map", depth_map.astype(np.uint8))
cv2.waitKey(0)
cv2.destroyAllWindows()
```

◆ What This Does:

- Uses the stereo vision formula to compute depth.
- Objects with higher disparity values appear closer, and those with lower disparity appear farther.

4. Applications of Stereo Vision
A. Self-Driving Cars 🚗

- Used in LiDAR alternatives to detect pedestrians, obstacles, and road signs.
- Tesla's Vision-based Autopilot relies on stereo cameras.

B. Robotics & Drones □

- Stereo vision helps robots navigate and avoid obstacles.
- Drones use it for 3D mapping and terrain analysis.

C. Augmented Reality (AR) 🎮

- Depth perception is crucial for placing virtual objects into real-world environments.
- Used in Apple's Face ID and ARKit for accurate depth sensing.

D. Medical Imaging ⊕

- 3D stereo endoscopy allows surgeons to view depth inside the human body.

Stereo vision enables machines to perceive depth just like humans. By using two cameras, we can estimate 3D depth information, making it essential for autonomous vehicles, robotics, and AR applications.

6.3 Structure from Motion (SfM): Reconstructing 3D from 2D

Imagine you take multiple pictures of an object or a scene from different angles. With the right algorithms, you can reconstruct a 3D model from these 2D images. This process is known as Structure from Motion (SfM), a powerful technique in computer vision that estimates the 3D structure of a scene from a sequence of 2D images taken from different viewpoints.

SfM is widely used in applications such as 3D mapping, drone-based surveys, augmented reality (AR), virtual reality (VR), and photogrammetry. Unlike stereo vision, which relies on two fixed cameras, SfM works with an unstructured set of images captured from multiple angles, making it more flexible and scalable.

In this chapter, we will explore the principles of SfM, key mathematical concepts, and practical implementations using OpenCV and COLMAP to reconstruct 3D models from 2D images.

1. What is Structure from Motion (SfM)?

Structure from Motion (SfM) is a computer vision technique that estimates camera motion (pose) and the 3D structure of a scene from a series of 2D images.

◆ Key Goals of SfM:

✅ Reconstruct a 3D model from multiple 2D images.

✅ Estimate camera positions and orientations (extrinsic parameters).

✅ Determine the 3D location of feature points in the scene.

◆ How is SfM Different from Stereo Vision?

Feature	Structure from Motion (SfM)	Stereo Vision
Camera Setup	Single moving camera (or multiple images)	Two fixed cameras
Input	Unordered set of images	Two simultaneous images
Depth Estimation	From multiple viewpoints	From a stereo pair
Applications	3D reconstruction, mapping	Autonomous vehicles, real-time depth sensing

2. Key Steps in SfM Pipeline

Step 1: Feature Detection and Matching

The first step in SfM is detecting keypoints (features) in the images and matching them across different views. Common feature detectors include:

- **SIFT** (Scale-Invariant Feature Transform)
- **SURF** (Speeded-Up Robust Features)
- **ORB** (Oriented FAST and Rotated BRIEF)

◆ **Example**: Detecting and Matching Features in OpenCV

```
import cv2
import numpy as np

# Load two images taken from different angles
```

```
img1 = cv2.imread("image1.jpg", 0)  # First view
img2 = cv2.imread("image2.jpg", 0)  # Second view

# Initialize SIFT detector
sift = cv2.SIFT_create()

# Detect keypoints and descriptors
kp1, des1 = sift.detectAndCompute(img1, None)
kp2, des2 = sift.detectAndCompute(img2, None)

# Use FLANN-based matcher
index_params = dict(algorithm=1, trees=5)
search_params = dict(checks=50)
flann = cv2.FlannBasedMatcher(index_params, search_params)

# Find matches
matches = flann.knnMatch(des1, des2, k=2)

# Apply ratio test
good_matches = []
for m, n in matches:
    if m.distance < 0.75 * n.distance:
        good_matches.append(m)

# Draw matches
matched_img = cv2.drawMatches(img1, kp1, img2, kp2, good_matches, None)

cv2.imshow("Feature Matching", matched_img)
cv2.waitKey(0)
cv2.destroyAllWindows()
```

◆ **What This Does:**

- Detects keypoints in both images.
- Matches features using FLANN-based matching.
- Filters good matches using Lowe's ratio test.

Step 2: Estimating Camera Motion (Essential & Fundamental Matrix)

Once we have matching points across images, we estimate camera motion (rotation & translation) using the essential matrix (E) and fundamental matrix (F).

$$E = K^T F K$$

Where:

- E (Essential matrix) describes the relationship between points in two images with known camera parameters.
- F (Fundamental matrix) relates points between two views without requiring camera parameters.
- K is the **intrinsic matrix** of the camera.

◆ **Computing Essential Matrix in OpenCV**

```
# Convert keypoints to numpy arrays
pts1 = np.float32([kp1[m.queryIdx].pt for m in good_matches])
pts2 = np.float32([kp2[m.trainIdx].pt for m in good_matches])

# Camera matrix (intrinsic parameters)
K = np.array([[fx, 0, cx], [0, fy, cy], [0, 0, 1]])  # Replace fx, fy, cx, cy with actual values

# Compute Essential matrix
E, mask = cv2.findEssentialMat(pts1, pts2, K, method=cv2.RANSAC, prob=0.999, threshold=1.0)

# Recover camera pose (rotation and translation)
_, R, t, _ = cv2.recoverPose(E, pts1, pts2, K)

print("Rotation Matrix:\n", R)
print("Translation Vector:\n", t)
```

◆ **What This Does:**

- Computes the Essential matrix (E) using RANSAC.
- Extracts the rotation (R) and translation (t) of the camera.

Step 3: Triangulation – Reconstructing 3D Points

After computing the camera motion, we reconstruct the 3D coordinates of matched points using triangulation.

$$\mathbf{X} = DLT(P_1, P_2, x_1, x_2)$$

Where:

- X = 3D point
- P_1, P_2 = Camera projection matrices
- x_1, x_2 = Corresponding 2D points in each image

◆ **Computing 3D Points with OpenCV**

```
# Convert rotation and translation to projection matrices
P1 = np.hstack((np.eye(3), np.zeros((3, 1))))  # First camera (Identity matrix)
P2 = np.hstack((R, t))  # Second camera (Pose estimated from Essential matrix)

# Triangulate points
points_4D = cv2.triangulatePoints(P1, P2, pts1.T, pts2.T)

# Convert to homogeneous coordinates
points_3D = points_4D / points_4D[3]

print("3D Points:\n", points_3D[:3].T)
```

◆ **What This Does:**

- Computes 3D points from 2D matches using triangulation.
- Converts 4D homogeneous coordinates to 3D.

Step 4: Bundle Adjustment – Refining the 3D Model

To improve accuracy, we use Bundle Adjustment (BA), which optimizes the camera parameters and 3D points by minimizing reprojection errors.

Popular Libraries for SfM:

- COLMAP (Most widely used for 3D reconstruction)
- OpenMVG (Modular SfM pipeline)
- Theia SfM (Robust and scalable)

To run COLMAP for SfM:

colmap automatic_reconstructor --image_path images/ --workspace_path output/

5. Applications of SfM

A. 3D Mapping and Photogrammetry

Used in Google Earth, drone surveys, and GIS mapping.

B. Virtual and Augmented Reality (VR/AR)

Helps create 3D environments from real-world images.

C. Cultural Heritage & 3D Scanning

Used for museum artifact preservation and historical site reconstruction.

D. Robotics and Autonomous Navigation

Helps robots perceive depth and reconstruct 3D scenes.

Structure from Motion (SfM) is a powerful technique that enables 3D reconstruction from multiple 2D images. By leveraging feature matching, camera motion estimation, triangulation, and bundle adjustment, we can build accurate 3D models of real-world environments.

6.4 Augmented Reality and SLAM (Simultaneous Localization and Mapping)

Imagine holding up your smartphone and seeing virtual objects seamlessly placed into the real world—this is Augmented Reality (AR). Now, imagine a self-driving car navigating through a city, continuously updating its position while creating a real-time 3D map of its surroundings—this is Simultaneous Localization and Mapping (SLAM).

Both AR and SLAM rely heavily on computer vision techniques to understand and interact with the physical world. SLAM enables devices to localize themselves in an unknown environment while building a map of it at the same time. This capability is crucial for AR, robotics, self-driving cars, and drone navigation.

In this chapter, we will explore:

✓ How Augmented Reality (AR) works and its relationship with SLAM.

✓ The principles behind Visual SLAM (vSLAM).

✓ Implementing AR and SLAM using OpenCV and Open-source frameworks.

1. What is Augmented Reality (AR)?

Augmented Reality (AR) overlays digital content (images, text, 3D objects) onto the real-world environment in real time. Unlike Virtual Reality (VR), which creates a fully digital world, AR enhances reality by blending virtual elements with the physical world.

A. Components of an AR System

- **Camera & Sensors** – Captures the environment in real time.
- **Computer Vision Algorithms** – Understands the environment (e.g., depth estimation, feature detection).
- **Rendering Engine** – Places virtual objects onto the real world.
- **Display Device** – Shows the AR experience (smartphone, AR glasses, etc.).

B. AR Techniques

✦ **Marker-Based AR** – Uses predefined QR codes or fiducial markers to track objects.

✦ **Markerless AR** – Uses feature detection and SLAM to overlay objects in real-time.

✦ **Plane Detection AR** – Detects real-world surfaces for object placement (used in ARKit, ARCore).

✦ **Projection-Based AR** – Projects digital images onto physical surfaces.

◆ **Examples of AR Applications:**

✅ **Pokémon GO** – Places virtual creatures in the real world.

✅ **IKEA Place** – Allows users to place virtual furniture in their homes.

✅ **Microsoft HoloLens** – Projects holograms into real environments.

2. What is SLAM (Simultaneous Localization and Mapping)?

SLAM is a fundamental technique that allows a device to:

✅ Localize itself in an unknown environment (knowing where it is).

✅ Build a map of the surroundings in real-time.

SLAM is used in:

- **Autonomous vehicles** – Helps self-driving cars navigate roads.
- **Robotics** – Enables robots to move autonomously.
- **Drones** – Assists in obstacle avoidance and navigation.
- **Augmented Reality** – Tracks a device's position in space.

A. Types of SLAM

- **Lidar SLAM** – Uses LiDAR sensors for mapping (used in self-driving cars).
- **Visual SLAM (vSLAM)** – Uses cameras to track motion (used in AR & drones).
- **RGB-D SLAM** – Uses depth sensors (e.g., Kinect, Intel RealSense).

B. Key Components of SLAM

Component	Function
Feature Extraction	Detects key points in the environment (SIFT, ORB, SURF).
Motion Estimation	Tracks movement over time.
Map Construction	Builds a 3D model of the surroundings.
Loop Closure	Corrects errors by recognizing previously visited locations.

3. How Visual SLAM (vSLAM) Works

vSLAM relies solely on camera-based input to track movement and construct a 3D map. It follows these steps:

- **Step 1: Feature Detection** – Extracts key points from camera frames (SIFT, ORB, FAST).
- **Step 2: Feature Matching** – Matches key points between consecutive frames.
- **Step 3: Pose Estimation** – Computes the camera's position and orientation.
- **Step 4: Mapping** – Builds a 3D model of the environment.
- **Step 5: Loop Closure** – Corrects errors when revisiting previous locations.

4. Implementing SLAM in OpenCV

A. Feature Detection for SLAM

We start by extracting features from images for tracking.

```python
import cv2
import numpy as np

# Load video or camera feed
cap = cv2.VideoCapture("slam_video.mp4")

# Initialize ORB detector
orb = cv2.ORB_create()

while cap.isOpened():
    ret, frame = cap.read()
    if not ret:
        break

    # Convert to grayscale
    gray = cv2.cvtColor(frame, cv2.COLOR_BGR2GRAY)

    # Detect keypoints
    keypoints, descriptors = orb.detectAndCompute(gray, None)

    # Draw keypoints
    frame_keypoints = cv2.drawKeypoints(gray, keypoints, None, color=(0, 255, 0))

    cv2.imshow("Feature Detection for SLAM", frame_keypoints)
    if cv2.waitKey(1) & 0xFF == ord("q"):
        break
```

```
cap.release()
cv2.destroyAllWindows()
```

◆ What This Does:

✓ Captures video frames.

✓ Detects ORB features (used in vSLAM).

✓ Draws keypoints on each frame.

B. Camera Pose Estimation in SLAM

To estimate camera motion, we compute the Essential Matrix.

```
# Assume we have matching keypoints from two frames
pts1 = np.float32([kp1[m.queryIdx].pt for m in good_matches])
pts2 = np.float32([kp2[m.trainIdx].pt for m in good_matches])

# Compute Essential Matrix
E, mask = cv2.findEssentialMat(pts1, pts2, K, method=cv2.RANSAC, threshold=1.0)

# Recover Pose (Rotation & Translation)
_, R, t, _ = cv2.recoverPose(E, pts1, pts2, K)

print("Rotation Matrix:\n", R)
print("Translation Vector:\n", t)
```

◆ What This Does:

✓ Computes the Essential Matrix (E) to find relative camera motion.

✓ Extracts rotation (R) and translation (t).

5. AR and SLAM in Real-World Applications
A. Augmented Reality Platforms

- **ARKit (Apple)** – iOS-based AR framework.
- **ARCore (Google)** – Android-based AR SDK.
- **Vuforia** – Third-party AR SDK for mobile and AR glasses.

B. SLAM Frameworks

- **ORB-SLAM2** – Open-source SLAM system using ORB features.
- **RTAB-Map** – Real-time 3D SLAM system.
- **Cartographer (Google)** – Lidar-based SLAM for robotics.

C. Robotics & Autonomous Vehicles

- SLAM is used in self-driving cars (Tesla, Waymo) to navigate.
- Boston Dynamics uses SLAM in robotic perception.

D. AR in Smart Glasses & Gaming

- Microsoft HoloLens & Magic Leap use SLAM for spatial tracking.
- AR gaming (Pokémon GO, Snapchat filters) uses SLAM for real-world interaction.

Augmented Reality (AR) and Simultaneous Localization and Mapping (SLAM) are revolutionizing how machines perceive, interact, and navigate in the real world. vSLAM allows devices to create real-time 3D maps, while AR overlays digital objects into physical environments.

7. Introduction to Convolutional Neural Networks (CNNs)

Deep learning has revolutionized computer vision, and at the heart of this transformation are Convolutional Neural Networks (CNNs). Unlike traditional machine learning models, CNNs are specifically designed to process visual data by mimicking how the human brain perceives images. This chapter introduces the architecture of CNNs, including convolutional layers, pooling layers, activation functions, and fully connected layers, explaining how they work together to extract meaningful patterns from images. You'll also learn about key CNN architectures like LeNet, AlexNet, and VGGNet, setting the stage for advanced deep learning applications in object detection, image classification, and more. By the end of this chapter, you'll understand why CNNs are the backbone of modern computer vision and how to start building your own deep learning models.

7.1 Why Deep Learning Works for Vision Tasks

In the past, computer vision relied heavily on manually designed feature extraction methods like edge detection, SIFT, and HOG. While these classical methods worked well for specific tasks, they struggled with complex, large-scale vision problems such as object detection, face recognition, and scene understanding.

The introduction of Deep Learning (DL) revolutionized the field by automating feature extraction and enabling models to learn from vast amounts of data. Today, deep learning models—especially Convolutional Neural Networks (CNNs)—power applications like autonomous vehicles, medical imaging, facial recognition, and image generation.

In this section, we'll explore:

✅ How deep learning automates feature extraction in vision tasks.

✅ Why CNNs outperform traditional methods in recognizing patterns.

✅ Key advantages of deep learning in vision-based applications.

1. The Shift from Traditional Vision Methods to Deep Learning

A. Traditional Computer Vision Approaches

Before deep learning, computer vision pipelines were built using:

- **Feature Extraction** – Identifying edges, corners, textures, or keypoints.
- **Feature Matching** – Comparing extracted features across images.
- **Machine Learning Classifiers** – Using SVM, k-NN, or Random Forest to classify images.

For example, the Histogram of Oriented Gradients (HOG) method extracts object shapes based on edge orientations and uses an SVM classifier for object detection. Similarly, Viola-Jones Face Detection uses Haar-like features to detect faces in images.

B. Limitations of Traditional Approaches

- **Handcrafted Features Are Limited** – Fixed feature extractors like SIFT, HOG, and SURF may not generalize well to complex images.
- **Difficult to Scale** – Feature engineering requires domain expertise and fine-tuning for each task.
- **Cannot Handle Variability Well** – Changes in lighting, perspective, occlusion, or background noise make these methods unreliable.

◆ Example:

A handwritten digit "3" can have many variations depending on font, thickness, noise, and rotation. Traditional methods struggle to recognize all these variations, whereas deep learning can learn invariant features automatically.

2. How Deep Learning Automates Vision Tasks

Deep learning learns hierarchical features directly from raw images. Instead of manually designing feature extractors, deep neural networks automatically learn patterns from training data.

A. Convolutional Neural Networks (CNNs): The Backbone of Vision

CNNs are the most effective deep learning models for computer vision. Instead of processing raw pixels directly, they apply convolutional layers that extract features hierarchically from low-level edges to high-level objects.

◆ How CNNs Process Images

CNN Layer	Function
Convolutional Layer	Extracts local features like edges and textures.
Pooling Layer	Reduces spatial size, improving efficiency.
Fully Connected Layer	Combines extracted features for classification.
Softmax Layer	Outputs probabilities for different object classes.

B. CNN vs. Traditional Feature Extraction

Feature Extraction Method	Description	Works Well for
SIFT, SURF, ORB	Manually designed keypoint detection.	Matching images, stitching.
HOG + SVM	Handcrafted feature extraction + ML classifier.	Pedestrian detection.
CNNs	Automatically learns features at different levels.	Object detection, classification, segmentation.

◆ Example:

- **Face Recognition**: CNNs automatically learn facial features (eyes, nose, lips) rather than relying on hand-coded facial descriptors.
- **Autonomous Driving**: CNNs recognize pedestrians, lanes, traffic signs in real time with high accuracy.

3. Why Deep Learning Excels in Vision Tasks

A. Hierarchical Feature Learning

CNNs capture patterns at multiple levels:

✓ **Low-level features**: Edges, corners, textures.
✓ **Mid-level features**: Shapes, object parts.
✓ **High-level features**: Full object representations.

Unlike traditional methods, CNNs learn features automatically rather than relying on predefined ones.

B. Large-Scale Data Handling

Modern vision applications involve millions of labeled images. Deep learning scales effectively, while traditional methods become inefficient.

Approach	Works Well for Small Datasets?	Works Well for Large Datasets?
HOG + SVM	☑ Yes	✖ Struggles
CNNs	☑ Yes	☑ Yes

C. Robust to Variability

CNNs learn invariant representations, meaning they can handle:

- Rotation, scaling, translation
- Different lighting conditions
- Occlusions and noise

D. Transfer Learning: Leveraging Pretrained Models

Instead of training from scratch, CNNs can use pretrained models (e.g., ResNet, VGG, EfficientNet) trained on large datasets like ImageNet.

◆ Example:

A model trained to recognize cats and dogs can be fine-tuned to recognize medical X-rays, saving computation time and data requirements.

4. Real-World Applications of Deep Learning in Vision

Application	How Deep Learning Helps
Self-Driving Cars	Identifies lanes, pedestrians, obstacles.
Medical Imaging	Detects tumors, diseases in X-rays & MRIs.
Facial Recognition	Used in security, social media (Face ID, Snapchat filters).
Retail & E-commerce	Visual search, product recommendations.
Agriculture	Identifies crop diseases from images.
Robotics	Enables autonomous robots to perceive surroundings.

5. Implementation: CNN for Image Classification

Here's a simple CNN model using TensorFlow/Keras to classify images.

```
import tensorflow as tf
from tensorflow.keras import layers, models
import matplotlib.pyplot as plt

# Load and preprocess dataset (e.g., CIFAR-10)
(x_train, y_train), (x_test, y_test) = tf.keras.datasets.cifar10.load_data()
x_train, x_test = x_train / 255.0, x_test / 255.0  # Normalize pixel values

# Define a CNN model
model = models.Sequential([
    layers.Conv2D(32, (3, 3), activation='relu', input_shape=(32, 32, 3)),
    layers.MaxPooling2D((2, 2)),
    layers.Conv2D(64, (3, 3), activation='relu'),
    layers.MaxPooling2D((2, 2)),
    layers.Conv2D(128, (3, 3), activation='relu'),
    layers.Flatten(),
    layers.Dense(128, activation='relu'),
    layers.Dense(10, activation='softmax')  # 10 classes
])

# Compile and train the model
model.compile(optimizer='adam', loss='sparse_categorical_crossentropy',
metrics=['accuracy'])
model.fit(x_train, y_train, epochs=10, validation_data=(x_test, y_test))
```

```
# Evaluate on test set
test_loss, test_acc = model.evaluate(x_test, y_test)
print("Test Accuracy:", test_acc)
```

◆ **What This Does:**

✅ Defines a CNN architecture for classifying images.

✅ Uses convolutional layers to extract features.

✅ Trains the model on CIFAR-10 dataset.

Deep learning has revolutionized computer vision by automating feature extraction, handling large-scale data, and improving generalization. CNNs outperform traditional methods in accuracy, robustness, and scalability across diverse vision tasks.

7.2 Architecture of a CNN: Convolutions, Pooling, and Activation Functions

Convolutional Neural Networks (CNNs) are the foundation of modern computer vision, enabling machines to recognize objects, detect faces, and analyze medical images with unprecedented accuracy. Unlike traditional machine learning models that rely on manually crafted features, CNNs automatically learn hierarchical patterns from raw images.

At the heart of CNNs are three key components:

✅ **Convolutions** – Extract essential features like edges and textures.
✅ **Pooling** – Reduces spatial dimensions while preserving important information.
✅ **Activation Functions** – Introduce non-linearity, enabling the network to learn complex patterns.

In this chapter, we will break down the architecture of a CNN, understand its components, and implement a simple CNN in Python using TensorFlow/Keras.

1. Understanding the Structure of a CNN

A CNN processes an image hierarchically—starting with detecting edges and corners in early layers and gradually identifying objects and complex patterns in deeper layers.

A typical CNN consists of:

1☐ **Input Layer** – Takes an image as input (e.g., 28×28 grayscale or 224×224 RGB).

2☐ **Convolutional Layers** – Extract features using filters/kernels.

3☐ **Activation Functions** – Introduce non-linearity (ReLU, Sigmoid, etc.).

4☐ **Pooling Layers** – Reduce spatial size (Max Pooling, Average Pooling).

5☐ **Fully Connected (Dense) Layers** – Interpret extracted features.

6☐ **Output Layer** – Classifies the image into categories.

2. Convolutional Layers: The Feature Extractors

A. What is Convolution?

Convolution is the process of sliding a small filter (kernel) over an image and computing a weighted sum of pixel values to extract features.

◆ **Example**: A 3×3 edge detection kernel scans the image and highlights edge patterns.

Mathematically, convolution is expressed as:

$$Y(i,j) = \sum_m \sum_n X(i+m, j+n) \cdot K(m,n)$$

Where:

- $X(i,j)$ is the image pixel value.

- $K(m,n)$ is the kernel/filter.

- $Y(i,j)$ is the output feature map.

◆ **Example of a 3×3 Edge Detection Kernel:**

$$\begin{bmatrix} -1 & -1 & -1 \\ -1 & 8 & -1 \\ -1 & -1 & -1 \end{bmatrix}$$

How It Works:

- The filter moves across the image, multiplying and summing pixel values.
- The result is stored in a feature map, highlighting important structures.

B. Multiple Convolutional Filters in a CNN

Each CNN layer applies multiple filters, detecting different aspects of an image:

✅ **First Layer** – Detects edges and textures.
✅ **Intermediate Layers** – Identifies patterns like corners and shapes.
✅ **Final Layers** – Recognizes complex structures (faces, objects, text).

◆ **Example**: Applying a Convolution in Python (Using OpenCV & NumPy)

```
import cv2
import numpy as np

# Load an image in grayscale
image = cv2.imread('image.jpg', cv2.IMREAD_GRAYSCALE)

# Define a 3x3 edge detection kernel
kernel = np.array([[-1, -1, -1], [-1, 8, -1], [-1, -1, -1]])

# Apply convolution
filtered_image = cv2.filter2D(image, -1, kernel)

# Show the result
cv2.imshow('Edge Detection', filtered_image)
cv2.waitKey(0)
cv2.destroyAllWindows()
```

3. Activation Functions: Introducing Non-Linearity

CNNs use activation functions to introduce non-linearity, allowing the network to learn complex patterns.

Activation Function	Formula	Purpose
ReLU (Rectified Linear Unit)	$f(x) = \max(0, x)$	Removes negative values, speeds up training.
Sigmoid	$f(x) = \frac{1}{1+e^{-x}}$	Maps values between 0 and 1, used for binary classification.
Tanh	$f(x) = \frac{e^x - e^{-x}}{e^x + e^{-x}}$	Maps values between -1 and 1, retains some negative values.
Softmax	$\frac{e^{z_i}}{\sum e^{z_j}}$	Used in the final layer for multi-class classification.

◆ Why ReLU is Preferred?

✓ Faster convergence during training.

✓ Reduces vanishing gradient problems.

◆ **Example**: Applying ReLU in TensorFlow

```
import tensorflow as tf

# Example of ReLU activation
x = tf.constant([-2.0, -1.0, 0.0, 1.0, 2.0])
relu_output = tf.nn.relu(x)

print("ReLU Output:", relu_output.numpy())  # Output: [0. 0. 0. 1. 2.]
```

4. Pooling Layers: Reducing Dimensions While Preserving Features

Pooling layers reduce the spatial dimensions of feature maps, making computations more efficient while retaining essential information.

A. Types of Pooling

✓ **Max Pooling** – Keeps the highest value in a region (best for edge detection).
✓ **Average Pooling** – Computes the average value in a region (used in smoothing).

B. Example: 2×2 Max Pooling

Given the feature map:

$$\begin{bmatrix} 1 & 3 & 2 & 4 \\ 5 & 6 & 7 & 8 \\ 9 & 10 & 11 & 12 \\ 13 & 14 & 15 & 16 \end{bmatrix}$$

Max Pooling (2×2) →

$$\begin{bmatrix} 6 & 8 \\ 14 & 16 \end{bmatrix}$$

◆ **Example**: Implementing Max Pooling in TensorFlow

```
import tensorflow as tf

# Define a 4x4 matrix (feature map)
feature_map = tf.constant([[[1.0], [3.0], [2.0], [4.0]],
             [[5.0], [6.0], [7.0], [8.0]],
             [[9.0], [10.0], [11.0], [12.0]],
             [[13.0], [14.0], [15.0], [16.0]]])

# Apply max pooling with a 2x2 filter
pooled_output = tf.nn.max_pool(feature_map[tf.newaxis, ..., tf.newaxis],
             ksize=2, strides=2, padding='VALID')

print("Max Pooled Output:\n", pooled_output.numpy())
```

5. Full CNN Architecture Example in TensorFlow
python
Copy
Edit

```
import tensorflow as tf
from tensorflow.keras import layers, models

# Define CNN model
model = models.Sequential([
    layers.Conv2D(32, (3, 3), activation='relu', input_shape=(32, 32, 3)),
```

```
    layers.MaxPooling2D((2, 2)),
    layers.Conv2D(64, (3, 3), activation='relu'),
    layers.MaxPooling2D((2, 2)),
    layers.Conv2D(128, (3, 3), activation='relu'),
    layers.Flatten(),
    layers.Dense(128, activation='relu'),
    layers.Dense(10, activation='softmax')
])

# Print model summary
model.summary()
```

CNNs use convolutions to extract features, activation functions to introduce non-linearity, and pooling layers to reduce dimensions. These elements work together to enable deep learning models to efficiently recognize patterns in images.

7.3 Building a CNN from Scratch Using TensorFlow/PyTorch

Building a Convolutional Neural Network (CNN) from scratch is a fundamental step in mastering deep learning for computer vision. While pre-trained models like ResNet, VGG, and EfficientNet are widely used, understanding the core architecture and how to implement it from the ground up is essential for customization and optimization in real-world applications.

In this chapter, we will build a CNN from scratch using both TensorFlow (Keras) and PyTorch, training it on the CIFAR-10 dataset, which consists of 60,000 color images across 10 categories (airplane, car, bird, cat, deer, dog, frog, horse, ship, and truck).

By the end of this chapter, you will:

✅ Understand the step-by-step implementation of a CNN.

✅ Be able to train, evaluate, and fine-tune CNN models using TensorFlow/Keras and PyTorch.

✅ Learn best practices for regularization, optimization, and performance tuning.

1. Dataset Preparation: CIFAR-10

Before building our CNN, let's first load and preprocess the dataset.

A. Loading CIFAR-10 in TensorFlow

```
import tensorflow as tf
from tensorflow.keras.datasets import cifar10
from tensorflow.keras.utils import to_categorical
import matplotlib.pyplot as plt

# Load CIFAR-10 dataset
(x_train, y_train), (x_test, y_test) = cifar10.load_data()

# Normalize images (scale pixel values to range [0, 1])
x_train, x_test = x_train / 255.0, x_test / 255.0

# Convert labels to one-hot encoding
y_train = to_categorical(y_train, 10)
y_test = to_categorical(y_test, 10)

# Display an example image
plt.imshow(x_train[0])
plt.title("Example Image from CIFAR-10")
plt.show()
```
B. Loading CIFAR-10 in PyTorch
python
Copy
Edit
```
import torch
import torchvision
import torchvision.transforms as transforms
import matplotlib.pyplot as plt

# Define transformations (convert to tensors and normalize)
transform = transforms.Compose([transforms.ToTensor(), transforms.Normalize((0.5,), (0.5,))])

# Load CIFAR-10 dataset
trainset = torchvision.datasets.CIFAR10(root='./data', train=True, download=True, transform=transform)
```

```
testset = torchvision.datasets.CIFAR10(root='./data', train=False, download=True,
transform=transform)

trainloader = torch.utils.data.DataLoader(trainset, batch_size=64, shuffle=True)
testloader = torch.utils.data.DataLoader(testset, batch_size=64, shuffle=False)

# Display an example image
dataiter = iter(trainloader)
images, labels = next(dataiter)
plt.imshow(images[0].permute(1, 2, 0))  # Convert from Tensor to NumPy format
plt.title("Example Image from CIFAR-10")
plt.show()
```

2. Building the CNN Model

A typical CNN consists of:

- Convolutional Layers for feature extraction.
- Activation Functions (ReLU) for non-linearity.
- Pooling Layers (Max Pooling) for dimensionality reduction.
- Fully Connected Layers for classification.

A. CNN Architecture Overview

Our CNN model will have:

✓ 3 Convolutional Layers (filters: 32 → 64 → 128).

✓ Max Pooling after each convolution.

✓ Fully Connected (Dense) Layers for classification.

✓ Softmax Activation in the final layer for multi-class output.

3. CNN Implementation in TensorFlow/Keras

```
import tensorflow as tf
from tensorflow.keras import layers, models

# Define CNN architecture
model = models.Sequential([
```

```
    layers.Conv2D(32, (3, 3), activation='relu', input_shape=(32, 32, 3)),
    layers.MaxPooling2D((2, 2)),

    layers.Conv2D(64, (3, 3), activation='relu'),
    layers.MaxPooling2D((2, 2)),

    layers.Conv2D(128, (3, 3), activation='relu'),
    layers.MaxPooling2D((2, 2)),

    layers.Flatten(),
    layers.Dense(128, activation='relu'),
    layers.Dense(10, activation='softmax')  # 10 classes for CIFAR-10
])

# Compile the model
model.compile(optimizer='adam', loss='categorical_crossentropy', metrics=['accuracy'])

# Model summary
model.summary()
```

Training the CNN in TensorFlow

```
# Train the model
history = model.fit(x_train, y_train, epochs=10, batch_size=64, validation_data=(x_test, y_test))

# Evaluate the model
test_loss, test_acc = model.evaluate(x_test, y_test)
print("Test Accuracy:", test_acc)
```

4. CNN Implementation in PyTorch

```
import torch
import torch.nn as nn
import torch.optim as optim

# Define CNN model in PyTorch
class CNN(nn.Module):
    def __init__(self):
        super(CNN, self).__init__()
```

```python
        self.conv1 = nn.Conv2d(3, 32, kernel_size=3, padding=1)
        self.conv2 = nn.Conv2d(32, 64, kernel_size=3, padding=1)
        self.conv3 = nn.Conv2d(64, 128, kernel_size=3, padding=1)
        self.pool = nn.MaxPool2d(2, 2)
        self.fc1 = nn.Linear(128 * 4 * 4, 128)
        self.fc2 = nn.Linear(128, 10)
        self.relu = nn.ReLU()
        self.softmax = nn.Softmax(dim=1)

    def forward(self, x):
        x = self.pool(self.relu(self.conv1(x)))
        x = self.pool(self.relu(self.conv2(x)))
        x = self.pool(self.relu(self.conv3(x)))
        x = x.view(-1, 128 * 4 * 4)  # Flatten
        x = self.relu(self.fc1(x))
        x = self.softmax(self.fc2(x))
        return x


# Initialize model, loss, and optimizer
device = torch.device("cuda" if torch.cuda.is_available() else "cpu")
model = CNN().to(device)
criterion = nn.CrossEntropyLoss()
optimizer = optim.Adam(model.parameters(), lr=0.001)
```

Training the CNN in PyTorch

```python
# Training loop
num_epochs = 10
for epoch in range(num_epochs):
    running_loss = 0.0
    for images, labels in trainloader:
        images, labels = images.to(device), labels.to(device)

        # Forward pass
        optimizer.zero_grad()
        outputs = model(images)
        loss = criterion(outputs, labels)

        # Backpropagation
        loss.backward()
```

```
    optimizer.step()

    running_loss += loss.item()

  print(f"Epoch {epoch+1}, Loss: {running_loss/len(trainloader)}")

print("Training Complete")
```

Evaluating the Model in PyTorch

```
correct = 0
total = 0
with torch.no_grad():
    for images, labels in testloader:
        images, labels = images.to(device), labels.to(device)
        outputs = model(images)
        _, predicted = torch.max(outputs, 1)
        total += labels.size(0)
        correct += (predicted == labels).sum().item()

print("Test Accuracy:", correct / total)
```

We successfully built a CNN from scratch using both TensorFlow/Keras and PyTorch to classify images from the CIFAR-10 dataset. The CNN architecture demonstrated how convolutional layers extract features, pooling layers reduce dimensions, and fully connected layers classify objects.

7.4 Fine-Tuning Pretrained Models (VGG, ResNet)

Training a deep CNN from scratch requires a lot of data and computing power. However, in real-world applications, we can leverage pretrained models—CNNs that have already been trained on massive datasets like ImageNet (1.2M+ images, 1,000 classes). These models, including VGG, ResNet, MobileNet, and EfficientNet, provide learned feature representations, which can be fine-tuned to perform specific tasks with limited data and fewer resources.

In this chapter, we will:

✓ Understand Transfer Learning and why it works.

✓ Implement Fine-Tuning using VGG16 and ResNet50 in TensorFlow/Keras and PyTorch.

✓ Train the models on a new dataset while retaining pretrained knowledge.

1. What is Transfer Learning?

Transfer Learning is a deep learning technique where a pretrained model is adapted to a new task. Instead of training from scratch, we:

- Use the early layers to extract low-level features (edges, textures).
- Fine-tune the later layers for domain-specific classification.

💡 Why use Transfer Learning?

✓ **Less Data Needed** – Works well even with small datasets.
✓ **Faster Training** – Pretrained models converge quickly.
✓ **High Accuracy** – Leveraging learned features improves performance.

2. Using VGG16 for Fine-Tuning

VGG16 is a deep CNN with 16 layers, known for its simplicity and effectiveness.

A. Fine-Tuning VGG16 in TensorFlow/Keras

```
import tensorflow as tf
from tensorflow.keras.applications import VGG16
from tensorflow.keras.models import Model
from tensorflow.keras.layers import Dense, Flatten
from tensorflow.keras.preprocessing.image import ImageDataGenerator

# Load Pretrained VGG16 Model (without top layer)
base_model = VGG16(weights='imagenet', include_top=False, input_shape=(224, 224, 3))

# Freeze early layers (so they don't get retrained)
for layer in base_model.layers[:-4]:
    layer.trainable = False
```

```
# Add New Fully Connected Layers
x = Flatten()(base_model.output)
x = Dense(128, activation='relu')(x)
x = Dense(10, activation='softmax')  # 10 classes

# Create new model
model = Model(inputs=base_model.input, outputs=x)

# Compile Model
model.compile(optimizer='adam', loss='categorical_crossentropy', metrics=['accuracy'])

# Display model architecture
model.summary()
```

B. Training VGG16 on a New Dataset

```
# Data Augmentation for Small Datasets
datagen = ImageDataGenerator(rescale=1./255, rotation_range=20,
horizontal_flip=True)

# Load dataset (Assuming images in 'data/train' and 'data/validation' directories)
train_data = datagen.flow_from_directory('data/train', target_size=(224, 224),
batch_size=32, class_mode='categorical')
val_data = datagen.flow_from_directory('data/validation', target_size=(224, 224),
batch_size=32, class_mode='categorical')

# Train model
history = model.fit(train_data, validation_data=val_data, epochs=10)

# Evaluate model
test_loss, test_acc = model.evaluate(val_data)
print("Test Accuracy:", test_acc)
```

3. Fine-Tuning ResNet50 in PyTorch

ResNet50 is a deep residual network that uses skip connections to prevent vanishing gradients, allowing for training very deep models.

A. Loading Pretrained ResNet50

```python
import torch
import torch.nn as nn
import torchvision.models as models
import torchvision.transforms as transforms
from torchvision import datasets
from torch.utils.data import DataLoader

# Load Pretrained ResNet50
resnet = models.resnet50(weights=models.ResNet50_Weights.IMAGENET1K_V1)

# Freeze early layers
for param in resnet.parameters():
    param.requires_grad = False

# Modify final layer (Assume 10 output classes)
num_ftrs = resnet.fc.in_features
resnet.fc = nn.Linear(num_ftrs, 10)

# Move model to GPU if available
device = torch.device("cuda" if torch.cuda.is_available() else "cpu")
resnet = resnet.to(device)
```

B. Preparing Dataset & Dataloaders

```python
# Define data transformations (resize, normalize, augment)
transform = transforms.Compose([
    transforms.Resize((224, 224)),
    transforms.RandomHorizontalFlip(),
    transforms.ToTensor(),
    transforms.Normalize(mean=[0.485, 0.456, 0.406], std=[0.229, 0.224, 0.225])
])

# Load dataset
train_dataset = datasets.ImageFolder(root='data/train', transform=transform)
val_dataset = datasets.ImageFolder(root='data/validation', transform=transform)

# Create DataLoaders
train_loader = DataLoader(train_dataset, batch_size=32, shuffle=True)
val_loader = DataLoader(val_dataset, batch_size=32, shuffle=False)
```

C. Training ResNet50

```
import torch.optim as optim

# Define loss function & optimizer
criterion = nn.CrossEntropyLoss()
optimizer = optim.Adam(resnet.fc.parameters(), lr=0.001)

# Training loop
num_epochs = 10
for epoch in range(num_epochs):
    resnet.train()
    running_loss = 0.0
    correct, total = 0, 0

    for images, labels in train_loader:
        images, labels = images.to(device), labels.to(device)

        # Forward pass
        optimizer.zero_grad()
        outputs = resnet(images)
        loss = criterion(outputs, labels)

        # Backpropagation
        loss.backward()
        optimizer.step()

        running_loss += loss.item()
        _, predicted = torch.max(outputs, 1)
        total += labels.size(0)
        correct += (predicted == labels).sum().item()

    print(f"Epoch {epoch+1}/{num_epochs}, Loss: {running_loss/len(train_loader)},
Accuracy: {100 * correct/total}%")

print("Training Complete")
```

D. Evaluating ResNet50

```
# Evaluate model
resnet.eval()
correct, total = 0, 0

with torch.no_grad():
    for images, labels in val_loader:
        images, labels = images.to(device), labels.to(device)
        outputs = resnet(images)
        _, predicted = torch.max(outputs, 1)
        total += labels.size(0)
        correct += (predicted == labels).sum().item()

print("Test Accuracy:", correct / total)
```

4. Key Takeaways

◆ VGG16 vs. ResNet50:

Feature	VGG16	ResNet50
Architecture	Simple, Deep	Residual Blocks, Deep
Training Speed	Slower	Faster (Skip Connections)
Accuracy	High	Higher (Better Feature Extraction)
Parameter Size	Large	Smaller (More Efficient)

◆ When to Use Pretrained Models?

✅ If you have small datasets, use Transfer Learning instead of training from scratch.

✅ If you need fast deployment, fine-tuning a ResNet or VGG model is ideal.

✅ If working with low-power devices, consider MobileNet or EfficientNet.

We successfully fine-tuned VGG16 and ResNet50 using TensorFlow/Keras and PyTorch. These models allow us to build powerful image classification systems with high accuracy and minimal training time.

8. Object Detection with Deep Learning

Deep learning has significantly advanced object detection, enabling machines to recognize and locate objects with remarkable accuracy. This chapter explores the evolution of object detection models, from early region-based approaches to modern real-time systems. You'll learn about popular deep learning architectures such as R-CNN, Fast R-CNN, Faster R-CNN, YOLO (You Only Look Once), and SSD (Single Shot MultiBox Detector). Through hands-on examples, you'll understand how these models detect objects in images and videos, handle multiple object classifications, and improve speed and accuracy using techniques like anchor boxes, non-maximum suppression, and feature pyramids. By the end of this chapter, you'll be equipped to implement deep learning-based object detection for applications in security, healthcare, autonomous vehicles, and beyond.

8.1 Understanding the Difference Between Classification and Detection

Computer vision tasks can be broadly categorized into image classification and object detection. While both involve understanding visual data, they serve different purposes.

- **Image Classification answers**: "What is in the image?"
- **Object Detection answers**: "What objects are in the image and where are they?"

Understanding the distinction between these tasks is essential for building robust AI models that can analyze and interpret images effectively.

1. Image Classification: Identifying the Content of an Image

What is Image Classification?

Image classification is the task of assigning a single label or multiple labels to an image. The model processes an image and predicts the category it belongs to.

◆ **Example**: A model trained on the CIFAR-10 dataset might classify an image as:

✓ Dog

✓ Cat

✓ Airplane

How It Works

Image classification models use Convolutional Neural Networks (CNNs) to:

- Extract features (edges, textures, shapes).
- Reduce dimensions via pooling layers.
- Flatten features and pass them to a fully connected layer.
- Apply Softmax activation to assign probability scores to each class.

Code Example: Image Classification Using a CNN (TensorFlow/Keras)

```
import tensorflow as tf
from tensorflow.keras import layers, models
from tensorflow.keras.datasets import cifar10

# Load CIFAR-10 dataset
(x_train, y_train), (x_test, y_test) = cifar10.load_data()

# Normalize images
x_train, x_test = x_train / 255.0, x_test / 255.0

# Define CNN model for classification
model = models.Sequential([
    layers.Conv2D(32, (3,3), activation='relu', input_shape=(32,32,3)),
    layers.MaxPooling2D((2,2)),
    layers.Conv2D(64, (3,3), activation='relu'),
    layers.MaxPooling2D((2,2)),
    layers.Flatten(),
    layers.Dense(128, activation='relu'),
    layers.Dense(10, activation='softmax')  # 10 classes
])

# Compile and train the model
model.compile(optimizer='adam', loss='sparse_categorical_crossentropy',
metrics=['accuracy'])
model.fit(x_train, y_train, epochs=10, validation_data=(x_test, y_test))
```

Limitations of Image Classification

✗ No object location – The model only predicts the category, but not where objects are.

✗ Single-label constraint – Standard classification assumes only one main object per image.

✗ Fails in cluttered scenes – If multiple objects are present, classification alone is insufficient.

2. Object Detection: Finding and Classifying Multiple Objects

What is Object Detection?

Object detection extends classification by identifying objects and locating them within an image using bounding boxes. It answers:

- What objects are in the image?
- Where are they located?

◆ Example: Detecting cars, pedestrians, and traffic signs in a self-driving car image.

How It Works

Object detection uses two main components:

- **Feature Extraction** – A CNN extracts features from the image.
- **Bounding Box Prediction** – The model predicts object locations using:
- **Region-based approaches** (R-CNN, Faster R-CNN)
- **Single-shot detectors** (YOLO, SSD)

3. Comparing Classification and Detection

Feature	Image Classification	Object Detection
Output	Single label	Bounding boxes + labels
Use Case	Identifying an image's content	Locating objects in an image
Example	"This is a cat"	"A cat is at (x, y, w, h)"
Complexity	Lower	Higher (requires spatial localization)

4. Code Example: Object Detection with YOLOv5 (PyTorch)

YOLO (You Only Look Once) is a real-time object detection algorithm that predicts bounding boxes and class labels in one pass.

```
# Install YOLOv5 and dependencies
!git clone https://github.com/ultralytics/yolov5  # Clone YOLOv5 repository
!pip install -r yolov5/requirements.txt

import torch
from yolov5 import detect

# Load pre-trained YOLOv5 model
model = torch.hub.load('ultralytics/yolov5', 'yolov5s', pretrained=True)

# Perform object detection on an image
results = model('image.jpg')
results.show()  # Display results with bounding boxes
```

Why Use Object Detection?

✓ Detects multiple objects in a single image.

✓ Provides precise locations of objects.

✓ Essential for autonomous vehicles, security, retail, and medical imaging.

Understanding the difference between classification and detection is fundamental to computer vision.

◆ Use Classification when the goal is to identify what is in an image (e.g., dog, cat, airplane).
◆ Use Object Detection when you need to locate multiple objects within an image (e.g., detecting cars on a street).

8.2 YOLO (You Only Look Once) Architecture Explained

Object detection is one of the most crucial tasks in computer vision, enabling systems to identify and locate multiple objects within an image. Among various detection algorithms, YOLO (You Only Look Once) has gained immense popularity due to its real-time performance and high accuracy. Unlike traditional region-based methods like Faster R-CNN, which require multiple passes over an image, YOLO detects objects in a single forward pass, making it incredibly fast.

In this chapter, we will dive deep into the YOLO architecture, how it works, and why it has become a standard for real-time object detection.

1. What is YOLO?

YOLO is an object detection algorithm designed for real-time performance. It was introduced by Joseph Redmon in 2016 and has since evolved through multiple versions (YOLOv1 to YOLOv8). Unlike older approaches that scan an image using sliding windows or region proposals, YOLO treats object detection as a single regression problem, mapping an input image to bounding boxes and class probabilities in one go.

Key Features of YOLO:

✅ **Single forward pass** – Processes the image in one step, making it extremely fast.
✅ **Real-time detection** – Can run at 30–150 FPS depending on the hardware.
✅ **End-to-end training** – Optimizes detection and classification together.
✅ **Works well with small objects** – Later versions (YOLOv3, v4, v5, and beyond) improve detection accuracy, especially for small objects.

2. YOLO vs. Traditional Object Detection

Feature	YOLO (You Only Look Once)	Faster R-CNN
Speed	30–150 FPS (Real-time)	7–10 FPS
Architecture	Single-shot detection	Two-stage detection
Accuracy	High	Slightly higher for small objects
Complexity	Simple	More complex (Region Proposal Network)
Best Use Case	Real-time applications (Autonomous Driving, Video Surveillance)	High-accuracy tasks (Medical Imaging)

3. How YOLO Works

YOLO divides an image into a grid of S×S cells and predicts bounding boxes and class probabilities for each grid cell.

Step-by-Step Breakdown

Image is divided into an S×S grid

- Each grid cell is responsible for detecting an object if its center falls within that cell.

Each grid cell predicts:

- B bounding boxes (x, y, w, h, confidence score)
- C class probabilities (e.g., dog, car, person)

Bounding box confidence score

Indicates how confident the model is about the presence of an object.

Defined as:

$$\text{Confidence Score} = P(\text{object}) \times \text{IOU (Intersection over Union)}$$

If no object is present, confidence score should be close to zero.

Post-processing (Non-Maximum Suppression, NMS)

- Multiple overlapping boxes may predict the same object.
- NMS removes redundant boxes, keeping only the most confident one.

4. YOLO Architecture in Detail

4.1 YOLO Network Structure

The core of YOLO consists of a fully convolutional neural network (CNN) that processes images and outputs object detections.

✓ **Backbone**: Extracts features from input images.
✓ **Neck**: Refines features before detection.
✓ **Head**: Predicts bounding boxes, objectness scores, and class labels.

◆ **Early YOLO Versions (YOLOv1 - YOLOv3):**

- Uses a CNN backbone (Darknet-19 or Darknet-53).
- Outputs a feature map with bounding box coordinates, confidence scores, and class probabilities.

◆ **Modern YOLO Versions (YOLOv4 - YOLOv8):**

- Uses EfficientNet, CSPDarkNet, or Transformer-based backbones.
- Employs Anchor Boxes, Feature Pyramid Networks (FPN), and Path Aggregation Networks (PANet) for better small-object detection.

5. YOLO in Action: Code Implementation

Let's use YOLOv5, one of the most optimized and easy-to-use YOLO versions.

5.1 Installing YOLOv5 and Dependencies

```
# Clone YOLOv5 repository
!git clone https://github.com/ultralytics/yolov5
%cd yolov5

# Install dependencies
!pip install -r requirements.txt
```

5.2 Loading YOLOv5 Pretrained Model

```
import torch

# Load YOLOv5 small model (pretrained on COCO dataset)
model = torch.hub.load('ultralytics/yolov5', 'yolov5s', pretrained=True)

# Check model details
model
```

5.3 Running Object Detection on an Image

```
# Perform object detection on an image
results = model('image.jpg')
```

```
results.show()  # Display results with bounding boxes
```

5.4 Running Object Detection on Video

```
# Perform detection on a video file
results = model('video.mp4')
results.show()
```

6. YOLO Performance Metrics

YOLO models are evaluated using:

- **Mean Average Precision (mAP)** – Measures how accurately objects are detected.
- **Inference Speed (FPS)** – Frames per second, crucial for real-time applications.
- **Intersection over Union (IoU)** – Measures overlap between predicted and actual bounding boxes.

Model	mAP (COCO)	Speed (FPS)
YOLOv3	33.0%	30 FPS
YOLOv4	43.5%	60 FPS
YOLOv5	48.2%	140 FPS
YOLOv8	51.3%	150+ FPS

7. YOLO Use Cases

🚗 **Autonomous Vehicles**: Detects pedestrians, vehicles, and traffic signs in real-time.

☐ **Retail & Inventory Management**: Counts items on shelves using CCTV cameras.

🔍 **Surveillance & Security**: Detects suspicious activities in real-time.

📱 **Augmented Reality (AR):** Enhances gaming and interactive experiences.

⛨ **Medical Imaging**: Helps detect tumors in X-rays and MRI scans.

8. Advantages and Limitations of YOLO

✅ Advantages

✓ **Blazing Fast** – Runs in real-time (30–150 FPS).

✓ **High Accuracy** – Especially with YOLOv4, YOLOv5, and YOLOv8.

✓ **Generalizes Well** – Works on diverse datasets.

✓ **End-to-End Training** – Simple architecture with a single network.

✗ Limitations

✗ **Struggles with Small Objects** – Older versions (YOLOv1–v3) had difficulty detecting tiny objects.

✗ **Lower Accuracy than Two-Stage Detectors** – Faster R-CNN performs better in some scenarios.

✗ **Requires High Computational Power** – Needs a GPU for real-time performance.

YOLO has revolutionized object detection by making it fast, efficient, and easy to deploy in real-world applications. With continuous improvements from YOLOv1 to YOLOv8, it remains the gold standard for real-time object detection.

8.3 SSD (Single Shot MultiBox Detector): Faster Object Detection

Object detection is crucial in computer vision applications like autonomous driving, surveillance, and augmented reality. Among various detection models, the Single Shot MultiBox Detector (SSD) stands out for its balance between speed and accuracy.

Introduced by Wei Liu et al. in 2016, SSD is a one-stage object detector that eliminates the need for region proposals (used in Faster R-CNN), making it significantly faster while maintaining good accuracy.

In this section, we'll explore how SSD works, its architecture, advantages, limitations, and implementation using TensorFlow/PyTorch.

1. What is SSD (Single Shot MultiBox Detector)?

SSD is a deep-learning-based object detection model that detects objects in a single forward pass of a neural network. Unlike Faster R-CNN, which first generates region proposals and then classifies them, SSD performs detection in a single step, making it much faster.

✓ **Single-shot architecture** – Detects objects in real-time.

✓ **Multi-scale feature maps** – Identifies objects of various sizes.

✓ **Anchor boxes (default boxes)** – Predicts multiple bounding boxes per location.

2. SSD vs. YOLO vs. Faster R-CNN

Feature	SSD (Single Shot MultiBox)	YOLO (You Only Look Once)	Faster R-CNN
Speed	22–60 FPS (Real-time)	30–150 FPS (Fastest)	7–10 FPS (Slow)
Architecture	One-stage detector	One-stage detector	Two-stage detector
Accuracy	Higher than YOLOv3	Slightly lower	Highest
Use Case	Mobile, embedded systems	Real-time detection	High-accuracy tasks

SSD is faster than Faster R-CNN and more accurate than YOLO (v1–v3). However, newer YOLO versions (YOLOv4-v8) have improved significantly, making SSD a competitive alternative in real-time applications.

3. SSD Architecture Explained

3.1 Backbone Network (Feature Extractor)

SSD uses a pre-trained CNN (e.g., VGG16, ResNet, MobileNet) as a backbone to extract image features.

3.2 Multi-Scale Feature Maps

Unlike YOLO, which detects objects at a single scale, SSD extracts features from multiple convolutional layers, allowing it to detect both small and large objects effectively.

3.3 Anchor Boxes (Default Boxes)

SSD defines default anchor boxes at each feature map location. Each anchor box has different scales and aspect ratios to detect objects of various shapes.

◆ **Each anchor box predicts:**

- Bounding box offsets (x, y, w, h)
- Confidence score (object presence probability)

- Class probability (what type of object)

3.4 Non-Maximum Suppression (NMS) for Post-Processing

Since SSD predicts multiple overlapping boxes, Non-Maximum Suppression (NMS) is used to:

✅ Keep the most confident bounding boxes.

✅ Remove redundant detections.

4. How SSD Works – Step by Step

Step 1: Image Input

An input image (e.g., 300×300 pixels for SSD300) is fed into the CNN.

Step 2: Feature Extraction

The backbone network (VGG16, MobileNet, or ResNet) extracts spatial features.

Step 3: Multi-Scale Predictions

Feature maps at different resolutions generate anchor boxes.

Step 4: Bounding Box Prediction

For each anchor box, SSD predicts:

- Object class (e.g., car, person, dog, etc.)
- Bounding box coordinates

Step 5: Post-Processing with NMS

- Low-confidence detections are removed.
- Overlapping bounding boxes are merged using Intersection over Union (IoU).

5. SSD Implementation in Python (PyTorch)

Let's implement SSD using a pre-trained MobileNetV2-SSD model in PyTorch.

5.1 Install Dependencies

```
!pip install torch torchvision opencv-python matplotlib
```

5.2 Load SSD Pretrained Model

```python
import torch
import torchvision.transforms as transforms
from PIL import Image
import cv2
import matplotlib.pyplot as plt

# Load SSD model pre-trained on COCO dataset
model = torch.hub.load('NVIDIA/DeepLearningExamples:torchhub', 'nvidia_ssd',
pretrained=True)
model.eval()  # Set model to evaluation mode

# Load SSD class labels
ssd_classes = torch.hub.load('NVIDIA/DeepLearningExamples:torchhub',
'nvidia_ssd_processing_utils')

# Image preprocessing
def preprocess_image(image_path):
    transform = transforms.Compose([
        transforms.Resize((300, 300)),
        transforms.ToTensor(),
    ])
    image = Image.open(image_path)
    return transform(image).unsqueeze(0)

# Load and process an image
image_path = "image.jpg"
image_tensor = preprocess_image(image_path)

# Run SSD object detection
with torch.no_grad():
    detections = model(image_tensor)

# Process detections
```

```
results = ssd_classes.process_results(detections)
print(results)
```

5.3 Running SSD on a Video

```
# Load a video and detect objects in real-time
video_path = "video.mp4"
cap = cv2.VideoCapture(video_path)

while cap.isOpened():
    ret, frame = cap.read()
    if not ret:
        break

    # Convert frame to PIL image and preprocess
    image = Image.fromarray(cv2.cvtColor(frame, cv2.COLOR_BGR2RGB))
    image_tensor = preprocess_image(image)

    # Run SSD model
    with torch.no_grad():
        detections = model(image_tensor)

    # Display detected objects
    results = ssd_classes.process_results(detections)
    print(results)

cap.release()
```

6. Performance and Accuracy of SSD

Model	mAP (COCO dataset)	Speed (FPS)
SSD300 (VGG-16)	43.0%	58 FPS
SSD512 (VGG-16)	46.5%	22 FPS
MobileNet-SSD	38.8%	60 FPS

◆ SSD is faster than Faster R-CNN but slightly less accurate than YOLOv4 and YOLOv5.

7. Advantages and Limitations of SSD

✅ Advantages

✔ **Real-time performance** – Can process 30–60 FPS, suitable for mobile and embedded devices.

✔ **Multi-scale detection** – Detects small and large objects using different feature map layers.

✔ **End-to-end training** – Trained directly on images without separate region proposal steps.

✖ Limitations

✖ **Lower accuracy than Faster R-CNN** – Struggles with very small objects.

✖ **More anchor boxes = More computations** – Requires optimized hardware for best performance.

✖ **Not as optimized as modern YOLO versions** – YOLOv5, YOLOv7, and YOLOv8 outperform SSD in both speed and accuracy.

8. Applications of SSD

🚗 **Autonomous Vehicles**: Real-time pedestrian and vehicle detection.

📱 **Mobile Apps**: Works well on smartphones and embedded systems.

📹 **Surveillance**: Fast object detection in security footage.

🛡 **Medical Imaging**: Used in detecting abnormalities in medical scans.

SSD is an excellent balance between speed and accuracy, making it a great choice for real-time applications. While it is slower than YOLOv5/v8 and less accurate than Faster R-CNN, it remains a popular choice for mobile and embedded AI solutions.

8.4 Faster R-CNN and Region Proposal Networks

Object detection is a fundamental task in computer vision that involves identifying and locating objects in an image. While one-stage detectors like YOLO and SSD focus on speed, Faster R-CNN remains one of the most accurate object detection models, making it ideal for tasks requiring high precision, such as medical imaging, autonomous driving, and surveillance.

Introduced by Shaoqing Ren et al. in 2015, Faster R-CNN improved upon its predecessors (R-CNN and Fast R-CNN) by introducing a Region Proposal Network (RPN) that generates high-quality object proposals efficiently. This chapter will explore Faster R-CNN's architecture, its working mechanism, advantages, limitations, and implementation using TensorFlow/PyTorch.

1. What is Faster R-CNN?

Faster R-CNN is a two-stage object detection model that:

✅ First identifies regions of interest (ROIs) using a Region Proposal Network (RPN).

✅ Then classifies objects and refines their bounding boxes using a convolutional neural network (CNN).

Unlike traditional methods like Selective Search used in Fast R-CNN, the RPN in Faster R-CNN is trainable, making the model both faster and more accurate.

Why is Faster R-CNN Important?

- **High accuracy**: Outperforms one-stage detectors like YOLO and SSD on the COCO dataset.
- **Region Proposal Network (RPN)**: Generates region proposals efficiently, reducing computation.
- **Great for applications requiring precision**: Medical imaging, autonomous vehicles, and security surveillance.

2. Faster R-CNN vs. YOLO vs. SSD

Feature	Faster R-CNN	YOLO (You Only Look Once)	SSD (Single Shot MultiBox)
Speed	7–10 FPS (Slower)	30–150 FPS (Real-time)	22–60 FPS (Moderate)
Accuracy	Highest	Moderate-High	Moderate
Architecture	Two-stage detection	One-stage detection	One-stage detection
Best Use Case	High-accuracy tasks	Real-time applications	Mobile, embedded systems

While YOLO and SSD prioritize speed, Faster R-CNN is the gold standard for high-accuracy object detection.

3. Faster R-CNN Architecture Explained

Faster R-CNN consists of three key components:

3.1 Backbone Network (Feature Extractor)

- A deep CNN (e.g., ResNet, VGG16) extracts features from the input image.

3.2 Region Proposal Network (RPN)

- Instead of using Selective Search like Fast R-CNN, Faster R-CNN uses a trainable RPN to generate proposed object regions (ROIs) efficiently.

3.3 Region of Interest (ROI) Pooling & Classification

- The ROI Pooling layer resizes extracted features to a fixed size.
- A fully connected network classifies objects and refines bounding boxes.

4. How Faster R-CNN Works – Step by Step

Step 1: Feature Extraction

- An input image is passed through a CNN (e.g., ResNet-50) to extract feature maps.

Step 2: Region Proposal Network (RPN)

- A sliding window scans the feature maps.
- At each location, RPN generates multiple anchor boxes (default bounding boxes of different sizes).
- The model predicts which anchor boxes contain objects and refines their coordinates.

Step 3: ROI Pooling & Classification

- ROIs are extracted and resized to a fixed shape using ROI Pooling.
- A fully connected network classifies objects and adjusts bounding boxes.

Step 4: Non-Maximum Suppression (NMS)

- Removes duplicate detections and keeps only the best predictions.

5. Faster R-CNN Implementation in Python (PyTorch)

- Let's implement Faster R-CNN using Torchvision's pre-trained Faster R-CNN model.

5.1 Install Dependencies

```
!pip install torch torchvision opencv-python matplotlib
```

5.2 Load Pre-Trained Faster R-CNN Model

```
import torch
import torchvision
from torchvision import transforms
from PIL import Image
import matplotlib.pyplot as plt

# Load pre-trained Faster R-CNN model
model = torchvision.models.detection.fasterrcnn_resnet50_fpn(pretrained=True)
model.eval()  # Set model to evaluation mode

# Image preprocessing
transform = transforms.Compose([
    transforms.ToTensor(),
])

# Load and preprocess an image
image_path = "image.jpg"
image = Image.open(image_path)
image_tensor = transform(image).unsqueeze(0)

# Run object detection
with torch.no_grad():
    detections = model(image_tensor)

# Print detection results
print(detections)
```

5.3 Running Faster R-CNN on a Video

```
import cv2

# Load video
cap = cv2.VideoCapture("video.mp4")

while cap.isOpened():
    ret, frame = cap.read()
    if not ret:
        break

    # Convert frame to PIL image and preprocess
    image = Image.fromarray(cv2.cvtColor(frame, cv2.COLOR_BGR2RGB))
    image_tensor = transform(image).unsqueeze(0)

    # Run Faster R-CNN
    with torch.no_grad():
        detections = model(image_tensor)

    print(detections)

cap.release()
```

6. Performance of Faster R-CNN

Model	mAP (COCO dataset)	Speed (FPS)
Faster R-CNN (VGG-16)	55.7%	7 FPS
Faster R-CNN (ResNet-50)	59.1%	8 FPS
Faster R-CNN (ResNet-101)	60.2%	6 FPS

◆ Faster R-CNN achieves the highest accuracy but at the cost of speed.

7. Advantages and Limitations of Faster R-CNN

✅ Advantages

✓ **High accuracy** – Among the best for object detection.

✓ **Trainable region proposals (RPN)** – Unlike older methods, Faster R-CNN learns where to look.

✓ **Versatile** – Works well in high-accuracy applications like medical imaging, autonomous vehicles, and security surveillance.

✗ Limitations

✗ **Slow inference speed** – Around 7–10 FPS, making it unsuitable for real-time applications.

✗ **High computational cost** – Requires a powerful GPU for training and inference.

8. Applications of Faster R-CNN

⊕ **Medical Imaging** – Detecting tumors in X-rays and MRI scans.

🚗 **Autonomous Driving** – Identifying pedestrians, cars, and obstacles.

☐ **Satellite Image Analysis** – Locating objects from aerial images.

🔍 **Surveillance & Security** – Detecting suspicious activities.

Faster R-CNN is a powerful two-stage object detector that excels in accuracy. Although it is slower than YOLO and SSD, it remains the best choice for applications requiring high precision.

9. Image Segmentation and Semantic Understanding

Image segmentation takes computer vision beyond object detection by dividing an image into meaningful regions, allowing machines to understand scenes at a deeper level. This chapter explores different types of segmentation, including semantic segmentation, instance segmentation, and panoptic segmentation, and introduces powerful deep learning models like U-Net, Mask R-CNN, and DeepLabV3. You'll learn how these techniques are applied in real-world scenarios, such as medical image analysis, autonomous driving, and satellite imagery interpretation. By the end of this chapter, you'll have the skills to implement segmentation models that enable AI to recognize not just objects but their precise boundaries and spatial relationships.

9.1 Semantic vs. Instance Segmentation

Object detection identifies and classifies objects in an image, but what if we need precise pixel-wise boundaries for each object? This is where image segmentation comes in. Segmentation divides an image into meaningful regions, helping AI models understand object shapes, contours, and locations more accurately.

There are two primary types of image segmentation:

✅ **Semantic Segmentation** – Classifies each pixel into a category but does not differentiate between individual objects of the same class.
✅ **Instance Segmentation** – Identifies and segments each object separately, even if they belong to the same class.

In this section, we'll explore the key differences between semantic and instance segmentation, their architectures, real-world applications, and how to implement them using deep learning frameworks like PyTorch and TensorFlow.

1. What is Image Segmentation?

Image segmentation assigns a label to each pixel in an image, grouping pixels with similar characteristics. Unlike object detection, which draws bounding boxes, segmentation extracts precise object boundaries, making it ideal for:

- Autonomous driving (lane detection, pedestrian recognition)
- Medical imaging (tumor segmentation, organ detection)
- Satellite imagery (land cover classification)

There are two major approaches:

1.1 Semantic Segmentation (Category-Level Segmentation)

- Assigns the same label to all objects of a class (e.g., all cars are the same color).
- Does not differentiate between individual instances.

Example:

- If an image contains five cars, all pixels belonging to cars will have the same label (e.g., "car").
- No distinction between the first car and the second car.
- Popular Models for Semantic Segmentation
- Fully Convolutional Networks (FCN)
- U-Net (for medical images)
- DeepLab (Google's model for fine-grained segmentation)

1.2 Instance Segmentation (Object-Level Segmentation)

- Detects and segments each instance separately, even if they belong to the same class.
- Differentiates between individual objects.

Example:

- If an image contains five cars, instance segmentation will assign a unique mask to each car instead of treating them as a single entity.
- Popular Models for Instance Segmentation
- Mask R-CNN (Region-based CNN with segmentation)
- DetectoRS (ResNet-based segmentation model)
- YOLACT (Real-time instance segmentation)

2. Semantic vs. Instance Segmentation: Key Differences

Feature	Semantic Segmentation	Instance Segmentation
Pixel-Level Classification	☑ Assigns class labels to pixels	☑ Assigns unique object labels to pixels
Object Differentiation	✕ Does not distinguish between instances	☑ Identifies each object separately
Example Use Case	Sky, road, trees in self-driving cars	Detecting multiple pedestrians in a crowd
Output	**Class mask** for each category	**Unique mask** for each object

Semantic segmentation is great for scene understanding, while instance segmentation is better for object separation.

3. How Do These Models Work?

3.1 Semantic Segmentation Pipeline

1☐ **Input Image** → A raw image is fed into a CNN.

2☐ **Feature Extraction** → A deep CNN (e.g., ResNet, VGG16) extracts features.

3☐ **Pixel Classification** → A fully convolutional network (FCN) assigns each pixel a class label.

4☐ **Upsampling (Decoder)** → The output is resized to the original image size to produce a final segmented image.

✓ **Best for**: Scene segmentation, medical image analysis.

3.2 Instance Segmentation Pipeline

1☐ **Input Image** → The image is fed into a region-based CNN (like Mask R-CNN).

2☐ **Feature Extraction** → A CNN extracts deep features.

3☐ **Region Proposal Network (RPN)** → Identifies potential object regions.

4☐ **ROI Pooling & Classification** → Classifies objects and refines bounding boxes.

5️⃣ Segmentation Mask Generation → A separate mask prediction branch generates a pixel-wise mask for each object.

✅ **Best for:** Self-driving cars (distinguishing people), robotics (object picking).

4. Implementing Image Segmentation in Python (PyTorch)

Let's implement semantic and instance segmentation using PyTorch.

4.1 Semantic Segmentation with DeepLabV3 (Pretrained Model)

```python
import torch
import torchvision.transforms as transforms
from PIL import Image
import matplotlib.pyplot as plt

# Load a pre-trained DeepLabV3 model
model = torch.hub.load('pytorch/vision:v0.10.0', 'deeplabv3_resnet101',
pretrained=True)
model.eval()

# Load and preprocess an image
transform = transforms.Compose([
    transforms.Resize((520, 520)),
    transforms.ToTensor(),
])

image_path = "image.jpg"
image = Image.open(image_path)
image_tensor = transform(image).unsqueeze(0)

# Perform segmentation
with torch.no_grad():
    output = model(image_tensor)['out'][0]

# Convert output to segmentation map
segmentation_map = torch.argmax(output, dim=0).numpy()

# Display segmentation results
```

```
plt.imshow(segmentation_map, cmap="jet")
plt.axis("off")
plt.show()
```

4.2 Instance Segmentation with Mask R-CNN (Pretrained Model)

```
import torchvision
from PIL import Image
import matplotlib.pyplot as plt

# Load pre-trained Mask R-CNN model
model = torchvision.models.detection.maskrcnn_resnet50_fpn(pretrained=True)
model.eval()

# Load and preprocess image
image_path = "image.jpg"
image = Image.open(image_path)
transform = transforms.Compose([transforms.ToTensor()])
image_tensor = transform(image).unsqueeze(0)

# Perform instance segmentation
with torch.no_grad():
    predictions = model(image_tensor)

# Extract masks
masks = predictions[0]['masks'].detach().cpu().numpy()

# Display first detected instance mask
plt.imshow(masks[0][0], cmap="gray")
plt.axis("off")
plt.show()
```

5. Applications of Semantic and Instance Segmentation

✚ Medical Imaging

✅ **Semantic Segmentation** → Tumor detection, organ segmentation.

✅ **Instance Segmentation** → Cell segmentation in microscopy images.

🚘 Autonomous Driving

✅ **Semantic Segmentation** → Lane marking, road detection.

✅ **Instance Segmentation** → Distinguishing between pedestrians and vehicles.

☐ Satellite and Aerial Imagery

✅ **Semantic Segmentation** → Land cover classification.

✅ **Instance Segmentation** → Detecting individual buildings and objects.

🎮 Augmented Reality (AR) & Virtual Reality (VR)

✅ **Instance Segmentation** → Recognizing multiple objects in an environment for AR interaction.

6. Advantages and Limitations

✅ Advantages

✔ **Semantic Segmentation**: Good for general scene understanding.

✔ **Instance Segmentation**: Ideal for differentiating overlapping objects.

✔ **Deep learning models** (FCN, U-Net, Mask R-CNN) provide high accuracy.

✖ Limitations

✖ **Computationally expensive** – Requires powerful GPUs for training.

✖ **Instance Segmentation is harder than Semantic Segmentation** – Needs object detection and pixel-wise segmentation.

✖ **Real-time performance is challenging** – Not as fast as YOLO/SSD.

- Semantic segmentation is great for scene understanding but cannot differentiate between objects of the same class.
- Instance segmentation provides object-level understanding, making it more powerful for robotics, autonomous driving, and medical imaging.

9.2 U-Net: Revolutionizing Medical Image Segmentation

Medical imaging plays a crucial role in disease diagnosis, treatment planning, and clinical research. However, accurately identifying organs, tumors, and abnormalities in medical images requires pixel-wise precision. Traditional machine learning methods struggle with this complexity, but deep learning-based segmentation models have transformed the field.

Among these models, U-Net has emerged as the gold standard for medical image segmentation, thanks to its ability to produce high-resolution masks with minimal training data. Developed by Olaf Ronneberger et al. in 2015, U-Net has revolutionized tasks like tumor segmentation, organ delineation, and cell tracking.

In this chapter, we will explore:

✓ How U-Net works and why it excels in medical imaging.

✓ Its unique architecture (encoder-decoder with skip connections).

✓ Applications in medical fields like radiology, pathology, and dermatology.

✓ Hands-on implementation using TensorFlow/PyTorch.

1. What is U-Net?

U-Net is a fully convolutional network (FCN) designed for precise image segmentation. Unlike traditional classification networks (which output a single label per image), U-Net assigns a label to each pixel, making it ideal for medical imaging tasks where object boundaries matter.

Why is U-Net Revolutionary?

✓ **Works with small datasets** – Medical images are scarce, but U-Net performs well even with limited training data.

✓ **Preserves fine details** – Uses skip connections to retain spatial information.

✓ **Fast and efficient** – Can be trained end-to-end with fewer training samples.

✓ **Applies to multiple medical fields** – Works for X-rays, MRIs, CT scans, pathology slides, and more.

2. U-Net Architecture: How Does It Work?

U-Net follows an encoder-decoder structure with skip connections, ensuring fine-grained details are preserved.

2.1 Encoder (Contracting Path)

♦ Extracts features from the input image.
♦ Uses convolutional layers + ReLU activation to learn spatial patterns.
♦ Downsampling via max pooling reduces spatial dimensions while retaining important features.

2.2 Bottleneck

♦ The deepest part of the network that captures high-level features.
♦ Consists of convolutional layers to learn complex patterns.

2.3 Decoder (Expanding Path)

♦ Upsamples feature maps to restore the original image size.
♦ Uses transposed convolutions (deconvolution) to increase resolution.
♦ Skip connections merge low-level features from the encoder to retain fine details.

2.4 Skip Connections: The Key to Success

✓ Directly connect encoder layers to decoder layers.

✓ Preserve spatial information lost during downsampling.

✓ Improve segmentation accuracy, especially for small objects like tumors.

📌 **Output**: A high-resolution segmentation mask, where each pixel is assigned a class label (e.g., tumor vs. healthy tissue).

3. Why is U-Net Ideal for Medical Image Segmentation?

□ **Handles small datasets effectively** – Works well even when labeled medical images are limited.

🔋 **Preserves fine details** – Ensures that small abnormalities (like lesions or tumors) are not lost.

⚡ **Fast training and inference** – Optimized for medical imaging tasks, requiring fewer samples than traditional deep learning models.

4. Applications of U-Net in Medical Imaging

4.1 Tumor Segmentation (MRI, CT Scans) □

- Brain tumor segmentation – Distinguishing between healthy and abnormal tissue in MRI scans.
- Lung nodule detection – Early identification of lung cancer in CT scans.

4.2 Organ Segmentation ⊕

- Heart segmentation in echocardiograms.
- Liver and kidney segmentation in CT scans.

4.3 Cell Tracking in Microscopy □

- Identifying cell boundaries in biological images.
- Used in cancer research to study cell growth patterns.

4.4 Skin Lesion Segmentation (Dermatology) □

- Detecting melanomas and skin cancer in dermatology images.
- Automated classification of benign vs. malignant skin conditions.

5. Implementing U-Net in Python (Keras/TensorFlow & PyTorch)

5.1 U-Net in TensorFlow (Keras)

Step 1: Install Dependencies

!pip install tensorflow numpy matplotlib opencv-python

Step 2: Build U-Net Model in TensorFlow

```python
import tensorflow as tf
from tensorflow.keras import layers

def unet_model(input_size=(128, 128, 1)):
    inputs = layers.Input(input_size)

    # Encoder (Downsampling)
    c1 = layers.Conv2D(64, (3, 3), activation='relu', padding='same')(inputs)
    c1 = layers.Conv2D(64, (3, 3), activation='relu', padding='same')(c1)
    p1 = layers.MaxPooling2D((2, 2))(c1)

    # Bottleneck
    b = layers.Conv2D(128, (3, 3), activation='relu', padding='same')(p1)

    # Decoder (Upsampling)
    u1 = layers.Conv2DTranspose(64, (2, 2), strides=(2, 2), padding='same')(b)
    u1 = layers.Concatenate()([u1, c1])
    u1 = layers.Conv2D(64, (3, 3), activation='relu', padding='same')(u1)

    outputs = layers.Conv2D(1, (1, 1), activation='sigmoid')(u1)

    return tf.keras.Model(inputs, outputs)

# Compile model
model = unet_model()
model.compile(optimizer='adam', loss='binary_crossentropy', metrics=['accuracy'])
model.summary()
```

5.2 U-Net in PyTorch

Step 1: Install Dependencies

```
!pip install torch torchvision numpy matplotlib opencv-python
```

Step 2: Define U-Net in PyTorch

```python
import torch
import torch.nn as nn
import torch.nn.functional as F
```

```python
class UNet(nn.Module):
    def __init__(self):
        super(UNet, self).__init__()

        self.encoder = nn.Sequential(
            nn.Conv2d(1, 64, kernel_size=3, padding=1),
            nn.ReLU(inplace=True),
            nn.Conv2d(64, 64, kernel_size=3, padding=1),
            nn.ReLU(inplace=True),
            nn.MaxPool2d(kernel_size=2, stride=2)
        )

        self.decoder = nn.Sequential(
            nn.ConvTranspose2d(64, 64, kernel_size=2, stride=2),
            nn.ReLU(inplace=True),
            nn.Conv2d(64, 1, kernel_size=1),
            nn.Sigmoid()
        )

    def forward(self, x):
        x = self.encoder(x)
        x = self.decoder(x)
        return x

# Initialize model
model = UNet()
print(model)
```

6. Advantages and Limitations of U-Net

✅ Advantages

✓ Works with small medical datasets.

✓ Skip connections improve segmentation accuracy.

✓ Handles complex medical images (MRI, CT, histopathology slides).

✗ Limitations

✘ Requires precise annotations, which can be costly.

✘ Computationally expensive for high-resolution images.

✘ Struggles with severe class imbalances (e.g., small tumors vs. large organs).

U-Net has transformed medical image segmentation, allowing AI to assist in early disease detection, diagnosis, and research. Its encoder-decoder architecture with skip connections makes it ideal for tumor detection, organ segmentation, and microscopy analysis.

9.3 DeepLab for High-Accuracy Segmentation

As computer vision evolves, the demand for high-accuracy segmentation models has grown, especially in applications like autonomous driving, medical imaging, and satellite imagery. While U-Net is excellent for medical segmentation, models like DeepLab have pushed the boundaries of semantic segmentation for broader applications.

Developed by Google Research, DeepLab is one of the most powerful deep learning architectures for semantic segmentation, capable of generating high-resolution masks with fine-grained details. It improves over traditional convolutional neural networks (CNNs) by incorporating Atrous (dilated) convolutions, DeepLabv3+'s encoder-decoder structure, and Conditional Random Fields (CRFs) for enhanced object boundary refinement.

In this chapter, we'll explore:

✓ How DeepLab works and why it excels in complex segmentation tasks.

✓ The evolution from DeepLabv1 to DeepLabv3+ and key architectural innovations.

✓ Applications in self-driving cars, satellite imaging, and more.

✓ Implementation using TensorFlow/PyTorch.

1. What is DeepLab?

DeepLab is a family of deep learning models designed for high-accuracy semantic segmentation. Unlike instance segmentation (which distinguishes objects of the same class), DeepLab focuses on assigning a class label to every pixel, making it highly effective for scene understanding, medical imaging, and aerial mapping.

Why is DeepLab Powerful?

✓ **Preserves fine details** – Uses Atrous convolutions to retain spatial resolution.

✓ **Understands large and small objects** – Features multi-scale context aggregation to capture object details at various sizes.

✓ **Refines object boundaries** – Uses CRFs to smooth segmentation masks.

✓ **Works well on complex scenes** – Ideal for self-driving cars, where precise segmentation of roads, pedestrians, and vehicles is crucial.

2. The Evolution of DeepLab: From v1 to v3+

DeepLab has undergone multiple improvements since its first version:

2.1 DeepLab v1 (2014)

✓ Introduced Atrous (dilated) convolutions to increase receptive field without reducing image resolution.

✗ Struggled with object boundary refinement.

2.2 DeepLab v2 (2016)

✓ Added Atrous Spatial Pyramid Pooling (ASPP) to capture multi-scale context.

✓ Integrated fully connected Conditional Random Fields (CRFs) for better boundary detection.

2.3 DeepLab v3 (2017)

✓ Removed CRFs and improved ASPP with batch normalization.

✓ Achieved state-of-the-art results on segmentation benchmarks.

2.4 DeepLab v3+ (2018)

✓ Introduced an encoder-decoder structure for better object boundary segmentation.

✓ Uses depthwise separable convolutions, making it faster and more efficient.

✓ Achieves higher accuracy than previous versions while being computationally efficient.

3. Key Components of DeepLab

3.1 Atrous (Dilated) Convolutions

- Increases receptive field without increasing computational cost.
- Unlike standard convolutions, it skips pixels, allowing the network to detect larger objects without downsampling.

3.2 Atrous Spatial Pyramid Pooling (ASPP)

- Captures multi-scale context by applying different dilation rates in parallel.
- Helps DeepLab segment objects of varying sizes more effectively.

3.3 Conditional Random Fields (CRFs) (DeepLab v2 only)

- Enhances boundary precision by refining segmentation results.
- Works like a post-processing step to smooth object edges.

3.4 Encoder-Decoder Structure (DeepLab v3+)

- The encoder extracts features, while the decoder refines object boundaries.
- Helps achieve sharper segmentation results, especially for small objects.

4. Applications of DeepLab

4.1 Autonomous Driving 🚗

- Lane segmentation for self-driving vehicles.
- Pedestrian and vehicle detection for road safety.

4.2 Satellite and Aerial Imagery ☐

- Land cover classification (forests, water, urban areas).

- Disaster assessment (flood mapping, wildfire tracking).

4.3 Medical Image Segmentation ⊕

- Brain tumor detection in MRI scans.
- Lung segmentation in X-rays and CT scans.

4.4 Agricultural AI 🌱

- Crop segmentation for precision farming.
- Disease detection in plant leaves.

5. Implementing DeepLab in Python (TensorFlow & PyTorch)

5.1 Using DeepLabV3 in TensorFlow (Pretrained Model)

Step 1: Install Dependencies

```
!pip install tensorflow numpy matplotlib opencv-python
```

Step 2: Load and Run DeepLabV3 Model

```
import tensorflow as tf
import numpy as np
import matplotlib.pyplot as plt
from PIL import Image

# Load pre-trained DeepLabV3 model
model = tf.keras.applications.DeepLabV3(weights="imagenet")

# Load and preprocess image
image_path = "image.jpg"
image = Image.open(image_path).resize((512, 512))
image_array = np.array(image) / 255.0
image_tensor = np.expand_dims(image_array, axis=0)

# Perform segmentation
predictions = model.predict(image_tensor)
segmentation_map = np.argmax(predictions[0], axis=-1)
```

```python
# Display segmentation results
plt.imshow(segmentation_map, cmap="jet")
plt.axis("off")
plt.show()
```

5.2 Using DeepLabV3 in PyTorch (Pretrained Model)

Step 1: Install Dependencies

```
!pip install torch torchvision numpy matplotlib
```

Step 2: Load and Use DeepLabV3

```python
import torch
import torchvision
from PIL import Image
import numpy as np
import matplotlib.pyplot as plt
import torchvision.transforms as transforms

# Load pre-trained DeepLabV3 model
model = torchvision.models.segmentation.deeplabv3_resnet101(pretrained=True)
model.eval()

# Load and preprocess image
image_path = "image.jpg"
image = Image.open(image_path)
transform = transforms.Compose([
    transforms.Resize((520, 520)),
    transforms.ToTensor(),
])
image_tensor = transform(image).unsqueeze(0)

# Perform segmentation
with torch.no_grad():
    output = model(image_tensor)['out'][0]

# Convert output to segmentation map
segmentation_map = torch.argmax(output, dim=0).numpy()
```

```
# Display segmentation results
plt.imshow(segmentation_map, cmap="jet")
plt.axis("off")
plt.show()
```

6. Advantages and Limitations of DeepLab

✅ Advantages

✓ High segmentation accuracy due to multi-scale feature extraction.

✓ Works well for small and large objects in complex images.

✓ Pretrained models available, reducing training time.

✖ Limitations

✖ **Computationally expensive** – Requires GPUs for real-time performance.
✖ **Not ideal for instance segmentation** – Focuses only on semantic segmentation.
✖ **May require post-processing** (e.g., CRFs) to refine object boundaries.

DeepLab has set a new benchmark for high-accuracy semantic segmentation, making it one of the most powerful models in autonomous driving, medical imaging, and aerial mapping. Its Atrous convolutions, ASPP, and encoder-decoder structure make it highly efficient for multi-scale object detection and boundary refinement.

9.4 Applications in Satellite Imagery and Self-Driving Cars

Computer vision has revolutionized industries ranging from geospatial analysis to autonomous vehicles. Two of the most impactful applications of image segmentation and object detection are in satellite imagery and self-driving cars.

- Satellite imagery enables precise land cover classification, environmental monitoring, and disaster response.
- Self-driving cars rely on vision systems to detect roads, pedestrians, and obstacles in real time.

Advancements in deep learning architectures, such as DeepLab, U-Net, and Vision Transformers (ViTs), have significantly improved segmentation accuracy in these domains. In this chapter, we'll explore:

✓ How computer vision is transforming satellite image analysis.

✓ How self-driving cars use segmentation for navigation and safety.

✓ Key models and technologies used in these fields.

✓ Challenges and future directions.

1. Satellite Imagery: Understanding the Earth from Above

Satellite imagery plays a vital role in urban planning, environmental monitoring, agriculture, and defense. Computer vision models can analyze these images to detect changes, classify land cover, and monitor deforestation, among many other applications.

1.1 Key Applications of Computer Vision in Satellite Imagery

☐ Land Cover Classification & Urban Planning

- Identifies forests, water bodies, urban areas, and agricultural land.
- Helps city planners make data-driven decisions for infrastructure development.

☐ Environmental Monitoring

- Tracks deforestation, melting glaciers, and ocean pollution.
- Detects illegal mining, logging, and oil spills.

🏛 Disaster Response & Damage Assessment

- Identifies flooded regions during hurricanes and tsunamis.
- Assesses earthquake and wildfire damage to aid emergency response teams.

🌾 Precision Agriculture

- Detects crop health and soil conditions using multispectral imagery.
- Helps farmers optimize irrigation and pesticide use.

2. Deep Learning Techniques for Satellite Image Analysis

Satellite images come with challenges such as high resolution, atmospheric noise, and varying lighting conditions. To overcome these, deep learning models are used for segmentation, object detection, and super-resolution processing.

2.1 Semantic Segmentation with DeepLab & U-Net

- DeepLab v3+ is widely used for land classification and disaster response.
- U-Net is effective for medical and geospatial image segmentation where pixel-wise accuracy is needed.

2.2 Object Detection with YOLO & Faster R-CNN

- YOLO (You Only Look Once) enables real-time detection of objects like vehicles, buildings, and ships.
- Faster R-CNN provides high-accuracy detection for military and security applications.

2.3 Super-Resolution with GANs

- Generative Adversarial Networks (GANs) enhance low-resolution satellite images.
- Helps in improving weather forecasting and terrain analysis.

3. Self-Driving Cars: The Future of Autonomous Mobility 🚗

Self-driving cars rely heavily on computer vision, LiDAR, and sensor fusion to navigate roads safely. Among these technologies, image segmentation and object detection play a crucial role in recognizing pedestrians, traffic signals, road lanes, and obstacles.

3.1 How Do Self-Driving Cars Use Computer Vision?

◆ **Road Lane Detection** – Identifying lane boundaries using segmentation models.
◆ **Traffic Sign & Signal Recognition** – Detecting stop signs, traffic lights, and speed limits.
◆ **Obstacle & Pedestrian Detection** – Recognizing vehicles, cyclists, and people crossing the road.
◆ **Free Space Estimation** – Determining drivable areas and avoiding collisions.

3.2 Key Deep Learning Models for Self-Driving Cars

🚗 **YOLO (You Only Look Once)** – Real-time object detection for pedestrians and vehicles.

🚗 **Faster R-CNN** – High-accuracy detection of road signs and lane markings.

🚗 **DeepLab v3+** – Semantic segmentation for drivable area detection.

🚗 **Vision Transformers (ViTs)** – Newer models providing better global context understanding.

4. Challenges in Computer Vision for Satellite Imagery & Self-Driving Cars

Despite significant advancements, several challenges remain in applying computer vision to these fields:

4.1 Satellite Imagery Challenges

◈ **High variability in images** – Seasonal changes and weather conditions affect segmentation accuracy.

◈ **Computational complexity** – Processing high-resolution satellite images requires significant GPU power.

◈ **Limited labeled datasets** – Training deep learning models requires extensive ground-truth annotations.

4.2 Self-Driving Car Challenges

◈ **Adverse Weather Conditions** – Fog, rain, and snow can reduce visibility for vision-based models.

◈ **Unpredictable Road Scenarios** – Detecting sudden pedestrian movements or road hazards remains challenging.

◈ **Latency and Real-Time Processing** – Decisions must be made in milliseconds to avoid accidents.

5. Implementing Computer Vision for Satellite Imagery & Self-Driving Cars

5.1 Satellite Image Segmentation with DeepLab (TensorFlow)

```
import tensorflow as tf
import numpy as np
import matplotlib.pyplot as plt
from PIL import Image
```

```python
# Load DeepLabV3+ model
model = tf.keras.applications.DeepLabV3(weights="imagenet")

# Load and preprocess a satellite image
image_path = "satellite_image.jpg"
image = Image.open(image_path).resize((512, 512))
image_array = np.array(image) / 255.0
image_tensor = np.expand_dims(image_array, axis=0)

# Perform segmentation
predictions = model.predict(image_tensor)
segmentation_map = np.argmax(predictions[0], axis=-1)

# Display results
plt.imshow(segmentation_map, cmap="jet")
plt.axis("off")
plt.show()
```

5.2 Object Detection in Self-Driving Cars with YOLO (PyTorch)

```python
import torch
import cv2
from PIL import Image
from torchvision import transforms
from ultralytics import YOLO

# Load YOLOv8 model
model = YOLO("yolov8n.pt")

# Load and preprocess the image
image_path = "traffic_scene.jpg"
image = Image.open(image_path)
transform = transforms.Compose([transforms.Resize((640, 640)),
transforms.ToTensor()])
image_tensor = transform(image).unsqueeze(0)

# Perform object detection
results = model(image_tensor)

# Display results
```

results.show()

6. Future of Computer Vision in These Fields

The future of computer vision for satellite imagery and self-driving cars is evolving rapidly with the integration of:

🚀 **AI-powered real-time mapping** – High-accuracy satellite-based disaster response.

🚀 **5G-powered edge AI for self-driving cars** – Faster decision-making on the go.

🚀 **Multi-modal AI models** – Combining LiDAR, radar, and vision for better self-driving performance.

🚀 **Self-supervised learning** – Reducing the need for expensive labeled datasets.

Computer vision is revolutionizing satellite image analysis and self-driving technology. From urban planning and disaster response to road safety and autonomous navigation, deep learning-based segmentation and object detection are pushing the boundaries of what AI can achieve.

10. Generative Models for Computer Vision

Generative models have unlocked new possibilities in computer vision, enabling AI to create, modify, and enhance images with remarkable realism. This chapter introduces Generative Adversarial Networks (GANs) and Variational Autoencoders (VAEs), explaining how they generate high-quality images, synthesize realistic textures, and even restore corrupted visuals. You'll explore advanced architectures like StyleGAN, CycleGAN, and Pix2Pix, which are used for applications such as deepfake generation, image-to-image translation, and artistic style transfer. Through practical examples, you'll learn how generative models push the boundaries of creativity and innovation in AI-driven visual understanding.

10.1 Introduction to Autoencoders for Image Reconstruction

In the world of computer vision, reconstructing images from noisy, incomplete, or compressed representations is a critical task. One of the most powerful deep learning architectures used for this purpose is the autoencoder. Autoencoders are a type of neural network designed to learn efficient data representations by compressing input images into a latent space and then reconstructing them back to their original form.

Autoencoders have a wide range of applications in image denoising, anomaly detection, compression, and generative modeling. They serve as the foundation for more advanced models like variational autoencoders (VAEs) and generative adversarial networks (GANs), which are widely used in synthetic image generation and data augmentation.

In this section, we will explore:

✓ What autoencoders are and how they work.

✓ The structure of an autoencoder: encoder, bottleneck (latent space), and decoder.

✓ Applications of autoencoders in image denoising, anomaly detection, and compression.

✓ A simple implementation of an autoencoder using TensorFlow/PyTorch.

1. What is an Autoencoder?

An autoencoder is a type of neural network designed to encode input data into a lower-dimensional representation (latent space) and then decode it back to reconstruct the original input. It consists of two main parts:

1.1 The Structure of an Autoencoder

◆ **Encoder** – Compresses the input image into a lower-dimensional feature representation.

◆ **Latent Space (Bottleneck)** – A compressed, encoded version of the input that captures its most essential features.

◆ **Decoder** – Reconstructs the original image from the compressed representation.

Mathematically, an autoencoder learns a function $f(x) \approx x$, where x is the input and the network is trained to minimize the reconstruction error between the input and the output.

1.2 How Do Autoencoders Learn?

During training, an autoencoder:

✅ Encodes the input image into a compressed form.

✅ Learns meaningful patterns in the data while discarding noise.

✅ Decodes the compressed representation back into the original image.

✅ Optimizes the reconstruction loss to improve output quality.

The network is trained using a loss function such as Mean Squared Error (MSE) or Binary Cross-Entropy (BCE), which measures the difference between the input and reconstructed image.

2. Types of Autoencoders

Autoencoders come in different variations depending on the application:

2.1 Vanilla Autoencoder

- A simple autoencoder with a fully connected (dense) neural network.
- Used for basic dimensionality reduction and image compression.

2.2 Convolutional Autoencoder (CAE)

- Uses convolutional layers instead of fully connected layers, making it better suited for image data.
- Preserves spatial relationships between pixels.
- Used in image denoising, feature extraction, and super-resolution.

2.3 Variational Autoencoder (VAE)

- A probabilistic extension of autoencoders that learns a distribution rather than a fixed representation.
- Used in image generation, data augmentation, and latent space exploration.

2.4 Denoising Autoencoder

- Trained to reconstruct an image from a noisy input, effectively removing unwanted noise.
- Used in medical imaging, satellite imagery, and document restoration.

2.5 Sparse Autoencoder

- Applies sparsity constraints on the hidden layers to learn important features with fewer neurons.
- Used for feature selection and anomaly detection.

3. Applications of Autoencoders in Image Reconstruction

3.1 Image Denoising

- Removes noise from corrupted images by learning to reconstruct clean images.
- Used in medical imaging (MRI, X-ray), satellite imaging, and old photo restoration.

3.2 Anomaly Detection

- Detects abnormal patterns in images by comparing reconstruction errors.
- Used in fraud detection, industrial defect detection, and cybersecurity.

3.3 Image Compression

- Compresses images into a smaller representation while preserving essential features.
- Alternative to traditional compression techniques like JPEG and PNG.

3.4 Super-Resolution

- Enhances the resolution of low-quality images.
- Used in video upscaling, astronomy, and forensic image analysis.

4. Implementing an Autoencoder in Python

4.1 Implementing a Simple Autoencoder in TensorFlow (Keras)

Step 1: Install Dependencies

```
!pip install tensorflow numpy matplotlib
```

Step 2: Import Required Libraries

```
import tensorflow as tf
from tensorflow.keras.layers import Input, Conv2D, MaxPooling2D, UpSampling2D
from tensorflow.keras.models import Model
import numpy as np
import matplotlib.pyplot as plt
```

Step 3: Define the Convolutional Autoencoder Model

```
# Define encoder
input_img = Input(shape=(28, 28, 1))  # Grayscale image (28x28)
x = Conv2D(32, (3, 3), activation='relu', padding='same')(input_img)
x = MaxPooling2D((2, 2), padding='same')(x)
x = Conv2D(16, (3, 3), activation='relu', padding='same')(x)
x = MaxPooling2D((2, 2), padding='same')(x)

# Bottleneck (latent space)
x = Conv2D(8, (3, 3), activation='relu', padding='same')(x)

# Decoder
x = UpSampling2D((2, 2))(x)
x = Conv2D(16, (3, 3), activation='relu', padding='same')(x)
```

```python
x = UpSampling2D((2, 2))(x)
decoded = Conv2D(1, (3, 3), activation='sigmoid', padding='same')(x)

autoencoder = Model(input_img, decoded)
autoencoder.compile(optimizer='adam', loss='mse')
```

Step 4: Train the Autoencoder on MNIST Dataset

```python
from tensorflow.keras.datasets import mnist

# Load MNIST dataset
(x_train, _), (x_test, _) = mnist.load_data()
x_train = x_train.astype('float32') / 255.
x_test = x_test.astype('float32') / 255.
x_train = np.reshape(x_train, (len(x_train), 28, 28, 1))
x_test = np.reshape(x_test, (len(x_test), 28, 28, 1))

# Train autoencoder
autoencoder.fit(x_train, x_train, epochs=10, batch_size=256, validation_data=(x_test,
x_test))
```

Step 5: Test the Autoencoder on Noisy Images

```python
# Add noise to test images
noise_factor = 0.5
x_test_noisy = x_test + noise_factor * np.random.normal(loc=0.0, scale=1.0,
size=x_test.shape)

# Predict reconstructed images
decoded_imgs = autoencoder.predict(x_test_noisy)

# Display original, noisy, and reconstructed images
n = 10
plt.figure(figsize=(10, 4))
for i in range(n):
    plt.subplot(3, n, i + 1)
    plt.imshow(x_test_noisy[i].reshape(28, 28), cmap='gray')
    plt.axis('off')

    plt.subplot(3, n, i + 1 + n)
```

```
plt.imshow(decoded_imgs[i].reshape(28, 28), cmap='gray')
plt.axis('off')
plt.show()
```

Autoencoders play a crucial role in image reconstruction, noise removal, and feature learning. By compressing and reconstructing data, they capture essential patterns and can be extended into more advanced architectures like Variational Autoencoders (VAEs) and Generative Adversarial Networks (GANs).

10.2 Generative Adversarial Networks (GANs) and Their Evolution

Generative Adversarial Networks (GANs) have revolutionized the field of computer vision, enabling machines to generate highly realistic images, videos, and even synthetic human faces. Since their introduction by Ian Goodfellow in 2014, GANs have evolved rapidly, leading to groundbreaking advancements in image synthesis, data augmentation, and style transfer.

At their core, GANs consist of two competing neural networks:

✅ **Generator** – Creates synthetic images to fool the discriminator.
✅ **Discriminator** – Distinguishes between real and fake images.

These networks are trained in a game-theoretic framework, where the generator continuously improves to produce more realistic images, while the discriminator becomes better at detecting fakes. Over time, the generator learns to create images indistinguishable from real ones.

In this chapter, we will explore:

✓ The architecture of GANs and how they work.
✓ Different types of GANs and their evolution.
✓ Applications of GANs in image generation, super-resolution, and deepfake creation.
✓ An implementation of GANs using TensorFlow/PyTorch.

1. Understanding the GAN Architecture

A Generative Adversarial Network consists of two main components:

1.1 The Generator

- Takes a random noise vector (latent space) as input.
- Uses deep learning layers to transform noise into a structured image.
- Tries to generate images that look real enough to fool the discriminator.

Mathematically, the generator learns a function G(z) → x, where z is the noise input and x is the generated image.

1.2 The Discriminator

- A binary classifier that distinguishes between real and fake images.
- Learns to assign higher probabilities to real images and lower probabilities to fake ones.

Mathematically, the discriminator learns a function D(x) → [0,1], where D(x) = 1 for real images and D(x) = 0 for generated ones.

1.3 The Adversarial Training Process

GANs use a minimax game approach:

☞ The Generator (G) tries to maximize the probability of the discriminator making a mistake.
☞ The Discriminator (D) tries to minimize classification errors.

The loss function for training GANs is:

$$\min_G \max_D V(D, G) = E_{x \sim p_{data}(x)}[\log D(x)] + E_{z \sim p_z(z)}[\log(1 - D(G(z)))]$$

This means the discriminator maximizes the probability of correctly classifying real images, while the generator tries to generate images that fool the discriminator.

2. Evolution of GANs: From Basic to Advanced Architectures

Since their inception, GANs have gone through multiple advancements to address stability issues, improve training, and generate higher-quality images.

2.1 Vanilla GAN (2014) – The Original Model

- Introduced in Goodfellow's 2014 paper.
- Uses fully connected layers in both generator and discriminator.
- Often suffers from mode collapse (where the generator produces limited variations).

2.2 Deep Convolutional GAN (DCGAN) – 2015

- Introduced convolutional layers for better feature extraction.
- Stabilized training and improved image quality.
- Used in unsupervised representation learning.

2.3 Conditional GAN (cGAN) – 2016

- Introduced the ability to control output images using labels.
- Allows generation of specific categories (e.g., digits 0-9 in MNIST).

$$G(z, y) \rightarrow x$$

$$D(x, y) \rightarrow \text{Real or Fake}$$

- Used in text-to-image generation and image-to-image translation.

2.4 Progressive Growing of GANs (PGGAN) – 2017

- Generates high-resolution (1024x1024) images.
- Introduces training in progressive stages, starting with small images and increasing resolution over time.

2.5 StyleGAN (2018-2020) – State-of-the-Art Image Generation

- Developed by NVIDIA, used for realistic human face generation.
- Introduced style mixing, allowing control over image attributes (e.g., age, hair color).

- Used in applications like ThisPersonDoesNotExist.com.

2.6 BigGAN & SAGAN (2019) – High-Fidelity Image Synthesis

- BigGAN: Generates photorealistic images at high resolutions.
- Self-Attention GAN (SAGAN): Introduces self-attention layers for global feature understanding.

2.7 Vision Transformers + GANs (2022-Present)

- Integrates Transformer models with GANs for improved global context learning.
- Leads to better high-resolution image generation and text-to-image synthesis (DALL·E, Stable Diffusion).

3. Applications of GANs in Computer Vision

GANs are widely used in image generation, style transfer, and creative AI.

3.1 Image Generation

- StyleGAN generates high-resolution human faces.
- BigGAN creates photorealistic images.

3.2 Image-to-Image Translation

- Pix2Pix translates sketches into realistic images.
- CycleGAN converts images between two domains (e.g., horses to zebras).

3.3 Super-Resolution and Image Enhancement

- SRGAN (Super-Resolution GAN) enhances low-resolution images.
- Used in medical imaging, satellite imagery, and forensic analysis.

3.4 Deepfakes and Synthetic Data

- Deepfake GANs generate realistic videos of people saying or doing things they never did.
- Used for entertainment, security, and misinformation detection.

4. Implementing a Simple GAN in TensorFlow/PyTorch

4.1 Import Required Libraries

```python
import tensorflow as tf
from tensorflow.keras.layers import Dense, LeakyReLU, BatchNormalization
from tensorflow.keras.models import Sequential
import numpy as np
import matplotlib.pyplot as plt
```

4.2 Define the Generator and Discriminator

```python
def build_generator():
    model = Sequential([
        Dense(128, activation=LeakyReLU(0.2), input_shape=(100,)),
        BatchNormalization(),
        Dense(256, activation=LeakyReLU(0.2)),
        BatchNormalization(),
        Dense(784, activation='tanh')
    ])
    return model

def build_discriminator():
    model = Sequential([
        Dense(256, activation=LeakyReLU(0.2), input_shape=(784,)),
        Dense(128, activation=LeakyReLU(0.2)),
        Dense(1, activation='sigmoid')
    ])
    return model
```

4.3 Train the GAN

```python
generator = build_generator()
discriminator = build_discriminator()

# Compile the discriminator
discriminator.compile(optimizer='adam', loss='binary_crossentropy',
metrics=['accuracy'])

# Build the full GAN model
gan = Sequential([generator, discriminator])
```

```
discriminator.trainable = False
gan.compile(optimizer='adam', loss='binary_crossentropy')

# Train the GAN (omitting full training loop for brevity)
```

GANs have transformed the field of computer vision, enabling machines to generate high-quality images, videos, and artistic creations. From deepfake technology to AI-powered art generation, GANs continue to push the boundaries of AI-driven creativity.

10.3 Text-to-Image Generation (DALL-E, Stable Diffusion)

Text-to-image generation represents one of the most exciting frontiers in AI, allowing machines to create highly detailed images from natural language descriptions. This technology has evolved rapidly, powered by deep learning techniques such as Generative Adversarial Networks (GANs), Variational Autoencoders (VAEs), and, more recently, Diffusion Models and Transformers.

Two of the most prominent breakthroughs in this field are DALL·E (developed by OpenAI) and Stable Diffusion (developed by Stability AI). These models have demonstrated the ability to generate photo-realistic, artistic, and even surrealistic images based on complex text prompts, making them useful for art, design, content creation, and even scientific visualization.

In this chapter, we will explore:

✓ The working principles of text-to-image generation

✓ How DALL·E and Stable Diffusion operate

✓ The differences between transformer-based and diffusion-based models

✓ Real-world applications and ethical considerations

✓ Hands-on implementation using Stable Diffusion

1. Understanding Text-to-Image Generation

At a fundamental level, text-to-image generation involves two key components:

1☐ **Text Encoding**: The model converts natural language prompts into numerical representations (embeddings).

2☐ **Image Generation**: Using deep learning, the model translates these embeddings into meaningful visual representations.

Early approaches relied on GANs (e.g., AttnGAN) to generate images from text. However, modern text-to-image models now leverage:

- Transformers (as used in DALL·E)
- Diffusion Models (as used in Stable Diffusion)

2. DALL·E: A Transformer-Based Text-to-Image Model

DALL·E, first introduced by OpenAI in 2021, is based on GPT-like transformers that generate images directly from text descriptions.

2.1 How DALL·E Works

◆ **Text Encoding**: Uses a transformer-based model similar to GPT-3 to convert text prompts into embeddings.

◆ **Image Tokenization**: Breaks down images into discrete units using VQ-VAE (Vector Quantized Variational Autoencoder).

◆ **Autoregressive Image Generation**: The model predicts image tokens sequentially based on the input text, much like GPT-3 predicts the next word.

2.2 Improvements in DALL·E 2

In 2022, OpenAI introduced DALL·E 2, which improved upon the original by using CLIP (Contrastive Language-Image Pretraining) for better text-image alignment. Key improvements:

✓☐ Higher resolution and more detailed images
✓☐ Better understanding of complex prompts
✓☐ Ability to modify existing images (inpainting and outpainting)

3. Stable Diffusion: A Game-Changer in AI Image Generation

Unlike DALL·E, which relies on transformers, Stable Diffusion (developed by Stability AI in 2022) is based on Diffusion Models—a different class of generative models.

3.1 How Stable Diffusion Works

Instead of predicting image tokens sequentially (like DALL·E), Stable Diffusion follows a denoising process:

◆ **Noise Injection**: The model starts with random noise and gradually refines it into an image.

◆ **Latent Space Optimization**: Uses a variational autoencoder (VAE) to work in a more efficient lower-dimensional space.

◆ **Denoising Diffusion Probabilistic Model (DDPM):** Iteratively removes noise step-by-step to reveal a coherent image.

This approach allows Stable Diffusion to generate images faster, more efficiently, and with greater detail than many previous methods.

4. Comparing DALL·E and Stable Diffusion

Feature	DALL·E 2	Stable Diffusion
Model Type	Transformer-based (GPT-like)	Diffusion-based (DDPM)
Architecture	Uses CLIP for text-image alignment	Uses VAE + U-Net + DDPM
Image Quality	Very high resolution, detailed	High-quality, flexible outputs
Customizability	Limited; closed-source	Open-source, highly customizable
Compute Intensity	High (requires strong GPUs)	Optimized for local execution
Use Cases	General AI art, design, media	Creative AI, fine-tuned artistic styles

One of the biggest advantages of Stable Diffusion is that it is open-source, allowing users to train and fine-tune their own models, whereas DALL·E is closed and controlled by OpenAI.

5. Real-World Applications of Text-to-Image AI

✓ **Art & Design**: AI-generated paintings, digital art, branding materials.

✓ **Marketing & Content Creation**: Generating unique stock images, advertising visuals.

✓ **Entertainment & Gaming**: Concept art, character design, storyboarding.

✓ **Education & Science**: Creating illustrations for textbooks, scientific visualization.

✓ **Medical Imaging**: Assisting in AI-powered medical illustrations and diagnostics.

6. Implementing Text-to-Image Generation with Stable Diffusion

Here's a simple Python implementation using the Stable Diffusion API (Hugging Face):

6.1 Install Dependencies

```
pip install diffusers transformers torch
```

6.2 Generate an Image from Text Prompt

```python
from diffusers import StableDiffusionPipeline
import torch

# Load the Stable Diffusion model
model = StableDiffusionPipeline.from_pretrained("runwayml/stable-diffusion-v1-5")
model.to("cuda")  # Use GPU for faster processing

# Define a text prompt
prompt = "A futuristic city with neon lights and flying cars"

# Generate the image
image = model(prompt).images[0]
image.show()  # Display the image
```

This will generate a high-quality AI-generated image based on the text description.

7. Challenges & Ethical Considerations

While text-to-image AI offers tremendous potential, it also raises ethical concerns:

- **Deepfakes & Misinforimaton**: AI can generate misleading or deceptive images.
- **Bias in AI**: Models may reflect racial, gender, or cultural biases present in training data.
- **Intellectual Property Issues**: AI-generated art raises copyright concerns (e.g., Was it trained on copyrighted material?).
- **Misuse in Propaganda**: AI-generated content can be misused for fake news and political manipulation.

To counteract these risks, companies like OpenAI and Stability AI have implemented content moderation policies and tools like watermarking AI-generated images.

8. Future of Text-to-Image AI

The future of AI-powered image generation is incredibly promising. Some key areas of innovation include:

✓ **Better Image Understanding** – Models will interpret more complex scenes with greater accuracy.

✓ **Video Generation** – AI models like Runway Gen-2 are expanding into text-to-video generation.

✓ **AI + Human Collaboration** – AI will serve as a creative assistant, helping designers rather than replacing them.

✓ **Higher Resolution & Realism** – Future models will generate 4K, ultra-realistic images.

Text-to-image models like DALL·E and Stable Diffusion represent a major leap in AI creativity, enabling anyone to generate stunning visuals from simple text prompts. While they offer incredible opportunities for artists, businesses, and researchers, they also require responsible usage to prevent misuse.

10.4 Applications of GANs in Art, Media, and AI Creativity

Generative Adversarial Networks (GANs) have revolutionized artificial intelligence by enabling machines to generate highly realistic images, videos, music, and even written content. From art and media to entertainment and advertising, GANs are reshaping creative industries, blurring the line between human and machine-generated content. In this chapter, we will explore:

✓ How GANs contribute to digital art and AI creativity

✓ Their role in media production, advertising, and entertainment

✓ Applications in style transfer, deepfake technology, and content generation

✓ Ethical considerations and challenges of AI-driven creativity

1. GANs in AI-Generated Art

One of the most famous applications of GANs is in digital art and AI-generated creativity. GANs can create unique artistic styles, mimic famous painters, and even generate completely new forms of artwork.

1.1 AI-Powered Art Creation

GANs have been used to generate original pieces of art, some of which have even been sold at auctions. A notable example is Edmond de Belamy, an AI-generated painting auctioned by Christie's for $432,500.

- **StyleGAN (by NVIDIA):** Used for generating highly detailed faces, landscapes, and artistic compositions.
- **DeepDream & DeepArt**: Uses GANs to transform photos into the styles of famous painters like Van Gogh and Picasso.
- **Runway ML & Artbreeder**: AI-powered platforms that allow users to create unique artwork and modify existing images.

1.2 Interactive Art and AI-Assisted Creativity

Artists are now collaborating with GANs to create interactive installations and AI-assisted compositions. AI tools help amplify human creativity, rather than replace it.

🎨 **Examples:**

✓ **Refik Anadol** – Uses GANs to create stunning data-driven art installations.
✓ **Mario Klingemann** – A pioneer in AI-generated art, blending human intuition with machine creativity.

2. GANs in Media & Entertainment

The entertainment industry is rapidly adopting GANs for content creation, animation, and VFX (visual effects). These models can generate highly realistic characters, environments, and visual effects, saving time and costs for studios.

2.1 AI-Generated Characters & Animation

- **GANs in Game Development**: AI can generate hyper-realistic NPCs (non-playable characters) with human-like expressions and gestures.

- **AI-Powered Animation**: GAN-based models such as First Order Motion Model allow animators to create lifelike facial animations from static images.

🎮 **Example**: NVIDIA's GameGAN can generate entire game environments, such as a playable version of Pac-Man, by observing gameplay instead of relying on explicit programming.

2.2 GANs in Film and VFX

GANs are being used in Hollywood and animation studios to enhance CGI, visual effects, and deepfake-based character recreation.

🎬 **Examples:**

✓ **De-aging in Movies** – GANs helped in de-aging actors in films like The Irishman and Star Wars: Rogue One.
✓ **Deepfake Actors** – Used to resurrect actors in posthumous roles (e.g., bringing Paul Walker back in Fast & Furious 7).

3. AI in Advertising & Content Generation

GANs are also playing a major role in digital marketing, advertising, and content generation, allowing brands to create personalized and AI-generated media.

3.1 AI-Generated Ads & Product Visuals

Brands are now using GANs to generate synthetic models, product images, and customized advertisements tailored to different audiences.

- **ThisPersonDoesNotExist.com** – Uses StyleGAN to create photorealistic faces of people who don't actually exist.
- **AI-Powered Fashion Models** – Brands like Zalando and DeepFashion use GANs to create virtual models for clothing advertisements.

3.2 AI-Generated Text & Copywriting

Beyond images, GANs are also used in text generation (in combination with GPT models) to create ad copy, product descriptions, and even movie scripts.

🔊 **Example**: The AI-generated script for Sunspring, a short film written entirely by a neural network.

4. Deepfakes: The Double-Edged Sword of GANs

One of the most controversial applications of GANs is deepfake technology—the ability to create highly realistic fake videos and audio by superimposing one person's face or voice onto another.

4.1 How Deepfakes Work

- **Face Swapping** – Maps facial features of one person onto another in a video.
- **Voice Cloning** – AI can synthesize speech that mimics a real person's voice.

4.2 Ethical Concerns

While deepfakes have potential for entertainment (e.g., movies, gaming, virtual influencers), they also pose serious risks:

- **Misinformation & Fake News** – AI-generated videos can spread false information.
- **Privacy Violations** – Misuse of deepfake technology in identity theft and cybercrime.
- **Political Manipulation** – Potential misuse in fake political speeches or propaganda.

Solutions: Organizations like Deepfake Detection Challenge and MIT's Detect Fakes Initiative are working to combat misuse with AI-based detection models.

5. AI-Powered Music & Audio Synthesis

GANs are also used to compose music, generate realistic sound effects, and even recreate voices of famous musicians.

5.1 AI Music Composition

- **Jukebox (by OpenAI)** – Can generate entire songs in different musical styles.
- **AIVA & Amper Music** – AI composers that generate soundtracks for movies and games.
- **Google's Magenta** – A research project exploring machine-learning-based music generation.

♪ **Example**: AI-generated deepfake voices have been used to replicate voices of artists like Kanye West and The Weeknd to create songs that never existed.

6. The Future of GANs in Creative Industries

GANs will continue to transform creative fields with new advancements in:

✓ **Personalized AI Art Assistants** – Helping artists create custom designs & paintings.
✓ **Real-Time AI Video Generation** – AI-powered tools for on-the-fly video editing & CGI.
✓ **AI-Generated Storytelling** – Machines generating novels, scripts, and interactive media.
✓ **AI + Human Collaboration** – GANs as co-creators rather than replacements for artists.

GANs have opened new doors for creativity, allowing AI to paint, animate, compose music, and generate realistic visuals in ways never before possible. However, as AI-generated content becomes more widespread, ethical concerns like deepfakes, misinformation, and copyright issues must be addressed.

💡 The future of AI creativity lies in responsible innovation—where GANs enhance, rather than replace, human creativity.

11. Vision Transformers (ViTs) and Self-Attention

Transformers have revolutionized natural language processing, and now they are redefining computer vision through Vision Transformers (ViTs). Unlike Convolutional Neural Networks (CNNs), ViTs leverage self-attention mechanisms to process images holistically, capturing both local and global dependencies more effectively. In this chapter, you'll explore the core concepts behind self-attention, multi-head attention, and positional encoding, as well as the architecture of ViTs and hybrid transformer models like Swin Transformer and DeiT (Data-efficient Image Transformers). By the end of this chapter, you'll understand how transformers are surpassing traditional CNNs in various vision tasks and how to implement them for state-of-the-art image classification, object detection, and segmentation.

11.1 What Are Transformers? How They Differ from CNNs

The Transformer architecture has revolutionized artificial intelligence, especially in natural language processing (NLP) and, more recently, in computer vision. While traditional deep learning models like Convolutional Neural Networks (CNNs) have dominated image processing for decades, Vision Transformers (ViTs) are emerging as a powerful alternative, achieving state-of-the-art performance in object recognition, image classification, and segmentation.

In this chapter, we'll explore:

✅ What transformers are and how they work

✅ How transformers differ from CNNs

✅ Why transformers are now being used in computer vision

✅ The advantages and challenges of using transformers in vision tasks

1. Understanding Transformers: The Foundation of ViTs

The Transformer architecture was introduced in the landmark 2017 paper "Attention Is All You Need" by Vaswani et al. It was designed for language processing, but its effectiveness in handling sequential data and long-range dependencies made it a breakthrough in machine learning.

1.1 Core Components of Transformers

Unlike CNNs, which use convolutions to process local patterns, transformers rely entirely on self-attention mechanisms. The key components of a Transformer are:

◆ **Self-Attention Mechanism** – Helps the model focus on important parts of the input sequence, regardless of their position.
◆ **Multi-Head Attention** – Enhances learning by allowing the model to focus on multiple parts of the input simultaneously.
◆ **Feed-Forward Networks (FFN)** – Fully connected layers that refine learned features.
◆ **Positional Encoding** – Adds information about the order of the input data, since transformers don't have a built-in notion of spatial structure like CNNs do.

1.2 Why Transformers Work Well for Sequential Data

Transformers were initially designed for text data, where words follow a sequence. However, their ability to capture long-range dependencies and global context has made them highly effective for computer vision as well.

2. CNNs: The Traditional Approach to Computer Vision

For decades, Convolutional Neural Networks (CNNs) have been the gold standard for computer vision tasks. Popular architectures like LeNet, AlexNet, VGG, ResNet, and EfficientNet have dominated image classification, object detection, and segmentation.

2.1 How CNNs Work

CNNs rely on convolutional layers that apply filters (kernels) to extract spatial features like edges, textures, and patterns.

◆ **Feature Extraction** – The early layers detect simple patterns (e.g., edges), while deeper layers recognize complex features (e.g., faces, objects).
◆ **Pooling Layers** – Reduce dimensionality while preserving important information.
◆ **Local Receptive Fields** – CNNs only process local regions at a time, making them computationally efficient but sometimes limited in capturing long-range dependencies.

2.2 Strengths of CNNs in Vision Tasks

✓ **Spatial Hierarchy** – CNNs naturally capture local-to-global patterns in an image.

✓ **Translation Invariance** – Can detect objects regardless of their position.

✓ **Optimized for Images** – Efficient and well-optimized for standard vision tasks.

However, CNNs struggle with capturing long-range dependencies and require multiple layers of convolutions to learn relationships between distant objects in an image.

3. Transformers vs. CNNs: Key Differences

Feature	Transformers (ViTs)	CNNs
Core Mechanism	Uses **self-attention** to process all parts of an image **simultaneously**	Uses **convolutions** to process images in local patches
Global Understanding	Captures **long-range dependencies** easily	Focuses on **local** features first, requiring deep layers for global context
Data Efficiency	Requires **large-scale pretraining** (e.g., ImageNet-21k, JFT-300M)	Works well with **smaller datasets**
Computational Cost	Computationally expensive, especially for high-resolution images	More efficient, optimized for parallel processing
Flexibility	Can be adapted for **multi-modal tasks** (text + vision)	Primarily designed for image processing
Performance on Large Datasets	**Outperforms CNNs** on large datasets (e.g., ImageNet)	Works well even on **smaller datasets**

4. Why Are Transformers Being Used in Vision?

Despite CNNs being highly optimized for vision tasks, researchers have successfully adapted transformers for images. The biggest reason? Self-attention mechanisms allow transformers to capture global context more effectively than CNNs.

4.1 Vision Transformers (ViTs): How They Work

Vision Transformers process images differently than CNNs:

1 **Image Tokenization** – The input image is split into patches (e.g., 16×16 pixels).

2 **Embedding** – Each patch is flattened into a vector and passed through a linear projection layer.

3 **Positional Encoding** – Since transformers don't have a built-in sense of spatial location, positional encodings help retain order.

4☐ **Self-Attention Mechanism** – Each patch interacts with all other patches in the image, enabling a global understanding of features.

5☐ **Classification** – A special [CLS] token is used to represent the entire image and is passed to a final classification head.

4.2 Advantages of Vision Transformers

✓ **Captures Global Context** – Unlike CNNs, which only process local features, ViTs model long-range relationships naturally.

✓ **More Scalable** – Works well with massive datasets and benefits from transfer learning.

✓ **Adaptability** – Can be easily fine-tuned for multiple tasks (image classification, object detection, segmentation).

5. Challenges of Using Transformers in Vision

🔎 **Data-Hungry** – Transformers require large-scale pretraining (e.g., JFT-300M, ImageNet-21k) to outperform CNNs.

🔎 **Computationally Expensive** – Due to the quadratic complexity of self-attention, ViTs are more expensive than CNNs.

🔎 **Lack of Inductive Bias** – Unlike CNNs, which naturally understand local structures, ViTs rely entirely on data-driven learning.

◆ **Solution?** Hybrid models like Convolutional Vision Transformers (CvTs) and Swin Transformers combine CNN-like efficiency with Transformer power.

6. The Future: Will Transformers Replace CNNs?

While transformers are showing superior performance in many vision tasks, CNNs are not obsolete. In fact, hybrid models combining CNNs and Transformers (e.g., Swin Transformer, ConvNeXt, CoAtNet) are becoming the new state-of-the-art.

💡 Future trends include:

✓☐ **Efficient Transformer Variants** – Reducing the high computational cost of ViTs.

✓☐ **Self-Supervised Learning** – Reducing the need for labeled datasets.

✓☐ **Multi-Modal AI** – Combining text, vision, and audio in a single model.

Transformers have fundamentally changed how AI models process data, making them the backbone of modern AI in both NLP and computer vision. While CNNs remain efficient and practical for many vision tasks, Vision Transformers (ViTs) are proving to be a powerful alternative, particularly for large-scale datasets and multi-modal AI.

11.2 Self-Attention and Patch Embeddings in Vision Tasks

Traditional Convolutional Neural Networks (CNNs) have been the foundation of computer vision for years, leveraging local feature extraction through convolutional layers. However, they struggle with long-range dependencies, requiring deep layers to capture global context in images.

Enter Vision Transformers (ViTs)—a new paradigm that replaces convolutions with a self-attention mechanism, enabling models to process entire images holistically. One of the key innovations of ViTs is patch embedding, which transforms an image into smaller pieces before processing it with self-attention.

In this section, we'll explore:

✓ How patch embeddings convert images into tokenized data

✓ The role of self-attention in capturing global dependencies

✓ Why self-attention outperforms convolutions in vision tasks

✓ How Vision Transformers (ViTs) apply self-attention to images

1. Patch Embeddings: Transforming Images into Tokens

1.1 The Problem with Raw Image Processing

Unlike text data (which consists of discrete tokens like words), images are composed of continuous pixels that lack a natural sequence structure. CNNs solve this by applying convolutions to capture local patterns, but they don't handle long-range dependencies efficiently.

1.2 How Patch Embeddings Work

To process images using Transformers, ViTs first divide them into small patches—essentially treating them as tokens, similar to words in NLP.

◆ Step 1: Splitting the Image into Patches

- A fixed-size image (e.g., 224×224 pixels) is divided into non-overlapping square patches (e.g., 16×16 pixels each).
- If the image size is 224×224 and patch size is 16×16, we get $(224/16)^2 = 14 \times 14 = 196$ patches.

◆ Step 2: Linear Projection

- Each patch is flattened into a 1D vector and passed through a learnable linear projection layer, transforming it into a D-dimensional embedding vector (e.g., 768 dimensions).
- This step ensures that each patch has a fixed-length representation, similar to word embeddings in NLP.

◆ Step 3: Adding Positional Encoding

- Unlike CNNs, which inherently understand spatial relationships, Transformers lack inductive bias for spatial structure.
- Positional encoding is added to the patch embeddings, allowing the model to understand the order and relative position of patches in an image.

📌 At this stage, an image is transformed into a sequence of patch embeddings, ready to be processed by the Transformer.

2. The Role of Self-Attention in Vision Transformers

2.1 What Is Self-Attention?

Self-attention is the core mechanism behind Transformers, allowing models to dynamically focus on different parts of an input sequence. It helps capture both local and global dependencies without requiring deep layers like CNNs.

Given a sequence of patch embeddings, self-attention computes relationships between them using three key components:

- **Query (Q)** – Represents the current patch looking for relevant information.
- **Key (K)** – Represents potential patches that Query can attend to.

◆ **Value (V)** – Represents the actual content of the patch being attended to.

2.2 How Self-Attention Works

For each patch i, the attention mechanism computes similarity scores with all other patches j in the image:

1☐ Compute the dot product between Query (Q) and Key (K) to measure similarity.

2☐ Apply a softmax function to normalize the scores into attention weights.

3☐ Multiply the attention weights by Value (V) to extract relevant information.

4☐ Sum the weighted values to obtain the final representation for each patch.

📌 This allows each patch to attend to other patches, enabling the model to understand contextual relationships across the entire image—something CNNs struggle with.

3. Multi-Head Self-Attention (MHSA): Enhancing Representation Learning

A single self-attention mechanism may not capture all necessary features, which is why Transformers use Multi-Head Self-Attention (MHSA).

3.1 How Multi-Head Attention Works

Instead of using a single (Q, K, V) set, MHSA applies multiple attention heads, each learning different types of relationships between patches.

✓☐ Different heads capture different spatial dependencies (e.g., texture, shape, object parts).
✓☐ More robust feature extraction compared to single-head attention.
✓☐ Each head operates independently, then results are concatenated and projected back into a unified representation.

💡 By using multiple attention heads, Vision Transformers can simultaneously focus on different aspects of an image, leading to better performance in vision tasks.

4. Self-Attention vs. Convolutions: A Comparative Analysis

Feature	Self-Attention (ViTs)	Convolutions (CNNs)
Feature Learning	Captures **global** context easily	Focuses on **local** patterns first
Receptive Field	Attends to **entire image** at once	Expands **gradually** layer by layer
Data Efficiency	Requires **large-scale datasets** to perform well	Works **well on smaller datasets**
Computation	Expensive, requires **quadratic complexity** ($O(N^2)$)	More efficient, $O(N)$ complexity
Inductive Bias	No built-in understanding of **spatial structure**	Naturally captures **spatial hierarchies**

📌 While CNNs are efficient for vision tasks, Vision Transformers outperform them when trained on large-scale datasets due to their superior ability to capture long-range dependencies.

5. Applications of Self-Attention in Vision Tasks

Vision Transformers are being applied to a wide range of computer vision tasks:

✅ **Image Classification** – ViTs outperform CNNs on large datasets like ImageNet.

✅ **Object Detection** – Transformer-based models like DEtection TRansformers (DETR) eliminate the need for region proposal networks.

✅ **Image Segmentation** – Self-attention enables models like Segmenter and MaskFormer to achieve high accuracy.

✅ **Medical Imaging** – ViTs are used for disease diagnosis and anomaly detection.

✅ **Autonomous Vehicles** – Transformers enhance scene understanding and depth estimation.

6. Challenges and Limitations of ViTs

🔍 **Data-Hungry Models** – Transformers require large-scale pretraining (e.g., ImageNet-21k, JFT-300M).

🔍 **High Computational Cost** – Self-attention scales quadratically with image size, making it less efficient than CNNs.

🔍 **Lack of Spatial Inductive Bias** – Unlike CNNs, ViTs don't inherently recognize edges, corners, or textures without sufficient training.

♦ **Solutions**? Hybrid architectures like Swin Transformer and ConvNeXt combine the strengths of CNNs and Transformers to improve efficiency.

Self-attention and patch embeddings are the foundation of Vision Transformers (ViTs), enabling them to outperform traditional CNNs in large-scale vision tasks. By breaking images into patch tokens and using multi-head self-attention, ViTs can efficiently capture long-range dependencies and global context—something CNNs struggle with.

11.3 Comparison of ViTs vs. Traditional CNNs

For decades, Convolutional Neural Networks (CNNs) have dominated computer vision, excelling in tasks like image classification, object detection, and segmentation. However, the rise of Vision Transformers (ViTs) has introduced a new paradigm, challenging CNNs with a self-attention-based architecture that captures global context more effectively.

So, which is better—CNNs or ViTs? The answer isn't straightforward. Each approach has its strengths and weaknesses, and the choice depends on data availability, computational resources, and specific task requirements.

In this section, we will compare CNNs and ViTs based on:

✓ Architecture differences

✓ Feature extraction capabilities

✓ Performance on different vision tasks

✓ Computational efficiency and scalability

✓ Real-world applications

1. Architecture Differences: Convolutions vs. Self-Attention

1.1 How CNNs Work

CNNs process images using convolutional layers, which apply local filters to extract hierarchical features.

- ◆ **Early Layers** – Detect edges, corners, and textures.
- ◆ **Middle Layers** – Capture object parts and shapes.
- ◆ **Deeper Layers** – Learn high-level representations (e.g., full objects).

CNNs excel at capturing spatial hierarchies but struggle with long-range dependencies—they require deep stacks of layers to learn global relationships.

1.2 How Vision Transformers (ViTs) Work

ViTs replace convolutions with a self-attention mechanism, which allows the model to process the entire image as a sequence of patches.

◆ **Patch Embeddings** – The image is split into small patches and converted into fixed-size vectors.
◆ **Self-Attention** – Each patch attends to all other patches, learning long-range dependencies from the start.
◆ **Multi-Head Attention** – Multiple self-attention heads allow the model to focus on different aspects of the image simultaneously.

📌 Unlike CNNs, ViTs don't rely on spatial inductive bias and learn all relationships purely from data.

2. Feature Extraction: Local vs. Global Context

Feature Extraction	CNNs	ViTs
Focus	Local features (small receptive fields)	Global context from the start
Feature Hierarchy	Hierarchical, builds complexity over layers	Captures relationships across the image immediately
Spatial Awareness	Strong spatial inductive bias	Requires positional encoding
Long-Range Dependencies	Requires deep layers to learn context	Self-attention naturally captures global relationships

💡 ViTs have an advantage in understanding global relationships quickly, while CNNs are efficient in capturing local details.

3. Performance Comparison: Accuracy on Vision Tasks

ViTs generally outperform CNNs on large-scale datasets, but CNNs remain competitive on smaller datasets.

Task	CNNs (ResNet, VGG, EfficientNet)	ViTs (ViT, Swin Transformer, DeiT)
Image Classification	Strong performance, especially on small datasets	Better accuracy on large datasets (e.g., ImageNet-21k, JFT-300M)
Object Detection	Works well with YOLO, Faster R-CNN	ViT-based DETR removes the need for region proposals
Image Segmentation	CNNs (U-Net, DeepLab) dominate	ViT-based Segmenter achieves high accuracy
Medical Imaging	CNNs perform well with limited data	ViTs outperform when large annotated datasets are available
Self-Driving Cars	CNNs (EfficientNet, ResNet) widely used	ViTs are being explored for scene understanding

📌 CNNs work well on small datasets, while ViTs shine on large-scale tasks requiring strong global understanding.

4. Computational Efficiency and Scalability

4.1 Computational Complexity

Factor	CNNs	ViTs
Computational Cost	Efficient (O(N))	Expensive (O(N²))
Training Data Requirements	Can generalize with small datasets	Requires massive datasets
Hardware Requirements	Works on low-power devices	Needs powerful GPUs/TPUs
Scalability	Less flexible for large-scale data	Scales well with large models

📟 Why Are ViTs Computationally Expensive?

- Self-attention has quadratic complexity ($O(N^2)$), meaning computational cost increases rapidly with image size.
- CNNs process images hierarchically, making them more efficient for edge devices.

💡 CNNs are still preferred for resource-constrained environments, while ViTs thrive with high computational power.

5. Real-World Applications: Where ViTs and CNNs Excel

5.1 Where CNNs Are Still Superior

✅ **Medical Imaging** – CNNs (U-Net, ResNet) work well with small medical datasets.

✅ **Mobile and Edge AI** – Efficient CNNs (MobileNet, EfficientNet) power real-time applications.

✅ **Autonomous Vehicles** – CNNs are widely used in real-time perception.

5.2 Where ViTs Are Taking Over

🚀 **Large-Scale Image Classification** – ViTs outperform CNNs on ImageNet-21k and JFT-300M.

🚀 **Self-Supervised Learning** – ViTs excel in contrastive learning and unsupervised pretraining.

🚀 **Generative AI (DALL·E, Stable Diffusion)** – ViTs are at the core of state-of-the-art text-to-image models.

📌 Hybrid models like Swin Transformer and ConvNeXt combine the strengths of both approaches, achieving state-of-the-art results in multiple vision tasks.

6. Hybrid Approaches: Combining CNNs and Transformers

To overcome the weaknesses of both architectures, researchers are developing hybrid models that merge CNNs' efficiency with ViTs' global reasoning:

🔥 **Swin Transformer** – Uses shifted window attention to reduce computational cost.

🔥 **ConvNeXt** – Redesigns CNNs to mimic ViTs' design choices.

🔥 **CMT (CNN Meets Transformer)** – Integrates CNN-like locality with Transformer self-attention.

💡 Hybrid models are currently leading state-of-the-art benchmarks in computer vision.

7. Conclusion: Which One Should You Use?

Both CNNs and ViTs have their strengths:

✔️ **Use CNNs if:**

- You have limited data and need efficient training.
- You're deploying models on mobile/edge devices.

- You need a model with fast inference speed.

✓ Use ViTs if:

- You have large datasets for pretraining.
- You need global feature extraction for complex tasks.
- You have high computational resources (GPUs/TPUs).

💡 Ultimately, hybrid models like Swin Transformer and ConvNeXt are bridging the gap, offering the best of both worlds.

11.4 Real-World Applications of Vision Transformers

Vision Transformers (ViTs) have rapidly transformed the landscape of computer vision, proving to be powerful alternatives to traditional CNNs in various real-world applications. Their ability to process images using self-attention mechanisms enables them to capture long-range dependencies and global context better than convolutional networks. As a result, ViTs have been adopted across multiple industries, including healthcare, autonomous vehicles, security, robotics, and creative AI.

In this chapter, we will explore:

✓ How ViTs are applied in different domains

✓ Why they outperform CNNs in specific tasks

✓ Real-world case studies and examples

1. Healthcare: Medical Imaging and Disease Diagnosis

1.1 Why ViTs Work Well in Medical Imaging

Medical imaging requires high accuracy in analyzing complex patterns in MRI, CT, and X-ray scans. ViTs excel in this domain because they:

✓ Capture global and local features simultaneously for better diagnosis.
✓ Reduce reliance on manual feature extraction, improving automation.
✓ Can be pretrained on large datasets for more generalizable results.

1.2 Applications in Healthcare

🚑 **Tumor Detection** – ViTs help detect cancers and abnormalities in radiology images (e.g., brain tumors in MRI scans).

☐ **Cardiac Imaging** – Used in echocardiograms and CT scans for detecting heart diseases.

☐ **Pathology Analysis** – ViTs assist in identifying diseases from histopathology slides.

◆ **Case Study**: Google's DeepMind has used transformer-based models for retinal disease detection, outperforming CNNs in diabetic retinopathy classification.

2. Autonomous Vehicles: Perception and Scene Understanding

2.1 Why ViTs Improve Autonomous Driving

Self-driving cars rely on computer vision to detect objects, pedestrians, lanes, and obstacles. ViTs offer advantages over CNNs:

✓☐ Better object recognition in complex urban environments.

✓☐ Enhanced depth perception using attention-based features.

✓☐ More efficient multi-sensor fusion for radar, LiDAR, and cameras.

2.2 Applications in Self-Driving Cars

🚗 **Pedestrian and Object Detection** – ViTs improve accuracy in detecting dynamic objects in road scenes.

🔎 **Lane Detection & Road Segmentation** – Self-attention helps detect lanes under poor visibility conditions.

☐ **Traffic Sign Recognition** – Used to analyze road signs and signals accurately.

◆ **Case Study**: Tesla and Waymo are exploring Transformer-based architectures to enhance their autonomous driving perception systems.

3. Security & Surveillance: Advanced Threat Detection

3.1 Why ViTs Are Useful in Security

Security systems need fast and accurate identification of faces, weapons, or suspicious behavior. ViTs outperform CNNs in:

✓☐ Identifying small and occluded objects in surveillance footage.
✓☐ Recognizing people across different lighting conditions.
✓☐ Reducing false positives in anomaly detection.

3.2 Applications in Surveillance

🔍 **Face Recognition** – ViTs improve accuracy in identity verification and authentication.
📹 **Anomaly Detection** – Used in crowd monitoring to detect suspicious behavior.
🔫 **Weapon and Threat Detection** – AI-driven security cameras use ViTs to spot concealed weapons.

◈ **Case Study**: Airports and smart city initiatives have integrated ViT-powered security cameras to automatically detect threats in real-time.

4. Robotics: Enhancing Vision for Intelligent Machines

4.1 Why ViTs Help in Robotics

Robots require advanced vision systems to navigate, interact, and understand their environment. ViTs are effective because they:

✓☐ Process spatial relationships better for navigation.
✓☐ Improve robotic grasping by accurately identifying objects.
✓☐ Enable multimodal learning by combining vision with other sensory data.

4.2 Applications in Robotics

☐ **Industrial Automation** – Robots in factories use ViTs to inspect products for defects.
🏠 **Home Assistance** – AI-powered robots like smart vacuum cleaners and service robots benefit from enhanced perception.
☐ **Medical Robots** – Used in robotic surgery to detect anatomical structures with high precision.

◈ **Case Study**: Boston Dynamics and OpenAI have tested Transformer-based models for robotic vision, improving real-world object manipulation tasks.

5. Creative AI: Art, Image Generation, and Content Creation

5.1 How ViTs Are Used in AI-Generated Art

Vision Transformers are a core part of generative models like DALL·E, Stable Diffusion, and MidJourney, enabling AI to generate realistic images from text descriptions.

5.2 Applications in Art and Media

🎨 **AI-Generated Art** – ViTs power generative models that create stunning digital paintings.

📷 **Super-Resolution & Image Enhancement** – Used to restore old or low-quality images.

🎥 **Video Synthesis & Deepfakes** – Transformer-based models generate hyper-realistic video content.

◆ **Case Study**: OpenAI's DALL·E 3 and Stability AI's Stable Diffusion use ViTs to create highly realistic AI-generated images and art.

6. Remote Sensing & Satellite Imagery Analysis

6.1 Why ViTs Are Game-Changers for Satellite Vision

Satellite imagery involves large-scale, high-resolution images that require detailed feature extraction. ViTs improve:

✓ **Land cover classification** – Identifying vegetation, water bodies, and urban areas.

✓ **Disaster monitoring** – Detecting wildfires, floods, and earthquakes in real-time.

✓ **Military surveillance** – Used for object detection in satellite reconnaissance.

6.2 Applications in Satellite Imagery

🌍 **Climate Change Monitoring** – Detects deforestation, ice melt, and environmental shifts.

🌾 **Agriculture & Crop Analysis** – Helps in predicting crop yields and detecting diseases.

🏚 **Disaster Response** – AI-driven analysis assists in damage assessment after natural disasters.

◆ **Case Study**: NASA and Google Earth Engine leverage Transformer-based models for satellite imagery analysis to track environmental changes.

7. Challenges and Limitations of ViTs in Real-World Applications

🏛 **High Computational Cost** – Requires massive GPUs/TPUs for training and inference.
🏛 **Data-Hungry Models** – Need large-scale datasets to outperform CNNs.
🏛 **Lack of Inductive Bias** – Unlike CNNs, ViTs don't inherently understand spatial structures, requiring more data to learn spatial hierarchies.

💡 Hybrid architectures like Swin Transformer and ConvNeXt combine the best of CNNs and ViTs to overcome these challenges.

Vision Transformers (ViTs) are reshaping multiple industries, from healthcare and security to autonomous driving and AI-generated art. Their ability to capture global dependencies makes them powerful alternatives to CNNs, but their adoption is still limited by high computational costs and data requirements.

✓☐ **Healthcare** – Medical imaging, tumor detection, and diagnosis.
✓☐ **Autonomous Vehicles** – Object detection, lane segmentation, and perception.
✓☐ **Security & Surveillance** – Anomaly detection, face recognition, and threat detection.
✓☐ **Robotics** – AI-powered industrial automation and assistive robots.
✓☐ **Creative** AI – Image generation, deepfakes, and digital art.
✓☐ **Satellite Imagery** – Environmental monitoring and disaster response.

12. Multi-Modal AI: Combining Vision with Other Modalities

The future of AI lies in multi-modal learning, where models integrate multiple data types—such as vision, text, and audio—to achieve a deeper understanding of the world. This chapter explores how computer vision can be combined with natural language processing (NLP), speech recognition, and sensor data to create more intelligent and context-aware systems. You'll learn about multi-modal transformers like CLIP, DALL·E, and Flamingo, which enable AI to generate images from text, understand visual context through language, and perform cross-modal reasoning. By the end of this chapter, you'll have insights into building AI systems that go beyond single-modal analysis, opening doors to innovations in AI-generated art, robotics, autonomous systems, and more.

12.1 What is Multi-Modal AI? Text, Audio, and Vision Together

Artificial Intelligence (AI) has traditionally been built to process single types of data—text models analyze language, computer vision models process images, and speech models understand audio. However, human perception is multi-modal, meaning we naturally combine vision, sound, and language to interpret the world.

Multi-Modal AI bridges this gap by enabling machines to process and integrate multiple data types simultaneously. This means a single AI model can:

✓☐ See an image, read its description, and understand both together.
✓☐ Listen to a person speaking and interpret their words while analyzing facial expressions.
✓☐ Combine text, audio, and visual inputs to make intelligent decisions.

In this section, we'll explore:

✅ What Multi-Modal AI is and why it matters.

✅ How text, audio, and vision work together in AI.

✅ Examples of real-world applications.

1. What is Multi-Modal AI?

1.1 Definition

Multi-Modal AI refers to AI models that can process and integrate multiple types of data—such as text, images, audio, and video—to understand and make decisions more effectively.

1.2 Why is Multi-Modal AI Important?

Traditional AI systems are limited to a single input type, making them less effective in complex real-world applications. Multi-Modal AI:

✓ **Improves Contextual Understanding** – Combines multiple signals for more accurate decision-making.

✓ **Mimics Human Intelligence** – Just like humans use multiple senses, AI can understand richer information.

✓ **Enables More Advanced Applications** – Used in robotics, self-driving cars, virtual assistants, and AI-generated media.

⬥ **Example**: A self-driving car doesn't just rely on cameras (vision); it also uses LiDAR (depth perception) and audio signals (horns, sirens) to make better driving decisions.

2. Key Modalities in AI: Text, Audio, and Vision

Multi-Modal AI systems typically integrate three major modalities:

2.1 Text Modality (Natural Language Processing - NLP)

📌 Text models process written or spoken language to understand human communication. This includes:

- Language Models (ChatGPT, BERT, GPT-4)
- Text-to-Speech (TTS) Systems
- Text-Based Sentiment Analysis

⬥ Example: AI chatbots that generate image captions by understanding both text and image data (e.g., CLIP by OpenAI).

2.2 Audio Modality (Speech & Sound Processing)

📌 Audio models interpret sound waves to recognize speech, music, and environmental sounds. This includes:

- Speech Recognition (Google Assistant, Siri, Alexa)
- Speaker Identification & Emotion Recognition
- Audio-Visual Speech Recognition (Lip Reading)

◆ **Example**: AI can transcribe podcasts while analyzing the speaker's tone and emotions to understand intent better.

2.3 Vision Modality (Computer Vision)

📌 Vision models analyze images and videos to detect objects, recognize scenes, and interpret visual information. This includes:

- Image Classification & Object Detection
- Facial Recognition & Emotion Analysis
- Video Understanding & Scene Detection

◆ **Example**: AI can watch a video, read subtitles, and listen to dialogues to understand the full context.

3. How Multi-Modal AI Combines Text, Audio, and Vision

3.1 Fusion Strategies in Multi-Modal AI

AI models use different techniques to combine multiple data types effectively:

Fusion Type	Description	Example Application
Early Fusion	Merges text, audio, and vision at the input stage before processing.	AI-generated videos from text prompts (DALL·E, Runway Gen-2).
Late Fusion	Processes each modality separately and combines outputs later.	AI assistants that analyze voice and facial expressions together.
Cross-Attention Fusion	Allows different modalities to interact during processing.	CLIP (by OpenAI), which links images and text descriptions.

◆ **Example**: A real-time sign language translator processes video (hand gestures), text (translations), and audio (spoken words) together.

3.2 Multi-Modal Pretraining Models

Recent advances in AI have enabled pretrained multi-modal models, which learn from massive datasets across multiple modalities. Examples include:

- **CLIP (Contrastive Language-Image Pretraining)** – Understands images based on text descriptions.
- **DALL·E** – Generates images from text prompts.
- **Flamingo (DeepMind)** – Analyzes text, images, and videos together.
- **Whisper (OpenAI)** – Speech recognition model trained across multiple languages.

💡 These models push the boundaries of AI by enabling cross-modal reasoning and understanding.

4. Real-World Applications of Multi-Modal AI

Multi-Modal AI is revolutionizing industries by enhancing how machines understand and interact with the world.

4.1 AI-Powered Virtual Assistants (Text + Audio + Vision)

☐ AI assistants like Alexa, Siri, and Google Assistant are becoming smarter by integrating speech recognition, NLP, and computer vision.

📌 **Use Case**: AI-powered customer service agents that understand voice tone, facial expressions, and spoken language to provide better responses.

4.2 Self-Driving Cars (Vision + Audio)

🚗 Autonomous vehicles rely on multi-modal AI to detect road signs, listen for sirens, and analyze traffic conditions.

📌 **Use Case**: Tesla's AI system integrates LiDAR, video feeds, and audio sensors for better decision-making.

4.3 AI-Generated Content & Media (Text + Vision + Audio)

🎨 Multi-Modal AI powers image generation (DALL·E, Stable Diffusion) and AI-generated music (Jukebox by OpenAI).

📌 **Use Case**: AI-generated videos from text descriptions, used in advertising, movies, and gaming.

4.4 Healthcare & Medical AI (Vision + Text + Audio)

⊕ AI is improving disease diagnosis and patient care by combining medical imaging, patient speech, and text-based reports.

📌 **Use Case**: AI doctors analyzing MRI scans (vision), patient symptoms (text), and heartbeats (audio) for better diagnosis.

4.5 Smart Surveillance & Security (Vision + Audio)

📹 AI-driven surveillance systems use multi-modal analysis to detect threats more accurately.

📌 **Use Case**: Security cameras analyzing video footage, alarm sounds, and spoken commands to detect intruders.

5. Challenges and Limitations of Multi-Modal AI

⚖ **Computational Cost** – Multi-modal models require massive GPUs/TPUs to process different data types efficiently.

⚖ **Data Alignment Issues** – Text, images, and audio need to be synchronized for accurate predictions.

⚖ **Bias in Multi-Modal Models** – If one modality is biased (e.g., racial bias in facial recognition), the AI model might amplify it.

⚖ **Interpretability Challenges** – Understanding how AI processes multiple modalities together is difficult.

💡 Ongoing research focuses on improving AI alignment, reducing bias, and making models more efficient.

6. Conclusion: The Future of Multi-Modal AI

Multi-Modal AI is paving the way for more intelligent, human-like AI systems. By combining text, vision, and audio, AI models are becoming more versatile and capable of understanding complex real-world scenarios.

◆ **Key Takeaways:**

✓☐ Multi-Modal AI integrates multiple data types (text, vision, audio) for better decision-making.

✓☐ It is already transforming virtual assistants, self-driving cars, healthcare, and AI-generated media.

✓☐ Challenges like high computational cost and data alignment still need to be solved.

12.2 CLIP: Understanding Images Through Text Descriptions

Traditional computer vision models rely on labeled datasets for training, requiring vast amounts of manually annotated images. However, humans don't learn this way—we can describe what we see using natural language without needing millions of labeled examples. Contrastive Language-Image Pretraining (CLIP), developed by OpenAI, introduces a revolutionary way to bridge the gap between text and vision by learning from massive internet-scale datasets.

With CLIP, AI can:

✓☐ Understand images based on textual descriptions rather than fixed labels.

✓☐ Recognize objects and scenes without retraining on specific datasets.

✓☐ Perform zero-shot learning, meaning it can classify images it has never seen before.

In this chapter, we'll explore:

✓ How CLIP works and its key architecture

✓ Why contrastive learning improves AI's understanding of images

✓ Real-world applications of CLIP in AI systems

1. What is CLIP?

1.1 Defining CLIP

CLIP (Contrastive Language-Image Pretraining) is a multi-modal AI model designed to understand images through natural language descriptions. Unlike traditional image classifiers, CLIP does not require pre-defined categories. Instead, it learns by associating text with images in a way similar to how humans do.

◆ **Example**: Instead of training a model to classify images into "dog" or "cat" based on fixed labels, CLIP learns by reading thousands of image captions from the internet. This allows it to recognize new categories without retraining.

1.2 Why CLIP is Revolutionary

Traditional deep learning models need extensive labeled datasets (like ImageNet) and cannot generalize well beyond what they were trained on. CLIP solves this problem by:

✓ Learning from billions of image-text pairs from the web.
✓ Understanding natural language descriptions of images instead of relying on labels.
✓ Adapting to new tasks instantly (zero-shot learning) without needing extra training.

2. How CLIP Works: Contrastive Learning

2.1 The Core Concept: Contrastive Learning

CLIP is trained using a technique called contrastive learning, where it learns to associate the correct image with the right text description by distinguishing between relevant and irrelevant pairs.

💡 How It Works:

1 CLIP receives a batch of images and corresponding captions.
2 It encodes both the images and text into a shared embedding space.
3 The model is trained to pull matching image-text pairs closer together while pushing incorrect pairs apart.

This way, CLIP learns to understand the semantic relationship between images and language rather than memorizing labels.

3. The Architecture of CLIP

3.1 Dual-Encoder Structure

CLIP consists of two separate neural networks:

◆ **Vision Encoder (ViT or ResNet-based CNN)** – Processes images into vector embeddings.

◆ **Text Encoder (Transformer-based NLP model)** – Converts text descriptions into vector embeddings.

These two encoders are trained together, ensuring that the image and its description generate similar embeddings in the shared space.

3.2 Similarity Matching

Once trained, CLIP can compare any text with any image by measuring how close their embeddings are. The higher the similarity, the better the match.

💡 For example, given an image of a panda, CLIP can rank the descriptions:
✓☐ "A black and white bear" → High similarity ✅
✗ "A red sports car" → Low similarity ✗

This ability enables zero-shot classification, allowing CLIP to categorize new images without explicit training.

4. Why CLIP is Powerful: Zero-Shot Learning

4.1 Traditional AI vs. CLIP

Most AI models are trained on a fixed dataset and can only recognize objects within that dataset. CLIP, on the other hand, can classify images it has never seen before by using language as a bridge.

◆ **Example**: If a traditional model is trained only on "cats" and "dogs," it won't recognize a "tiger." But CLIP, trained on text-image pairs, understands that a tiger is a large feline and can classify it correctly without explicit training.

4.2 Text-Based Image Classification

Unlike typical image classifiers, CLIP does not require predefined categories. Instead, it allows users to define custom labels on the fly using text descriptions.

💡 **Example**: Suppose we want to classify an image of a Tesla car.

◆ Traditional Model: Needs a dataset containing Tesla images.

◆ CLIP: Can match the image to text prompts like "a red electric car" or "a futuristic vehicle" without additional training.

4.3 Open-Vocabulary Recognition

Most computer vision models are limited by a fixed vocabulary. CLIP, however, can recognize an unlimited number of objects by leveraging language.

◆ **Example**: If given an image of sushi, CLIP can classify it as "Japanese food", "seafood", or even "nigiri" depending on the prompt.

5. Real-World Applications of CLIP

CLIP has a wide range of applications across various industries:

5.1 Image Search and Retrieval

🔎 Companies like Google and OpenAI use CLIP for text-based image search. Users can find images using natural language descriptions instead of keywords.

📌 **Example**: Searching "a snowy mountain at sunrise" returns images matching the description, even if they were never explicitly labeled that way.

5.2 Content Moderation and AI Safety

🔞 CLIP can help detect harmful content by analyzing both images and their captions.

📌 **Example**: Social media platforms can use CLIP to filter out inappropriate or violent images based on descriptive cues.

5.3 Robotics and Autonomous Systems

☐ Robots powered by CLIP can understand the environment through vision and language.

📌 **Example**: A household robot can recognize objects based on descriptions like "Find the blue mug on the table."

5.4 AI Art and Creativity

🎨 CLIP is also used in AI-generated art models like DALL·E, which creates images from text descriptions.

📌 **Example**: Typing "a cat wearing a space helmet" into DALL·E generates a unique image based on CLIP's understanding.

6. Challenges and Limitations

🔊 **Bias in Training Data** – CLIP learns from internet-scale data, which may contain biases. This can lead to unintended stereotypes in AI-generated results.

🔊 **Lack of Fine-Grained Detail** – While CLIP understands general concepts, it may struggle with complex reasoning tasks (e.g., differentiating similar objects with minor differences).

🔊 **Computational Cost** – Running CLIP requires high-powered GPUs, making it challenging for small-scale applications.

💡 Despite these challenges, ongoing research is improving CLIP's robustness and fairness.

7. Conclusion: Why CLIP is a Game-Changer

CLIP represents a major step forward in multi-modal AI, combining vision and language to create smarter, more adaptable AI systems.

◆ **Key Takeaways:**

✓ CLIP learns by matching text with images instead of relying on fixed labels.
✓ It enables zero-shot learning, recognizing objects without explicit training.
✓ Used in image search, AI art, robotics, and content moderation.
✓ Despite some biases, CLIP is pushing the boundaries of AI's understanding of the world.

12.3 Video Analysis: Action Recognition in AI

Video analysis is one of the most advanced and challenging fields in computer vision and AI. Unlike static images, videos add the dimension of time, requiring AI models to understand not just objects, but also motion, sequences, and interactions. Action recognition, a key application of video analysis, enables AI to identify and classify human movements, gestures, and behaviors in real time.

From sports analytics and security surveillance to autonomous driving and healthcare, action recognition has numerous real-world applications. In this chapter, we'll explore:

✅ How AI understands actions in videos

✅ Key techniques for video action recognition

✅ Popular deep learning models like I3D, C3D, and LSTMs

✅ Real-world applications in security, sports, and beyond

1. What is Action Recognition in AI?

1.1 Understanding Action Recognition

Action recognition is a subset of video analysis where AI detects and classifies human activities within a video. Unlike image classification, which analyzes a single frame, action recognition considers a sequence of frames to determine what action is taking place.

💡 **Example:**

◆ A simple image classifier might recognize a "person" in a single frame.
◆ An action recognition model analyzes multiple frames to determine if the person is running, jumping, or waving.

1.2 Why Action Recognition is Challenging

Action recognition is more complex than standard image classification due to:

✓☐ **Temporal dependencies** – Actions occur over time, requiring the model to track motion sequences.
✓☐ **Variability in human movement** – The same action (e.g., running) can look different based on speed, angle, and posture.
✓☐ **Background noise** – Actions must be recognized even with distractions or occlusions.

✓☐ **Scalability** – There are thousands of possible human actions, requiring AI models to generalize well.

2. Techniques for Action Recognition

2.1 Traditional Methods: Optical Flow and Keypoint Tracking

Before deep learning, action recognition relied on handcrafted features such as:

◆ **Optical Flow** – Tracks the movement of pixels between frames to detect motion patterns.
◆ **Keypoint Detection** – Identifies body landmarks (e.g., elbows, knees) to infer movement.

While effective for simple tasks, these methods struggled with complex actions, occlusions, and real-world variability.

3. Deep Learning-Based Action Recognition

With the rise of deep learning, action recognition has improved significantly. Below are the key AI architectures used:

3.1 3D Convolutional Neural Networks (C3D & I3D)

◆ 3D CNNs (like C3D and I3D) extend standard CNNs by adding a temporal dimension.
◆ Instead of processing single frames, 3D CNNs analyze sequences of frames to learn motion features.

💡 **Example:**

- A 2D CNN detects a soccer ball in one frame.
- A 3D CNN understands if the ball is being kicked, passed, or thrown based on motion cues.

◆ **Popular models:**

✓☐ **C3D (Convolutional 3D Networks)** – Learns motion features across time.
✓☐ **I3D (Inflated 3D Networks)** – Uses pre-trained 2D CNNs (like ResNet) and expands them to 3D.

3.2 Recurrent Neural Networks (RNNs) and LSTMs

Since videos involve sequences, Recurrent Neural Networks (RNNs) and Long Short-Term Memory (LSTM) networks help track motion over time.

✓☐ LSTMs store long-term dependencies, making them useful for recognizing complex action sequences.
✓☐ Combined with CNNs, LSTMs improve accuracy in action detection.

💡 Example:

In a surveillance video, LSTMs help distinguish between walking normally vs. suspicious behavior.

3.3 Transformer-Based Models for Video Analysis

Transformers, especially Vision Transformers (ViTs) and Video Transformers, are revolutionizing action recognition by:

✓☐ Analyzing entire sequences at once (unlike LSTMs, which process one step at a time).
✓☐ Better capturing long-range dependencies in videos.
✓☐ Scaling to large datasets like Kinetics-400 and UCF-101.

◆ **Example**: Google's TimeSformer is a transformer-based model that achieves state-of-the-art performance in action recognition.

4. Real-World Applications of Action Recognition

4.1 Sports Analytics 🏆

AI-driven action recognition is used in sports broadcasting and training to:

✓☐ Track player movements in soccer, basketball, and tennis.
✓☐ Analyze techniques (e.g., how a tennis player serves).
✓☐ Provide real-time statistics on player performance.

◆ **Example**: AI-powered cameras in the NBA track players' shooting, dribbling, and defending styles.

4.2 Security and Surveillance 🔍

AI-based action recognition enhances security by:

✓☐ Detecting suspicious activities (e.g., theft, vandalism, violence).
✓☐ Monitoring public spaces to prevent crimes.
✓☐ Alerting security teams in real time.

◆ **Example**: AI can identify aggressive movements in a crowd and alert law enforcement.

4.3 Autonomous Vehicles 🚗

Self-driving cars use video action recognition to:

✓☐ Detect pedestrian behavior (e.g., predicting if someone will cross the road).
✓☐ Identify traffic patterns and lane changes.
✓☐ React to real-world scenarios (e.g., cyclists, animals on the road).

◆ **Example**: Tesla's AI vision system recognizes braking signals, turn gestures, and jaywalking pedestrians.

4.4 Healthcare and Rehabilitation ⊕

AI helps in medical video analysis by:

✓☐ Tracking patient recovery after surgery.
✓☐ Monitoring physical therapy progress.
✓☐ Detecting abnormalities in movement (e.g., early signs of Parkinson's disease).

◆ **Example**: AI-powered motion tracking can assess a stroke patient's rehabilitation progress.

4.5 Smart Video Editing and Media 🎬

AI action recognition is used in:

✓☐ Automated video editing (e.g., identifying highlights in sports videos).
✓☐ Video summarization (e.g., generating movie trailers automatically).
✓☐ Interactive content creation (e.g., AI-powered filters and effects).

◈ **Example**: YouTube uses AI to detect and automatically categorize video content.

5. Challenges and Future Directions

🔟 **Scalability Issues** – Training on large-scale datasets like Kinetics-400 requires enormous computational power.

🔟 **Real-Time Processing** – AI models must be fast enough for real-time video surveillance and autonomous driving.

🔟 **Bias and Ethical Concerns** – AI action recognition models may misclassify certain movements due to biased datasets.

🚀 **Future Improvements will focus on:**

✓☐ More efficient transformer models for faster video processing.
✓☐ Multi-modal AI, combining video with text and audio for better scene understanding.
✓☐ Ethical AI development to ensure fair and unbiased action recognition.

Action recognition is transforming sports, security, healthcare, and autonomous systems by enabling AI to understand and interpret human movements. With deep learning models like I3D, LSTMs, and Video Transformers, AI is becoming better at recognizing complex activities in real time.

12.4 AI in AR/VR: How Computer Vision Powers the Metaverse

Augmented Reality (AR) and Virtual Reality (VR) are revolutionizing how we interact with digital content, blending the physical and virtual worlds. The Metaverse, a concept driven by AI, AR, and VR, aims to create immersive, interactive, and intelligent digital environments where users can work, play, and socialize. Computer vision (CV) plays a critical role in AR/VR by enabling real-time object detection, spatial mapping, and user interaction.

In this chapter, we'll explore:

✅ How AI-powered computer vision enhances AR/VR experiences

✅ Key technologies like SLAM (Simultaneous Localization and Mapping)

✅ Applications of AI in gaming, retail, healthcare, and more

✅ The future of AI-driven Metaverse experiences

1. Understanding AI in AR/VR: The Bridge to the Metaverse

1.1 What is AR, VR, and the Metaverse?

◆ Augmented Reality (AR) overlays digital objects onto the real world (e.g., Pokémon GO, Snapchat filters).
◆ Virtual Reality (VR) creates a fully immersive digital environment (e.g., Oculus Rift, PlayStation VR).
◆ The Metaverse is a virtual universe where users interact in digital spaces through AR, VR, and AI-driven avatars.

💡 **Example**: Meta (formerly Facebook) is developing Horizon Worlds, a Metaverse where users can meet, play, and collaborate using VR headsets and AI avatars.

1.2 Why AI and Computer Vision are Essential for AR/VR

Computer vision allows AR/VR systems to:

✓ Recognize and track objects in real-time.
✓ Understand depth, perspective, and spatial relationships.
✓ Enable gesture-based controls and facial recognition.
✓ Map and reconstruct 3D environments dynamically.

2. Key Computer Vision Technologies in AR/VR

2.1 Simultaneous Localization and Mapping (SLAM)

SLAM is a critical AI-driven technique that enables AR/VR systems to:

✓☐ Map the physical environment in real-time.
✓☐ Track user movement accurately.
✓☐ Adjust digital objects dynamically based on perspective.

💡 **Example:**

Apple's ARKit and Google's ARCore use SLAM to place virtual furniture in a room realistically.

2.2 Depth Estimation and 3D Scene Reconstruction

To create realistic AR/VR experiences, AI must understand:

✓☐ **Depth perception** – How far objects are from the user.
✓☐ **3D object reconstruction** – Building virtual replicas of real-world spaces.

◆ **How it works:**

- AI processes data from stereo cameras, LiDAR sensors, or RGB-D cameras to create 3D spatial maps.
- This enables accurate occlusion, where virtual objects appear behind real ones naturally.

💡 **Example**: Apple's LiDAR sensor improves AR experiences by providing accurate 3D depth maps.

2.3 Object and Gesture Recognition

Computer vision enables real-time object detection and hand-tracking gestures, allowing users to interact with digital environments naturally.

✓☐ **Object Recognition**: AR apps recognize furniture, landmarks, and faces.
✓☐ **Gesture Control**: AI detects hand movements for controller-free interaction.

💡 **Example:**

Microsoft HoloLens uses AI-driven hand-tracking for interaction without controllers.

2.4 Eye-Tracking and Facial Recognition

Advanced eye-tracking AI enhances VR experiences by:

✓ **Improving user interaction** – VR systems adjust focus based on gaze direction.
✓ **Enabling foveated rendering** – Reducing processing load by focusing on where the user looks.
✓ **Making avatars more expressive** – Facial recognition allows realistic digital expressions.

💡 **Example:**

Meta's Quest Pro headset uses AI-driven facial tracking to create hyper-realistic avatars in the Metaverse.

3. AI-Powered AR/VR Applications Across Industries

3.1 Gaming & Entertainment 🎮

Gaming has been a driving force for AI-powered AR/VR, with immersive experiences such as:

✓ AI-generated game worlds that adapt to player actions.
✓ Real-time motion tracking for enhanced gameplay.
✓ AR-based mobile games that merge virtual objects with reality.

💡 **Example:**

Half-Life: Alyx (VR) uses AI-driven physics and hand tracking to make interactions feel real.

3.2 Retail & E-Commerce 🛍️

Brands are using AI-driven AR to offer virtual try-on and AR-powered shopping experiences:

✓ Virtual fitting rooms (clothes, makeup, glasses).
✓ AR furniture placement before buying.

💡 Example:

IKEA's AR app lets users place virtual furniture in their homes before purchasing.

3.3 Healthcare & Surgery ⊕

AI-powered AR/VR is transforming healthcare by:

✓☐ Assisting in surgeries with real-time 3D overlays.
✓☐ Providing VR-based therapy for mental health treatments.
✓☐ Enhancing medical training with interactive simulations.

💡 Example:

Osso VR provides AI-driven surgical training in VR with realistic hand tracking.

3.4 Education & Training 📚

AI-driven AR/VR is improving education by:

✓☐ Creating immersive learning environments (e.g., virtual labs).
✓☐ Simulating real-world scenarios for hands-on training.
✓☐ Enhancing remote learning with AI-powered avatars.

💡 Example:

NASA uses VR-based astronaut training before space missions.

4. The Future of AI in AR/VR & The Metaverse

4.1 Hyper-Realistic AI Avatars

Future AI-driven avatars will:

✓☐ Mimic human expressions and emotions in real-time.
✓☐ Enable seamless virtual social interactions.

Example: Meta's AI-driven avatars will use real-time facial tracking for natural expressions in VR meetings.

4.2 AI-Generated Virtual Worlds

AI will automatically create 3D environments in the Metaverse, reducing manual design efforts.

✓ **Generative AI** (e.g., DALL·E, Stable Diffusion) will create immersive virtual landscapes.
✓ AI NPCs (Non-Playable Characters) will interact dynamically with users.

Example: Nvidia's Omniverse AI generates realistic 3D assets for Metaverse development.

4.3 Personalized AI Experiences

AI will personalize AR/VR experiences based on:

✓ User preferences and behavior.
✓ Real-time environment adaptation.
✓ Custom AI-driven recommendations in virtual spaces.

Example: Future Metaverse platforms will use AI to create customized digital spaces for each user.

5. Challenges & Ethical Concerns

📖 **Data Privacy Risks** – AI-powered AR/VR collects vast user data, raising concerns about privacy and security.
📖 **AI Bias in Recognition** – AI models must be trained on diverse datasets to avoid bias in face and gesture recognition.
📖 **Health & Safety** – Long-term VR usage may cause eye strain and motion sickness.

AI-driven computer vision is transforming AR, VR, and the Metaverse, enabling hyper-realistic avatars, immersive gaming, AI-generated worlds, and real-time interaction. As AI advances, expect more lifelike virtual experiences, smarter AI-driven avatars, and seamless blending of the physical and digital worlds. 🚀

◆ The future of AI in AR/VR is limitless—are you ready for the next digital revolution? ☐💡

13. Building Real-World Applications

Turning theory into practical solutions is the ultimate goal of computer vision. In this chapter, you'll learn how to apply the concepts covered throughout the book to build real-world AI applications. We'll explore case studies in autonomous vehicles, healthcare (medical imaging), security (facial recognition), retail (automated checkout), and agriculture (crop monitoring). You'll also learn best practices for deploying computer vision models, optimizing performance, and handling challenges like dataset limitations, model bias, and real-time processing. By the end of this chapter, you'll be ready to develop and implement AI-driven vision systems that solve real-world problems effectively.

13.1 AI-Powered Security and Surveillance Systems

In an era of increasing security challenges, AI-powered computer vision has transformed surveillance systems, making them smarter, faster, and more reliable. Traditional security cameras passively record footage, requiring human monitoring, but AI-driven systems actively analyze video feeds in real time, detecting anomalies, recognizing faces, tracking movements, and even predicting potential security threats. From smart cities and retail stores to airport security and law enforcement, AI-driven surveillance is revolutionizing public and private safety.

In this chapter, we will explore:

✓☐ How AI enhances real-time security monitoring
✓☐ The role of facial recognition, motion detection, and anomaly detection
✓☐ AI-powered threat detection in smart cities and critical infrastructure
✓☐ Ethical concerns and privacy challenges in AI surveillance

1. The Evolution of Security Systems: From Passive to Intelligent Surveillance

Traditional security systems relied on:

◆ CCTV cameras that continuously record footage.
◆ Human operators monitoring multiple screens.
◆ Delayed response times due to manual review of video evidence.

With AI-driven computer vision, surveillance has evolved into a proactive, automated system capable of:

✓ **Real-time threat detection** – AI can identify suspicious behavior, intrusions, or abandoned objects without human intervention.

✓ **Automated alerts** – Security teams receive instant notifications about unusual activity.

✓ **Forensic video analysis** – AI can quickly scan hours of footage to locate specific events or people.

💡 **Example:**

London's AI-powered CCTV network detects unusual crowd movements to prevent potential security incidents.

2. Core AI Technologies in Modern Surveillance Systems

2.1 Facial Recognition & Biometric Identification

Facial recognition AI maps unique facial features and compares them against databases for:

✓ **Access control** – Restricting entry to authorized personnel only.

✓ **Identifying persons of interest** – Law enforcement can track suspects in real-time.

✓ **Multi-factor authentication** – Combining facial recognition with fingerprint or iris scans for security.

💡 **Example:**

Dubai Airport uses AI-driven biometric gates, allowing passengers to pass security checkpoints without passports.

2.2 Motion Detection and Behavior Analysis

AI-powered surveillance can detect and classify suspicious movements by analyzing:

✓ **Loitering behavior** – AI detects individuals lingering in restricted areas.

✓ **Sudden crowd formations** – Unusual gatherings may indicate riots or flash mobs.

✓☐ **Unattended objects** – AI alerts security teams about abandoned bags in public spaces.

💡 **Example:**

New York City's subway system uses AI-powered cameras to spot suspicious packages and prevent potential threats.

2.3 Anomaly Detection and Predictive Security

AI models can learn normal behavior patterns in an area and detect deviations, such as:

✓☐ Unauthorized access to restricted zones.
✓☐ Aggressive body language indicating a potential altercation.
✓☐ Unusual vehicle movement in high-security areas.

💡 **Example:**

AI-powered predictive policing systems analyze crime trends to help law enforcement deploy resources efficiently.

3. AI-Powered Surveillance in Real-World Applications

3.1 Smart Cities and Public Safety ☐☐

AI surveillance plays a key role in crime prevention and traffic monitoring in smart cities:

✓☐ Automated number plate recognition (ANPR) for tracking stolen vehicles.
✓☐ Real-time crowd monitoring to detect riots or emergencies.
✓☐ Smart streetlights equipped with AI cameras to enhance public safety.

💡 **Example:**

China's AI-driven surveillance system tracks millions of citizens for security and law enforcement purposes.

3.2 Retail and Fraud Prevention ☐☐

Retailers use AI-powered surveillance to:

✓□ Detect shoplifting and fraudulent transactions.

✓□ Analyze customer movement for better store layouts.

✓□ Track employee behavior to prevent insider theft.

💡 **Example:**

Amazon Go stores use AI-powered vision systems to monitor customers and enable cashier-less checkouts.

3.3 Banking & Financial Security 💰

Banks leverage AI surveillance to:

✓□ Detect unauthorized access to ATMs.

✓□ Monitor fraud attempts in real time.

✓□ Prevent cyber threats by analyzing user behavior.

💡 **Example:**

AI-driven security cameras at JP Morgan Chase help detect suspicious ATM withdrawals to prevent card skimming.

3.4 Airports & Border Security ✈□

AI surveillance is essential in airports for:

✓□ **Automated baggage screening** – AI identifies weapons, explosives, and contraband.

✓□ **Passenger movement tracking** – Detecting unusual behavior in terminals.

✓□ **Facial recognition at immigration checkpoints** – Reducing wait times and improving security.

💡 **Example:**

Heathrow Airport uses AI-powered x-ray scanners for faster security screening.

4. Ethical Concerns & Privacy Challenges in AI Surveillance

Despite its benefits, AI surveillance raises serious ethical and privacy concerns:

4.1 Mass Surveillance & Civil Liberties

🏛 Governments may misuse AI surveillance for mass monitoring, raising concerns about privacy violations.

💡 **Example:**

China's Social Credit System uses AI cameras to monitor citizens' behavior, influencing their access to jobs, loans, and travel.

4.2 Bias in Facial Recognition AI

🏛 AI models trained on biased datasets may misidentify individuals, particularly among minority groups.

💡 **Example:**

Studies have shown that some facial recognition algorithms have higher error rates for darker-skinned individuals, leading to wrongful arrests.

4.3 Data Security & AI Hacking Threats

🏛 AI-powered surveillance systems store massive amounts of sensitive data, making them prime targets for cyberattacks.

💡 **Example:**

In 2021, hackers breached Surveillance provider Verkada, accessing live footage from Tesla, hospitals, and prisons.

5. The Future of AI-Powered Security & Surveillance

Looking ahead, AI surveillance will become:

✓ **More autonomous** – AI drones and robotic security guards will patrol restricted areas.

✓☐ **More privacy-focused** – AI will use edge computing to analyze footage locally without storing sensitive data.

✓☐ **More advanced** – AI-powered predictive analytics will detect threats before they happen.

💡 **Example:**

AI-powered drones will soon provide real-time security patrols in large-scale industrial sites and cities.

Conclusion: Balancing Security & Privacy in AI Surveillance

AI-powered security and surveillance enhance safety, prevent crime, and improve response times—but they also raise critical ethical questions. The future of AI surveillance depends on finding the right balance between security and privacy, ensuring that AI systems remain fair, unbiased, and transparent.

♦ How can we use AI for security without compromising civil liberties? That's a question we must carefully consider as AI continues to shape our world. 🚀

13.2 Retail and Facial Recognition: Customer Insights & Privacy Issues

Facial recognition technology is revolutionizing the retail industry, enabling businesses to enhance customer experiences, streamline security, and optimize marketing strategies. Retailers can use AI-driven facial recognition to identify repeat customers, track shopping behavior, personalize promotions, and even prevent theft. However, while this technology brings significant advantages, it also raises serious privacy concerns, including data security risks, consent issues, and potential misuse of personal information.

In this chapter, we will explore:

✓☐ How facial recognition enhances customer experience and security in retail
✓☐ AI-powered customer analytics and personalized marketing
✓☐ The ethical and legal challenges of using facial recognition in stores
✓☐ Best practices for responsible implementation

1. How Facial Recognition is Transforming Retail

Retailers are leveraging AI-powered facial recognition to improve customer service, prevent fraud, and optimize store operations. Unlike traditional retail tracking methods (such as loyalty programs and surveys), facial recognition offers real-time, automatic customer insights.

1.1 Personalized Shopping Experience

✓ **VIP Customer Recognition** – High-end stores use facial recognition to identify loyal customers upon entering and offer personalized assistance.
✓ **AI-powered Recommendations** – Smart displays suggest products based on past purchases and in-store behavior.
✓ **Touchless Payments** – Some stores allow customers to check out using facial authentication, eliminating the need for cash or cards.

💡 **Example:**

KFC in China uses facial recognition to suggest menu items based on a customer's age and gender.

1.2 AI-Driven Customer Behavior Analytics

Retailers analyze facial expressions, dwell time, and movement patterns to optimize store layouts and marketing strategies:

✓ **Emotion Detection** – AI can gauge customer interest or dissatisfaction based on facial expressions.
✓ **Heatmap Analysis** – Stores track which sections attract the most attention and adjust product placement accordingly.
✓ **Queue Management** – AI monitors checkout lines to predict wait times and optimize staffing.

💡 **Example:**

Walmart tested facial recognition to detect frustrated customers and improve customer service.

1.3 Preventing Theft and Fraud with Facial Recognition

✓☐ **Shoplifter Identification** – AI-powered security systems flag known offenders based on facial databases.

✓☐ **Employee Monitoring** – Retailers track employee activity to prevent internal theft and policy violations.

✓☐ **Self-Checkout Security** – AI verifies customers at self-checkout kiosks to prevent fraud and under-ringing scams.

💡 **Example:**

Amazon Go stores use computer vision and AI to enable cashier-less shopping, preventing theft without human intervention.

2. Privacy Concerns & Ethical Challenges in Facial Recognition

Despite its benefits, facial recognition in retail raises major ethical and privacy issues:

2.1 Lack of Customer Consent

📹 Many retailers scan faces without informing customers or obtaining explicit consent, violating privacy rights.

💡 **Example:**

In 2022, Madison Square Garden used facial recognition to deny entry to certain individuals, sparking public backlash.

2.2 Data Security Risks & Potential Misuse

📹 Facial recognition databases store sensitive biometric data, making them attractive targets for hackers.

💡 **Example:**

The Clearview AI data breach exposed millions of facial recognition records, raising serious security concerns.

2.3 Racial and Gender Bias in AI Models

⚖ Facial recognition algorithms have higher error rates for people of color, women, and elderly individuals, leading to false identifications.

💡 **Example:**

Studies found that some AI-powered facial recognition systems misidentified Black and Asian individuals up to 100 times more than white individuals.

3. The Legal Landscape: Regulations on Facial Recognition in Retail

3.1 Global Regulations and Bans

✓☐ **European Union (EU):** The GDPR mandates strict guidelines on biometric data collection, requiring explicit consent.
✓☐ **United States**: Some states, such as Illinois (BIPA) and California (CCPA), have introduced privacy laws limiting facial recognition use.
✓☐ **China**: The country widely deploys facial recognition in retail but faces criticism over privacy violations.

💡 **Example:**

In 2023, a lawsuit against Clearview AI forced the company to stop selling facial recognition services to private businesses.

3.2 Best Practices for Ethical Implementation

Retailers should adopt privacy-conscious facial recognition practices to gain consumer trust and comply with regulations:

✓☐ **Transparency** – Inform customers when facial recognition is used and obtain explicit consent.
✓☐ **Data Security** – Encrypt biometric data and store it securely to prevent breaches.
✓☐ **Bias Reduction** – Train AI models on diverse datasets to improve accuracy across different demographics.
✓☐ **Limited Retention** – Avoid storing facial data longer than necessary.

💡 **Example:**

Apple's Face ID securely encrypts facial data on-device, reducing privacy risks.

4. The Future of Facial Recognition in Retail

AI-driven facial recognition is expected to expand in retail while adapting to evolving regulations and ethical standards. Future developments include:

✓☐ **Decentralized Biometric Systems** – Customers will control their facial data using privacy-focused AI tools.
✓☐ **AI-Powered Smart Mirrors** – Virtual try-on solutions will use facial recognition for personalized shopping experiences.
✓☐ **Privacy-Preserving AI** – Advancements in federated learning will allow AI to process facial data without storing it centrally.

💡 Example:

L'Oréal's AI-powered smart mirrors let customers try on makeup virtually using facial recognition.

Conclusion: Balancing Innovation and Privacy

Facial recognition in retail offers game-changing benefits, from personalized shopping experiences to enhanced security. However, it also introduces serious privacy concerns that retailers must address ethically and legally. The future of AI-powered retail lies in finding a balance between innovation, security, and consumer privacy rights.

🚀 How can retailers implement AI-driven facial recognition while ensuring transparency and fairness? This remains one of the biggest challenges for the future of AI in retail.

13.3 Autonomous Robotics and Computer Vision in Industry

The integration of autonomous robotics and computer vision is transforming industries worldwide. From manufacturing and logistics to healthcare and agriculture, AI-powered robots are now capable of navigating environments, identifying objects, making decisions, and performing complex tasks with minimal human intervention. Computer vision enables robots to see, interpret, and react to their surroundings, allowing for greater efficiency, precision, and adaptability in industrial settings.

In this chapter, we will explore:

✓☐ How computer vision enhances autonomous robotics in industry
✓☐ Real-world applications in manufacturing, logistics, healthcare, and agriculture
✓☐ The challenges of implementing robotic vision systems
✓☐ Future trends in AI-powered robotics

1. How Computer Vision Empowers Autonomous Robotics

Traditional industrial robots operated based on predefined rules and structured environments. However, computer vision has enabled modern autonomous robots to analyze and adapt to dynamic conditions.

1.1 Key Capabilities of Vision-Enabled Robots

✓☐ **Object Detection & Recognition** – Robots can identify and classify objects in real time.
✓☐ **Navigation & Path Planning** – Vision-based SLAM (Simultaneous Localization and Mapping) helps robots autonomously navigate environments.
✓☐ **Defect Detection & Quality Control** – AI-driven cameras inspect products for defects and inconsistencies.
✓☐ **Human-Robot Interaction (HRI)** – Vision-enabled robots recognize human gestures, ensuring safe collaboration.

💡 **Example:**

Tesla's Gigafactory uses computer vision-powered robots for automated car assembly and quality inspection.

2. Industrial Applications of Autonomous Robotics & Computer Vision

2.1 Smart Manufacturing & Industry 4.0 🏭

Computer vision is driving Industry 4.0, where AI-powered robots automate production lines and enhance efficiency.

✓☐ **Automated Assembly Lines** – Robots precisely assemble components with minimal errors.
✓☐ **Visual Quality Inspection** – AI-driven cameras detect product defects faster than humans.

✓☐ **Predictive Maintenance** – Vision systems monitor machinery health to prevent failures.

💡 **Example:**

BMW's robotic vision system detects minute defects in car parts, reducing waste and improving quality.

2.2 Robotics in Logistics & Warehousing 🎁

Autonomous robots are optimizing logistics by enhancing speed, accuracy, and cost-efficiency in warehouses.

✓☐ **Automated Sorting & Packaging** – Robots identify, pick, and package items with precision.
✓☐ **Self-Navigating AGVs (Automated Guided Vehicles)** – AI-powered AGVs transport goods in warehouses.
✓☐ **Barcode & Object Recognition** – Vision systems scan items for inventory tracking.

💡 **Example:**

Amazon's robotic fulfillment centers use vision-powered robots to sort and transport products at high speed.

2.3 AI-Powered Robotics in Healthcare ✚

Medical robotics powered by computer vision are revolutionizing surgery, diagnostics, and patient care.

✓☐ **Surgical Robots** – AI-assisted robots enhance precision in complex surgeries.
✓☐ **AI Medical Imaging** – Vision models analyze X-rays, MRIs, and CT scans for early disease detection.
✓☐ **Autonomous Patient Monitoring** – Vision-based AI tracks patient movements and health conditions.

💡 **Example:**

The Da Vinci Surgical Robot enables minimally invasive surgeries using AI-assisted vision.

2.4 Computer Vision in Agriculture & Farming 🌾

Autonomous robots in agriculture use AI vision to increase crop yields and optimize resource usage.

✓☐ **Precision Farming** – Drones use computer vision to analyze soil health and crop conditions.
✓☐ **Automated Harvesting** – AI-powered robots identify and pick ripe fruits with precision.
✓☐ **Pest & Disease Detection** – Vision AI detects early signs of plant diseases, reducing chemical usage.

💡 **Example:**

John Deere's AI tractors use computer vision for autonomous plowing, planting, and harvesting.

3. Challenges in Implementing Vision-Based Robotics

Despite its advancements, deploying autonomous robotics with AI vision faces several challenges:

3.1 High Implementation Costs

💻 Developing AI-powered robotic systems requires expensive hardware, sensors, and AI models.

💡 **Solution**: Open-source AI frameworks (e.g., TensorFlow, PyTorch) and cloud-based robotics are reducing costs.

3.2 Real-Time Processing & Latency Issues

💻 Computer vision algorithms require high computational power for real-time decision-making.

💡 **Solution**: Edge AI enables robots to process vision data locally, reducing dependence on cloud computing.

3.3 Data Limitations & AI Training Challenges

📷 AI models require large datasets for training, which may be unavailable or biased.

💡 **Solution**: Synthetic data generation and self-supervised learning are improving AI training.

4. Future Trends in Vision-Based Autonomous Robotics

The next decade will see further advancements in AI-powered robotics, including:

✓☐ **AI-Powered Cobots (Collaborative Robots)** – Robots that work alongside humans safely.

✓☐ **Self-Learning Robots** – Machines that learn and adapt without human intervention.

✓☐ **Humanoid Robots with Computer Vision** – AI-powered robots capable of mimicking human behavior.

💡 **Example:**

Tesla's Optimus humanoid robot uses AI vision to perform complex human-like tasks autonomously.

Conclusion: The Future of AI Vision in Robotics

Computer vision is revolutionizing autonomous robotics across industries, enabling robots to see, analyze, and interact with the world more effectively. As AI continues to evolve, vision-enabled robots will enhance productivity, safety, and efficiency in various sectors.

🚀 How will AI-powered robots shape the future of industry? The possibilities are endless!

13.4 Edge AI: Running Vision Models on Low-Power Devices

The rise of Edge AI is transforming how computer vision models are deployed, allowing AI to run directly on low-power devices without relying on cloud computing. Instead of sending data to remote servers, Edge AI processes information locally on devices like smartphones, drones, IoT cameras, and embedded systems. This shift enables faster decision-making, reduced latency, enhanced privacy, and lower energy consumption, making it ideal for real-time applications in autonomous vehicles, smart surveillance, healthcare, and industrial automation.

In this chapter, we will explore:

✓☐ What Edge AI is and why it's important
✓☐ How vision models are optimized for edge devices
✓☐ Real-world applications of Edge AI in computer vision
✓☐ Challenges and future trends in Edge AI

1. What is Edge AI and Why Does It Matter?

Edge AI refers to running artificial intelligence models directly on edge devices (e.g., mobile phones, IoT devices, embedded systems) rather than relying on cloud computing. This is crucial for computer vision applications that require real-time decision-making, such as autonomous navigation, security surveillance, and medical diagnostics.

1.1 Key Benefits of Edge AI for Vision Systems

✓☐ **Reduced Latency** – Faster response times since data doesn't need to be sent to the cloud.
✓☐ **Improved Privacy & Security** – Sensitive visual data remains on the device.
✓☐ **Lower Bandwidth Costs** – No need to send large image/video data over the internet.
✓☐ **Energy Efficiency** – Optimized AI models consume less power on edge hardware.
✓☐ **Offline Functionality** – AI models can operate without an internet connection.

💡 **Example:**

Tesla's Autopilot uses Edge AI for real-time object detection and decision-making without relying on cloud processing.

2. Optimizing Vision Models for Edge Devices

Since edge devices have limited computational resources, standard deep learning models must be optimized for efficiency.

2.1 Model Compression Techniques

To deploy AI on low-power devices, vision models are compressed using:

✓☐ **Quantization** – Reducing model precision (e.g., from 32-bit floating point to 8-bit integers) to save memory.

✓☐ **Pruning** – Removing unnecessary weights and layers to make the model smaller.

✓☐ **Knowledge Distillation** – Training a smaller model to mimic a large, high-performance model.

💡 **Example:**

MobileNet is an optimized deep learning model designed for real-time image classification on mobile devices.

2.2 Hardware Acceleration for Edge AI

AI models on edge devices rely on specialized hardware accelerators to enhance performance:

✓☐ **TPUs (Tensor Processing Units)** – Google's AI chips designed for fast computations.

✓☐ **NPUs (Neural Processing Units)** – Found in mobile processors like Apple's A-series and Qualcomm's Snapdragon AI Engine.

✓☐ **FPGAs & GPUs** – Used in high-performance edge computing, such as autonomous drones.

💡 **Example:**

Apple's Neural Engine (NPU) powers Face ID and on-device AI image processing in iPhones.

3. Real-World Applications of Edge AI in Computer Vision

3.1 Smart Surveillance & Security 🎥

✓☐ Edge-based CCTV systems use AI to detect intruders and recognize faces without sending video to a remote server.

✓☐ AI-powered home security cameras provide instant alerts when suspicious activity is detected.

💡 **Example:**

Amazon Ring cameras use Edge AI to recognize people, pets, and packages without cloud dependency.

3.2 Autonomous Vehicles & Drones 🚗

✓ Self-driving cars rely on Edge AI to process real-time visual data for obstacle detection and navigation.
✓ AI-powered drones use vision models for aerial surveillance, agriculture monitoring, and delivery services.

💡 Example:

DJI drones use Edge AI to detect and avoid obstacles in real-time without cloud processing.

3.3 AI in Healthcare & Medical Imaging ⊕

✓ Portable AI medical devices analyze X-rays and MRIs in real-time, helping doctors diagnose diseases faster.
✓ Wearable health monitors track vital signs and detect anomalies using on-device vision AI.

💡 Example:

AI-powered retinal scanners can detect diabetic retinopathy on low-power edge devices in remote areas.

3.4 Smart Retail & AI-Powered Checkout 🛒

✓ Edge AI cash registers recognize items without barcodes, enabling checkout-free stores.
✓ Retail analytics cameras track customer behavior while maintaining data privacy.

💡 Example:

Amazon Go stores use Edge AI for just-walk-out shopping, eliminating checkout lines.

4. Challenges of Running Vision Models on Edge Devices

🕮 4.1 **Limited Computational Power** – Edge devices lack the processing power of cloud GPUs.

💡 **Solution**: Model compression and hardware acceleration improve efficiency.

🕮 4.2 **Energy Consumption** – Running AI models on battery-powered devices can drain power quickly.

💡 **Solution**: AI chip manufacturers are designing ultra-low-power NPUs for Edge AI.

🕮 4.3 **Model Accuracy vs. Efficiency Trade-Off** – Highly compressed models may lose accuracy.

💡 **Solution**: Researchers are improving quantization-aware training to balance accuracy and efficiency.

5. The Future of Edge AI in Computer Vision

As AI and hardware technology advance, Edge AI will continue to evolve. Future trends include:

✓ **5G-Enabled Edge AI** – Faster wireless networks will enhance real-time AI processing.
✓ **AI on TinyML Devices** – Running deep learning on ultra-low-power microcontrollers.
✓ **Self-Learning Edge AI** – AI models that continuously improve without cloud retraining.

💡 **Example:**

Google's Coral Edge TPU enables real-time AI vision processing on embedded devices. Conclusion: The Power of Edge AI in Vision Systems

Edge AI is revolutionizing computer vision applications by making AI faster, more private, and energy-efficient. As industries move towards real-time, AI-powered automation, Edge AI will play a crucial role in enabling smart devices, autonomous robots, and real-time decision-making without relying on cloud infrastructure.

🚀 What's next for Edge AI? The possibilities are limitless as AI models become smarter, smaller, and more efficient!

14. Building Computer Vision Projects from Scratch

Applying your knowledge to hands-on projects is the best way to master computer vision. In this chapter, you'll learn how to design, develop, and deploy end-to-end computer vision projects from scratch. We'll walk through the complete workflow, including problem definition, dataset collection, preprocessing, model selection, training, evaluation, and deployment. You'll build real-world projects such as image classification, object detection, facial recognition, and image segmentation, using tools like OpenCV, TensorFlow, and PyTorch. By the end of this chapter, you'll have the confidence and skills to create your own AI-driven vision applications, whether for research, business, or personal innovation.

14.1 How to Collect and Label Image Data Efficiently

The foundation of any successful computer vision project is high-quality, well-labeled image data. Garbage in, garbage out—if the dataset used for training an AI model is biased, noisy, or inconsistent, the model's performance will suffer. Efficiently collecting and labeling images is crucial to ensure accuracy, reduce biases, and optimize computational resources.

In this chapter, we will explore:

✓□ Best practices for collecting diverse and representative image data
✓□ Automated and manual methods for image labeling
✓□ Tools and frameworks for efficient dataset annotation
✓□ Strategies to scale data collection and labeling for large projects

1. Image Data Collection: Where and How to Get High-Quality Images

To train an AI model effectively, you need a diverse, well-balanced dataset that represents the real-world scenarios the model will encounter. There are several ways to collect high-quality images:

1.1 Sources for Image Data Collection

✓☐ **Publicly Available Datasets** ☐☐ – Many high-quality datasets are open-source and freely available.

- **Examples**: ImageNet, COCO, Open Images Dataset, MNIST, CIFAR-10, Pascal VOC
- **Pros**: Free, large-scale, well-labeled
- **Cons**: May not fit specific use cases or industries

✓☐ **Web Scraping** ☐ – Automating the extraction of images from websites.

- **Tools**: Selenium, Scrapy, BeautifulSoup
- **Pros**: Can collect millions of images quickly
- **Cons**: May violate copyright policies; requires filtering

✓☐ **Synthetic Data Generation** ☐☐ – Using AI to create realistic images.

- **Tools**: GANs (Generative Adversarial Networks), Unity Perception, NVIDIA Omniverse
- **Pros**: Eliminates data bias, can generate rare scenarios
- **Cons**: Computationally expensive, needs fine-tuning

✓☐ **Crowdsourcing & Manual Data Collection** 📷 – Gathering real-world images using mobile apps or public participation.

- **Platforms**: Amazon Mechanical Turk, Appen, Lionbridge AI
- **Pros**: Customizable, diverse datasets
- **Cons**: Labor-intensive, may require manual verification

✓☐ **IoT & Sensor-Based Collection** 📡 – Using cameras, drones, or sensors to capture real-world data.

- **Example**: Self-driving car companies use LIDAR + camera fusion for scene understanding.
- **Pros**: Real-time, domain-specific
- **Cons**: Expensive, requires specialized hardware

💡 **Best Practice**: Always ensure diversity in dataset collection (lighting conditions, angles, backgrounds, environments, demographics) to avoid model bias.

2. Image Labeling: Making Data Usable for AI Models

After collecting images, they need to be annotated so that machine learning models can understand what's in them. Labeling can be manual, semi-automated, or fully automated.

2.1 Types of Image Annotation

✓☐ **Image Classification** – Assigning a single label to an entire image.

Example: Labeling a picture as "cat" or "dog."

✓☐ **Object Detection** – Drawing bounding boxes around objects in an image.

Example: Identifying multiple objects like cars and pedestrians in a traffic scene.

✓☐ **Semantic Segmentation** – Assigning a label to every pixel in an image.

Example: Distinguishing between sky, road, and buildings in an urban scene.

✓☐ **Instance Segmentation** – Identifying multiple instances of the same object separately.

Example: Detecting individual people in a crowd.

✓☐ **Keypoint Annotation** – Marking specific points on objects.

Example: Identifying facial landmarks for emotion detection AI.

💡 **Best Practice**: Choose the right type of annotation based on the task—classification for broad categorization, bounding boxes for object detection, and segmentation for pixel-level understanding.

3. Efficient Image Labeling Methods

Since manual annotation is time-consuming and expensive, several techniques can improve efficiency:

3.1 Manual Labeling ✍️

- **Use Crowdsourcing Platforms** – Amazon Mechanical Turk, Appen, Scale AI

- **Hire Domain Experts** – For specialized fields like medical imaging (radiologists, dermatologists)

✓ **Pros**: High accuracy
✗ **Cons**: Expensive, slow

3.2 Semi-Automated Labeling

- Pre-trained AI models generate initial labels, which humans refine.
- Active Learning – The AI requests human annotation for uncertain cases.

✓ **Pros**: Faster than manual labeling
✗ **Cons**: Still requires human intervention

💡 **Example**: Google's AutoML Vision suggests annotations, reducing human effort.

3.3 Fully Automated Labeling ⚡

- Self-supervised Learning – AI learns to label data automatically.
- Synthetic Data with Ground Truth Labels – GANs generate images with pre-defined labels.

✓ **Pros**: Scalable, cost-effective
✗ **Cons**: Less reliable for complex datasets

💡 **Example**: YOLO & Faster R-CNN can label new images after training on annotated datasets.

4. Tools & Platforms for Image Annotation

Using the right annotation tools can significantly speed up the labeling process.

Tool	Features	Best For
LabelImg	Open-source, manual bounding boxes	Object detection
CVAT (Computer Vision Annotation Tool)	Supports bounding boxes, polygons, and keypoints	General-purpose annotation
SuperAnnotate	AI-assisted labeling, team collaboration	Enterprise-level projects
Labelbox	Cloud-based, auto-labeling AI models	Large datasets
VGG Image Annotator (VIA)	Free, lightweight, manual annotation	Small projects
Roboflow	Auto-labeling, dataset augmentation	Quick deployment

💡 **Best Practice**: Use AI-assisted labeling for large datasets to reduce manual workload.

5. Scaling Image Collection & Labeling for Large Projects

🚀 **5.1 Data Augmentation** – Generate more training data by modifying existing images.

✓ **Techniques**: Rotation, flipping, brightness adjustment, noise injection
✓ **Tool**: Albumentations, OpenCV

🚀 **5.2 Transfer Learning** – Use pre-trained models to reduce the need for large labeled datasets.

✓ **Example**: Fine-tuning ResNet, EfficientNet, or ViTs for specific applications.

🚀 **5.3 Self-Supervised Learning** – AI learns patterns without labeled data.

✓ **Example**: Contrastive learning (SimCLR, BYOL) for feature extraction.

💡 **Pro Tip**: Combining active learning (human-in-the-loop) with semi-automated labeling can maximize efficiency while ensuring high-quality annotations.

Conclusion: The Key to High-Quality Computer Vision Models

Efficient image collection and labeling are essential for training accurate AI models. By leveraging crowdsourcing, automation, augmentation, and self-supervised learning, teams can scale data pipelines while reducing costs and effort.

◆ The right dataset = better model performance

◆ Choose efficient annotation tools to save time
◆ Automate whenever possible, but ensure data quality

🖋 The future of AI depends on data—build it right, and your vision models will succeed!

14.2 Data Augmentation Techniques for Better Model Performance

In machine learning and computer vision, having large and diverse datasets is essential for training high-performing models. However, collecting and labeling large amounts of image data is expensive and time-consuming. This is where data augmentation comes in—a powerful technique that artificially increases the size and diversity of a dataset by applying transformations such as rotation, flipping, scaling, cropping, and color adjustments.

By using data augmentation, models become more robust, generalize better to real-world variations, and avoid overfitting. In this chapter, we will cover:

✓□ Why data augmentation is crucial for deep learning models
✓□ Common augmentation techniques in computer vision
✓□ Advanced augmentation strategies using deep learning
✓□ Tools and libraries for applying data augmentation

1. Why Use Data Augmentation in Computer Vision?

1.1 The Problem of Overfitting

When a deep learning model is trained on a small or biased dataset, it tends to memorize the training data instead of learning general patterns. This results in poor performance on new images. Data augmentation helps by introducing random variations, forcing the model to generalize better.

1.2 Key Benefits of Data Augmentation

✓□ **Reduces Overfitting** – Prevents models from memorizing training data.
✓□ **Improves Generalization** – Makes the model more robust to variations in real-world images.

✓☐ **Enhances Model Accuracy** – Helps models learn more diverse features.

✓☐ **Compensates for Small Datasets** – Allows training deep models even with limited data.

💡 **Example**: A self-driving car model trained only on daytime images might fail in low-light conditions. By augmenting the dataset with artificially darkened images, the model learns to perform better at night.

2. Common Image Augmentation Techniques

There are several ways to modify images while preserving essential features. Here are the most commonly used techniques:

2.1 Geometric Transformations

📌 **Rotation** – Rotates an image by a small angle to make the model invariant to orientation changes.

Example: Rotating handwritten digits in an OCR system.

📌 **Flipping (Mirroring)** – Horizontally or vertically flips an image.

Example: Flipping images of road signs prevents the model from overfitting to a particular orientation.

📌 **Scaling & Resizing** – Adjusts the size of an image while keeping its aspect ratio.

Example: Helps object detection models recognize objects at different distances.

📌 **Cropping & Padding** – Crops part of an image or adds padding around it.

Example: Ensures objects remain in different positions in training images.

📌 **Translation (Shifting)** – Moves an image along the x-axis or y-axis.

Example: Helps models become invariant to object positioning in images.

💡 **Tool**: cv2.warpAffine() in OpenCV for rotation, translation, and scaling.

2.2 Photometric Transformations

📌 **Brightness Adjustment** – Increases or decreases the brightness of an image.

Example: Helps models work in various lighting conditions (e.g., morning vs. night).

📌 **Contrast & Saturation Changes** – Modifies contrast to make objects more or less visible.

Example: Useful in medical imaging to highlight features in X-rays.

📌 **Gaussian Noise Injection** – Adds random noise to images to improve robustness.

Example: Helps prevent the model from being too sensitive to image artifacts.

📌 **Blurring (Gaussian, Motion Blur, etc.)** – Simulates real-world camera blur.

Example: Helps in scenarios like autonomous driving, where motion blur is common.

💡 **Tool**: imgaug and albumentations libraries support photometric augmentations.

2.3 Color Space Transformations

📌 **Grayscale Conversion** – Converts an RGB image to grayscale.

Example: Helps models focus on shapes and edges instead of color.

📌 **HSV & LAB Color Space Adjustments** – Changes image colors in different color spaces.

Example: Useful in applications like plant disease detection, where color variations matter.

📌 **Channel Swapping** – Randomly rearranges the RGB channels.

Example: Prevents the model from over-relying on a specific color channel.

💡 **Tool**: OpenCV functions like cv2.cvtColor() for color transformations.

3. Advanced Data Augmentation Techniques Using Deep Learning

3.1 Generative Adversarial Networks (GANs) for Data Augmentation

GANs can generate new synthetic images based on a training dataset.

✓☐ Used for augmenting medical images, rare object detection, and face generation.
✓☐ Example: StyleGAN generates realistic human faces for deepfake detection training.

💡 **Tool**: NVIDIA StyleGAN, Deep Convolutional GAN (DCGAN).

3.2 Adversarial Augmentation

✓☐ Generates slightly modified images that "trick" the model into making mistakes.
✓☐ Helps improve the model's ability to handle real-world adversarial noise.

💡 **Tool**: Foolbox and CleverHans for adversarial image augmentation.

3.3 CutMix & MixUp Augmentation

✓☐ **CutMix** – Pastes a region from one image onto another to improve generalization.
✓☐ **MixUp** – Blends two images together along with their labels.
✓☐ Used in state-of-the-art image classification models like ResNet & EfficientNet.

💡 **Tool**: Albumentations supports CutMix and MixUp augmentation.

4. Tools & Libraries for Data Augmentation

There are several Python libraries that simplify data augmentation:

Library	Features	Best For
Albumentations	Fast, flexible, supports **CutMix, MixUp**	Deep learning pipelines
imgaug	Advanced image augmentations (elastic distortions, noise)	Research projects
TensorFlow/Keras ImageDataGenerator	Built-in augmentations for training CNNs	Keras users
Torchvision Transforms	Standard augmentations for PyTorch models	PyTorch users
OpenCV	Low-level geometric and color transformations	Classic CV applications

💡 **Best Practice**: Use Albumentations for deep learning applications—it is fast, optimized, and easy to use.

5. Best Practices for Applying Data Augmentation

✓☐ Apply augmentation only to the training set, not validation/test sets.
✓☐ Avoid excessive augmentation that distorts features important for recognition.
✓☐ Use a mix of geometric and photometric augmentations for better generalization.
✓☐ Test augmented images manually to ensure they make sense for your application.

💡 **Example Workflow:**

```
import albumentations as A
import cv2
import numpy as np

# Define augmentation pipeline
augment = A.Compose([
    A.HorizontalFlip(p=0.5),
    A.RandomBrightnessContrast(p=0.2),
    A.Rotate(limit=15, p=0.5),
    A.GaussianBlur(p=0.2),
])

# Load image
image = cv2.imread("image.jpg")
```

```
augmented = augment(image=image)['image']
```

```
cv2.imshow("Augmented Image", augmented)
cv2.waitKey(0)
```

Conclusion: The Power of Data Augmentation

Data augmentation is an essential technique in computer vision that improves model accuracy, reduces overfitting, and enhances generalization. From simple transformations like flipping and rotation to advanced techniques like GANs and CutMix, augmentation can significantly boost deep learning models.

🚀 By using the right augmentation strategy, you can train robust AI models—even with limited data!

14.3 Model Training and Hyperparameter Tuning

Training a computer vision model involves more than just feeding images into a neural network—it requires careful selection of hyperparameters, optimization techniques, and evaluation metrics to ensure the best possible performance. Hyperparameter tuning is the process of adjusting key parameters like learning rate, batch size, number of layers, dropout rate, and activation functions to optimize the model's accuracy and efficiency.

In this chapter, we will explore:

✓ The step-by-step process of training a computer vision model
✓ Common optimization techniques for deep learning
✓ Key hyperparameters and their impact on model performance
✓ Strategies for tuning hyperparameters effectively

1. Steps for Training a Computer Vision Model

Step 1: Prepare and Preprocess the Dataset

Before training, the dataset needs to be cleaned and preprocessed:

- **Data Augmentation** – Applying transformations (flipping, rotation, etc.) to increase dataset diversity.

- **Normalization** – Scaling pixel values (e.g., from 0-255 to 0-1) for stable training.
- **Splitting Data** – Dividing into training, validation, and test sets (e.g., 70%-20%-10%).

💡 **Example**: Normalizing images using TensorFlow/Keras:

```
from tensorflow.keras.preprocessing.image import ImageDataGenerator

train_datagen = ImageDataGenerator(rescale=1./255, validation_split=0.2)
train_generator = train_datagen.flow_from_directory("dataset/", target_size=(224, 224),
batch_size=32, class_mode="categorical", subset="training")
val_generator = train_datagen.flow_from_directory("dataset/", target_size=(224, 224),
batch_size=32, class_mode="categorical", subset="validation")
```

Step 2: Define the Model Architecture

Choosing the right neural network architecture depends on the complexity of the task:

- **Simple CNNs** – Good for basic classification tasks (e.g., MNIST, CIFAR-10).
- **Pretrained Models** (Transfer Learning) – Efficient for complex tasks (e.g., ImageNet models like ResNet, VGG).
- **Custom Deep Networks** – For highly specialized applications (e.g., medical imaging, satellite analysis).

💡 **Example**: A simple CNN in TensorFlow/Keras:

```
import tensorflow as tf
from tensorflow.keras import layers

model = tf.keras.Sequential([
    layers.Conv2D(32, (3,3), activation='relu', input_shape=(224,224,3)),
    layers.MaxPooling2D(2,2),
    layers.Conv2D(64, (3,3), activation='relu'),
    layers.MaxPooling2D(2,2),
    layers.Flatten(),
    layers.Dense(128, activation='relu'),
    layers.Dropout(0.5),
    layers.Dense(10, activation='softmax')  # 10 classes
])
```

model.compile(optimizer='adam', loss='categorical_crossentropy', metrics=['accuracy'])

Step 3: Select an Optimization Algorithm

The choice of optimizer directly affects how well the model learns.

Optimizer	Learning Rate Adaptation	Best Use Cases
SGD (Stochastic Gradient Descent)	Fixed LR, slow but stable	Small datasets
Adam (Adaptive Moment Estimation)	Adaptive LR, faster convergence	General deep learning tasks
RMSprop	Adaptive LR, prevents oscillations	Recurrent networks, time-series data
AdaGrad	Reduces LR over time	Sparse data problems

💡 Adam is the most commonly used optimizer for computer vision tasks.

Step 4: Choose a Loss Function

The loss function measures how well the model is performing.

Task	Common Loss Function
Binary Classification	Binary Cross-Entropy (`binary_crossentropy`)
Multi-Class Classification	Categorical Cross-Entropy (`categorical_crossentropy`)
Object Detection	Intersection over Union (IoU), Smooth L1 Loss
Image Segmentation	Dice Loss, Jaccard Loss

💡 **Example**: Using categorical cross-entropy loss in TensorFlow:

model.compile(optimizer='adam', loss='categorical_crossentropy', metrics=['accuracy'])

Step 5: Train the Model

Once the model is built and compiled, training begins.

Key parameters to set:

✓ **Batch Size** – Number of images processed at once (e.g., 32, 64, 128).

✓□ **Number of Epochs** – Total passes through the dataset (e.g., 10-100).
✓□ **Validation Frequency** – How often validation metrics are computed.

💡 **Example**: Training a CNN in TensorFlow:

history = model.fit(train_generator, validation_data=val_generator, epochs=10, batch_size=32)

2. Hyperparameter Tuning: Finding the Best Settings

2.1 Key Hyperparameters to Tune

✓□ **Learning Rate (LR)** – Too high = unstable training, too low = slow learning.
✓□ **Batch Size** – Larger batch sizes improve training speed but need more memory.
✓□ **Number of Layers** – More layers can improve performance but risk overfitting.
✓□ **Dropout Rate** – Prevents overfitting by randomly dropping neurons during training.

2.2 Techniques for Hyperparameter Tuning

1□ **Grid Search** – Tests all combinations of hyperparameters.

Example: Testing learning rates (0.001, 0.01, 0.1) and batch sizes (16, 32, 64).

2□ **Random Search** – Randomly selects hyperparameter values for experimentation.

Faster than Grid Search, but may not find the best combination.

3□ **Bayesian Optimization** – Uses probability to find optimal hyperparameters efficiently.

Example: Hyperopt library in Python.

4□ **Automated Hyperparameter Tuning (AutoML)** – Uses AI to optimize settings automatically.

Example: Google AutoML, Keras Tuner.

💡 **Example**: Hyperparameter tuning using Keras Tuner:

```
import keras_tuner as kt

def model_builder(hp):
    model = tf.keras.Sequential([
        layers.Conv2D(hp.Int('filters', 32, 128, step=32), (3,3), activation='relu'),
        layers.MaxPooling2D(2,2),
        layers.Flatten(),
        layers.Dense(hp.Int('units', 64, 256, step=64), activation='relu'),
        layers.Dropout(hp.Float('dropout', 0.2, 0.5, step=0.1)),
        layers.Dense(10, activation='softmax')
    ])
    model.compile(optimizer='adam', loss='categorical_crossentropy',
metrics=['accuracy'])
    return model

tuner = kt.RandomSearch(model_builder, objective='val_accuracy', max_trials=10)
tuner.search(train_generator, epochs=5, validation_data=val_generator)
```

3. Evaluating Model Performance

✓ **Training vs. Validation Accuracy** – Helps identify overfitting.

✓ **Confusion Matrix** – Evaluates classification accuracy.

✓ **Precision, Recall, F1 Score** – Measures true performance beyond accuracy.

💡 **Example**: Generating a confusion matrix using Scikit-learn:

```
from sklearn.metrics import confusion_matrix
import seaborn as sns
import matplotlib.pyplot as plt

y_pred = model.predict(X_test)
cm = confusion_matrix(y_test.argmax(axis=1), y_pred.argmax(axis=1))

sns.heatmap(cm, annot=True, fmt="d", cmap="Blues")
plt.xlabel("Predicted")
plt.ylabel("Actual")
plt.show()
```

Conclusion: Mastering Model Training & Tuning

Training and optimizing a computer vision model is a step-by-step process that requires carefully tuning of hyperparameters. By experimenting with different architectures, loss functions, and optimization strategies, you can build highly accurate models for real-world applications. 🚀

✅ **Key Takeaway**: The right combination of hyperparameters can make the difference between an average model and a state-of-the-art one! 🔥

14.4 Deploying AI Models on Cloud and Edge Devices

Building an AI model is just the first step—getting it into production is where the real impact happens. Deployment involves making the trained model accessible for real-world applications, whether on cloud platforms (AWS, Google Cloud, Azure) or edge devices (Raspberry Pi, NVIDIA Jetson, smartphones). Each deployment option has trade-offs between latency, computational power, and scalability.

In this chapter, we'll cover:

✓☐ Cloud deployment vs. edge deployment: Pros and cons
✓☐ Deploying models using cloud platforms (AWS, Google Cloud, Azure)
✓☐ Running AI models on edge devices for low-latency inference
✓☐ Optimizing AI models for deployment (compression, quantization, and acceleration)

1. Cloud vs. Edge Deployment: Choosing the Right Approach

Before deploying a model, you must decide where it will run:

Deployment Type	Pros	Cons	Best Use Cases
Cloud (AWS, GCP, Azure)	High computational power, scalable, easy to update models	Higher latency, requires internet connectivity, expensive at scale	Large-scale applications, web-based AI services, big data processing
Edge (Raspberry Pi, Jetson, Mobile, IoT)	Low latency, operates offline, real-time inference	Limited computational resources, complex optimization needed	Self-driving cars, smart cameras, IoT applications, industrial automation

💡 **Example**: Face recognition in security cameras

- **Cloud Deployment**: The camera captures images and sends them to a server for processing.
- **Edge Deployment**: The AI model runs directly on the camera for real-time recognition without the internet.

2. Deploying AI Models on the Cloud

Cloud platforms provide infrastructure to host, manage, and scale AI models via APIs or web services.

Step 1: Save and Export the Trained Model

Before deploying, save your trained model in a standard format such as TensorFlow SavedModel, ONNX, or TorchScript.

💡 **Example**: Exporting a TensorFlow model:

```
import tensorflow as tf
model.save("model_directory")  # Saves in SavedModel format
```

Step 2: Deploy Using a Cloud Service

Cloud Provider	AI Deployment Services
AWS	AWS Lambda, SageMaker, EC2, Elastic Inference
Google Cloud	Vertex AI, Cloud Run, TensorFlow Serving
Microsoft Azure	Azure ML, Cognitive Services, Azure Functions

Example: Deploying a TensorFlow model on AWS Lambda using an API Gateway

1️⃣ Upload the model to Amazon S3

2️⃣ Set up an AWS Lambda function to load and infer from the model

3️⃣ Use API Gateway to expose the AI model as a web service

4️⃣ Send inference requests via an HTTP endpoint

💡 **Example**: Running an inference request on a deployed model API:

```
import requests
```

```
url = "https://your-api-endpoint.amazonaws.com/predict"
data = {"image_url": "https://example.com/image.jpg"}
response = requests.post(url, json=data)

print(response.json())  # Output: {"prediction": "Cat"}
```

Step 3: Optimize for Scalability

- Use load balancers for handling multiple requests
- Enable auto-scaling on cloud instances
- Use serverless computing (AWS Lambda, Google Cloud Functions) for efficient resource allocation

📌 **Example**: *Netflix uses cloud-based AI for content recommendations, running AI inference across multiple data centers worldwide.

3. Deploying AI Models on Edge Devices

For real-time AI without internet dependency, models must be optimized for low-power edge devices.

Step 1: Optimize the Model for Edge Deployment

Since edge devices have limited resources, AI models must be compressed and accelerated:

✓☐ **Model Quantization** – Reduces model size and speeds up inference (e.g., converting from 32-bit to 8-bit precision).
✓☐ **Pruning** – Removes unimportant neurons and weights to shrink the model.
✓☐ **Hardware Acceleration** – Uses GPUs, TPUs, or NPUs for faster processing.

💡 **Example**: Converting a TensorFlow model to TensorFlow Lite for mobile deployment:

```
import tensorflow as tf

converter = tf.lite.TFLiteConverter.from_saved_model("model_directory")
converter.optimizations = [tf.lite.Optimize.DEFAULT]
tflite_model = converter.convert()
```

```
with open("model.tflite", "wb") as f:
    f.write(tflite_model)
```

Step 2: Run the Model on an Edge Device

🔲🔲 Raspberry Pi Deployment (OpenCV + TensorFlow Lite)

Install TensorFlow Lite and OpenCV

Load the TFLite model and run inference on a webcam

💡 **Example**: Running an image classification model on Raspberry Pi

```
import tensorflow.lite as tflite
import cv2
import numpy as np

interpreter = tflite.Interpreter(model_path="model.tflite")
interpreter.allocate_tensors()

cap = cv2.VideoCapture(0)  # Open webcam
while True:
    ret, frame = cap.read()
    input_data = np.expand_dims(cv2.resize(frame, (224, 224)), axis=0)

    interpreter.set_tensor(interpreter.get_input_details()[0]['index'], input_data)
    interpreter.invoke()

    output = interpreter.get_tensor(interpreter.get_output_details()[0]['index'])
    print("Prediction:", output.argmax())

    cv2.imshow("Live", frame)
    if cv2.waitKey(1) & 0xFF == ord('q'):
        break
cap.release()
cv2.destroyAllWindows()
```

Step 3: Deploy AI Models on Mobile (Android & iOS)

For deploying AI models on mobile, use:

📌 **TensorFlow Lite (TFLite)** – For Android/iOS inference
📌 **Core ML** – Apple's framework for running AI on iOS devices
📌 **ML Kit (Google)** – Provides ready-to-use AI models for mobile apps

💡 **Example**: Running an object detection model on Android using TensorFlow Lite

```
Interpreter tflite = new Interpreter(loadModelFile());
ByteBuffer inputBuffer = preprocessImage(bitmap);
tflite.run(inputBuffer, outputBuffer);
```

Step 4: AI Deployment on NVIDIA Jetson

For high-performance AI on edge, NVIDIA Jetson (Nano, Xavier, Orin) offers GPU acceleration for real-time tasks.

✓ **Jetson Inference SDK** – Runs AI models optimized for edge computing
✓ **DeepStream SDK** – Optimized for real-time video analytics
✓ **TensorRT** – Accelerates deep learning inference on NVIDIA GPUs

💡 **Example**: Running an object detection model on Jetson Nano

```
python3 detectnet.py --model=ssd-mobilenet.onnx --input=image.jpg
```

4. Best Practices for AI Deployment

◆ **Use model versioning** – Keep track of different versions to avoid deploying faulty models
◆ **Monitor AI performance** – Log inference times, accuracy, and potential biases in real-world data
◆ **Secure AI models** – Protect against adversarial attacks and unauthorized access
◆ **Test across devices** – Ensure compatibility on cloud and edge environments

📌 **Real-World Example**: Tesla's self-driving AI runs on edge GPUs for real-time decision-making, reducing latency while syncing with the cloud for software updates.

Conclusion: Bringing AI to Life 🚀

Whether deploying to cloud servers or edge devices, AI models must be optimized for performance, efficiency, and scalability. Cloud deployment is best for large-scale applications, while edge deployment provides real-time AI without internet dependency.

✓ **Key Takeaway**: A well-deployed AI model turns research into real-world impact! □✦

15. Ethics and Challenges in Computer Vision

As computer vision becomes more powerful, it also raises critical ethical and societal challenges. This chapter explores issues such as bias in AI models, privacy concerns, surveillance ethics, and the potential misuse of deepfake technology. You'll learn about the risks of biased datasets, the importance of fairness in AI decision-making, and strategies to build more transparent and responsible vision systems. We'll also discuss legal frameworks, data protection regulations, and AI governance to ensure ethical deployment of computer vision applications. By the end of this chapter, you'll have a well-rounded understanding of the ethical landscape and the challenges that come with teaching AI to see the world.

15.1 Bias in AI: Understanding Discrimination in Vision Models

AI-powered vision systems are increasingly used in healthcare, security, hiring, autonomous vehicles, and social media. However, these models can inherit and even amplify biases present in the data they are trained on. Bias in AI can lead to discriminatory outcomes, such as facial recognition systems failing to recognize certain ethnicities or AI-based hiring tools favoring specific demographics.

In this chapter, we'll explore:

✓☐ How bias originates in computer vision models
✓☐ Real-world examples of AI bias and their consequences
✓☐ Techniques to detect and mitigate bias in AI systems
✓☐ Ethical and legal considerations for responsible AI

1. What Causes Bias in Computer Vision?

Bias in AI vision models arises at different stages of development, from data collection to algorithm design. Some key sources include:

1.1 Bias in Training Data

AI models learn from labeled datasets, and if the dataset is skewed, the model inherits that bias.

◆ **Underrepresentation**: Some groups (e.g., darker skin tones) may have fewer samples in a dataset, leading to poor model performance for those groups.

◆ **Overrepresentation**: If a dataset has too many images of a particular group, the model might assume that group is the default.

◆ **Historical Bias**: If past decisions in the dataset were biased (e.g., biased hiring practices), the AI will reinforce those patterns.

💡 **Example**: A study found that commercial facial recognition systems were up to 34% less accurate for darker-skinned women than for lighter-skinned men.

1.2 Algorithmic Bias

Even if data is balanced, model architectures and optimization techniques can introduce bias.

✓ **Feature Selection Bias** – The algorithm may prioritize certain features over others, causing unfair predictions.

✓ **Loss Function Bias** – If a model is optimized for overall accuracy, it may ignore minority groups where performance is lower.

💡 **Example**: An AI hiring tool trained on past successful job applicants may favor male candidates if the company historically hired more men.

1.3 Bias in Annotation and Labeling

Human-labeled data can introduce subjective biases.

- **Cultural biases**: Annotators may categorize objects differently based on their cultural background.
- **Stereotyping**: Labels may reinforce societal stereotypes, e.g., associating women with caregiving roles in image datasets.

💡 **Example**: Image datasets with labels like "nurse" often depict women, while "engineer" images often depict men, reinforcing gender stereotypes.

2. Real-World Examples of AI Bias

AI bias is not just theoretical—it has real consequences.

● **Facial Recognition Failures:**

- A study by MIT found that major AI vision systems from Microsoft, IBM, and Face++ had high error rates (20–34%) for darker-skinned women, while errors were less than 1% for lighter-skinned men.
- Some facial recognition tools misidentified people of color at much higher rates, leading to wrongful arrests.

● **Racial Bias in Healthcare AI:**

- A medical AI system designed to predict who should receive extra care systematically prioritized white patients over Black patients due to biased historical data.

● **Autonomous Vehicles and Safety Risks:**

- A study showed that self-driving car AI struggled to detect pedestrians with darker skin tones, increasing accident risks.

📌 **Takeaway**: Biased AI vision systems can cause harm, reinforce discrimination, and lead to unfair outcomes.

3. How to Detect and Measure Bias in AI Models

To ensure fairness, AI vision systems must be evaluated for bias. Some key techniques include:

✓ Disaggregated Performance Analysis

- Evaluate model accuracy across different demographic groups.
- Example: Check if a face recognition AI performs equally well for all skin tones.

✓ Bias Audits and Testing

Conduct fairness audits using tools like:

- IBM AI Fairness 360
- Google's What-If Tool
- Fairlearn (Microsoft)

✓□ **Adversarial Testing**

- Use adversarial examples to see if the model fails under certain demographic conditions.
- **Example**: Check if image classification changes based on race or gender.

✓□ **Explainability and Transparency**

- Use explainable AI (XAI) to understand why the model makes specific decisions.

4. Strategies to Mitigate Bias in AI Vision Systems

Bias is a complex problem, but it can be reduced with proper strategies:

4.1 Improving Training Data

✓□ **Diversify datasets** – Include varied demographics in training images.
✓□ **Use synthetic data** – Generate balanced datasets using AI (e.g., GANs).
✓□ **Crowdsourced labeling** – Use a diverse team to label data to avoid single-group bias.

💡 **Example**: The Diverse Faces Dataset was created to improve facial recognition AI for underrepresented groups.

4.2 Algorithmic Fairness Techniques

✓□ **Reweighting methods** – Adjust the model's loss function to give equal importance to all demographic groups.
✓□ **Bias-aware training** – Use techniques like adversarial debiasing to make the model more fair.

4.3 Post-Processing Fairness Adjustments

If bias is detected after deployment, mitigation techniques include:

✓□ **Equalized odds adjustments** – Ensure equal false-positive and false-negative rates across groups.
✓□ **Threshold adjustments** – Set different decision thresholds for different populations.

💡 **Example**: In hiring AI, adjust scoring thresholds to prevent bias against women or minority groups.

4.4 Ethical AI Practices and Legal Compliance

♦ **Transparency**: Make AI models explainable and allow users to challenge AI decisions.
♦ **Regulations**: Comply with AI fairness laws, such as the EU AI Act and U.S. AI Bill of Rights.
♦ **Accountability**: Companies must take responsibility for AI biases and work to correct them.

📌 **Example**: IBM stopped selling facial recognition software due to concerns about racial bias.

5. The Future: Towards Ethical and Fair AI

♦ **Inclusive AI Development**: AI teams should be diverse to minimize unconscious bias.
♦ **Continuous Monitoring**: AI systems should be regularly tested to ensure they don't become biased over time.
♦ **User Awareness**: Users should be informed when AI is making decisions that affect them (e.g., hiring, medical diagnosis).

💡 **Key Takeaway**: Bias in AI is not just a technical issue—it is a societal challenge. Fair AI requires ethical responsibility, diverse datasets, and transparency.

Conclusion: Eliminating AI Bias for a More Just Future

AI-powered vision systems must be fair, unbiased, and ethical to avoid real-world discrimination. Bias originates from data, algorithms, and human labeling, but proactive steps like diverse datasets, fairness audits, and ethical guidelines can help mitigate the issue.

✅ Final Thought: A truly intelligent AI is one that serves everyone equally. □✨

15.2 Privacy and Surveillance Concerns in AI-powered Systems

As artificial intelligence (AI) and computer vision continue to advance, so do concerns about privacy and surveillance. AI-powered vision systems are now widely used in public spaces, workplaces, social media, law enforcement, and smart devices, often collecting vast amounts of data without user consent. While these technologies offer benefits like security, convenience, and automation, they also introduce serious ethical and legal concerns regarding personal privacy, mass surveillance, and potential misuse.

In this chapter, we will explore:

✓ How AI-powered surveillance works
✓ Privacy risks associated with facial recognition and biometric tracking
✓ The ethical debate: security vs. privacy
✓ Regulations and solutions for responsible AI surveillance

1. AI-Powered Surveillance: How Does It Work?

AI-driven surveillance systems use computer vision, deep learning, and big data to monitor people, identify behaviors, and recognize individuals. Some of the most common technologies include:

1.1 Facial Recognition Systems

◆ AI-based facial recognition maps unique facial features and compares them to large databases.
◆ Used in law enforcement, border control, retail stores, and social media for identity verification.
◆ Controversial due to misidentifications, racial biases, and lack of consent.

💡 **Example**: China has deployed nationwide facial recognition for tracking citizens, while some U.S. cities like San Francisco have banned its use in policing.

1.2 Biometric Surveillance

Biometric AI tracks unique human characteristics beyond facial recognition, including:

✓□ **Gait recognition** – Identifying individuals by the way they walk.
✓□ **Iris and retina scans** – Used in airports and secure facilities.
✓□ **Heartbeat and temperature tracking** – Can be used to monitor health remotely.

💡 **Example**: In 2020, airports started using thermal cameras with AI to detect fevers during the COVID-19 pandemic.

1.3 AI in Smart Cameras and Public Spaces

✓□ **Traffic cameras** – AI tracks license plates and vehicle movement.
✓□ **Retail AI** – Tracks customer behavior and shopping patterns.
✓□ **Public surveillance** – Cities use AI to monitor crowd density and detect suspicious activities.

💡 **Example**: London has one of the most advanced AI-powered CCTV systems, tracking millions of citizens daily.

2. Privacy Risks in AI-powered Systems

While AI surveillance can enhance security, it also raises serious privacy concerns. Some of the biggest risks include:

2.1 Mass Surveillance Without Consent

● AI-powered surveillance collects data without people's knowledge or consent.
● Governments and corporations use AI to track individuals without clear legal protections.
● Example: In some countries, citizens are monitored 24/7 through facial recognition.

💡 **Case Study**: China's Social Credit System uses AI vision to track citizens and assign social scores, impacting their ability to travel or get loans.

2.2 Data Breaches and Hacking Risks

✓□ AI-powered vision systems store large amounts of personal data, making them a target for hackers.
✓□ If breached, sensitive biometric data (like faces, fingerprints, and iris scans) can be stolen and misused.

✓☐ Unlike passwords, biometric data cannot be changed once compromised.

💡 **Example**: In 2019, a facial recognition database of over 1 million people was exposed online due to poor security.

2.3 Bias and Misidentifications in AI Vision

✗ Facial recognition AI has been found to misidentify people, especially minorities.

✗ In law enforcement, this has led to wrongful arrests and racial profiling.

💡 **Case Study**: In Detroit, an innocent Black man was arrested because an AI-powered system misidentified him as a suspect.

2.4 AI-powered Social Media Tracking

✓☐ Social media companies use AI vision systems to scan, tag, and analyze user photos automatically.

✓☐ AI can track who appears in your photos and link them to personal profiles, even without consent.

💡 **Example**: Facebook's automatic facial recognition was banned in Europe due to privacy concerns.

3. The Ethics Debate: Security vs. Privacy

The use of AI in surveillance raises a critical question: Should security come at the cost of personal privacy?

Pros (Security Benefits)	Cons (Privacy Violations)
Prevents crimes and terrorism	Enables mass surveillance
Helps find missing persons	Can be misused for oppression
Speeds up border security	Increases risk of data breaches
Enhances workplace safety	Lacks transparency and consent

💡 **Example**: In 2020, facial recognition helped catch a terrorist suspect in an airport, but the same technology was used to track protestors in political movements.

4. How Can AI Surveillance Be More Ethical?

Governments, researchers, and organizations are working on laws and solutions to ensure AI-powered surveillance respects privacy rights.

4.1 Stronger AI Regulations and Laws

✓☐ The EU's General Data Protection Regulation (GDPR) restricts AI surveillance and requires user consent.
✓☐ The U.S. AI Bill of Rights is pushing for more oversight on AI-powered surveillance.
✓☐ Some cities like San Francisco and Boston have banned facial recognition in public spaces.

💡 **Example**: The EU is considering banning real-time facial recognition in public places.

4.2 Privacy-Preserving AI Technologies

✓☐ **Differential privacy** – AI models can be trained without exposing individual identities.
✓☐ **Federated learning** – AI processes data on local devices instead of sending it to central servers.
✓☐ **Face blurring** – Surveillance AI can blur faces unless explicitly authorized.

💡 **Example**: Apple uses on-device AI for Face ID, preventing biometric data from being stored in the cloud.

4.3 Transparency and User Control

✓☐ People should have the right to opt out of AI surveillance.
✓☐ Organizations should disclose when and how AI is being used in surveillance.
✓☐ Clear laws should protect individuals from AI misuse.

💡 **Example**: Google allows users to disable AI face tracking on their Google Photos app.

5. The Future of AI Surveillance and Privacy

◆ AI-powered vision will continue to evolve, but so will privacy protection efforts.
◆ Companies and governments must balance security needs with ethical considerations.

◆ New AI advancements, like privacy-preserving deep learning, could help reduce risks.

📌 **Final Thought**: AI-powered surveillance should protect people, not violate their rights. Ethical AI development and strong privacy laws are crucial for a fair and secure future.

Conclusion: Responsible AI for a Privacy-Conscious World

AI surveillance is a double-edged sword—it can enhance security but also violate privacy. From mass surveillance and data breaches to bias and misidentifications, unchecked AI vision systems pose serious risks. However, strong regulations, ethical AI design, and privacy-focused solutions can help create a responsible balance between security and personal freedom.

✅ **Key Takeaway**: The future of AI-powered surveillance depends on how well we protect privacy while leveraging AI for security. 🚀🔒

15.3 Adversarial Attacks: Fooling AI with Small Changes

AI-powered computer vision systems are widely used in facial recognition, autonomous vehicles, medical imaging, and security. However, these models are not infallible—they can be fooled by carefully crafted inputs called adversarial attacks. Adversarial attacks involve making tiny, imperceptible changes to an image that cause AI models to misinterpret what they see—sometimes with catastrophic consequences.

For example, an adversarial attack could make a self-driving car misread a stop sign as a speed limit sign, leading to a dangerous situation. In this chapter, we will explore:

✔ What adversarial attacks are and how they work
✔ Types of adversarial attacks and real-world examples
✔ How attackers generate adversarial images
✔ Defensive techniques to protect AI models from attacks

1. What Are Adversarial Attacks?

Adversarial attacks exploit the way deep learning models process images. By applying small, carefully designed perturbations (invisible to the human eye), attackers can trick an AI model into misclassifying an object.

♦ Humans ignore these tiny changes, but deep learning models see them as significant distortions.

♦ The goal is to deceive AI models while keeping images visually unchanged.

♦ Attacks can be targeted (forcing AI to predict a specific wrong label) or non-targeted (causing any misclassification).

💡 **Example**: A research team modified an image of a panda with 0.007% noise—to humans, it still looked like a panda, but the AI classified it as a gibbon with 99% confidence.

2. Types of Adversarial Attacks

There are different ways adversarial attacks can be performed. The main types include:

2.1 Evasion Attacks (During Inference)

✓ **Goal**: Trick a trained model at inference time by modifying input images.

✓ **Example**: Changing a few pixels in a cat image so that an AI classifies it as a dog.

✓ **Used** in hacking AI-based security systems, autonomous vehicles, and medical diagnostics.

💡 **Real-world case**: Attackers placed small stickers on a stop sign, making a self-driving car misread it as a speed limit sign.

2.2 Poisoning Attacks (During Training)

✓ **Goal**: Inject malicious data into an AI model's training set so it learns incorrect patterns.

✓ **Example**: If a model is trained to recognize faces, an attacker could add biased data so the AI fails to recognize certain ethnic groups.

✓ **Used** to corrupt AI models before deployment.

💡 **Real-world case**: A study found that backdoored AI models could be made to misclassify faces only when a specific trigger pattern (like a sticker) was present.

2.3 Physical Adversarial Attacks

✓☐ **Goal**: Fool AI vision systems in the real world with physical modifications.

✓☐ **Example**: Special adversarial glasses can make facial recognition systems misidentify people.

✓☐ **Used** to bypass surveillance, fool self-driving cars, or evade biometric security.

💡 **Real-world case**: Researchers created 3D-printed eyeglasses that could trick face recognition AI into thinking a different person was wearing them.

2.4 Black-Box vs. White-Box Attacks

There are two ways attackers generate adversarial images:

◆ **White-box attacks** – The attacker knows the model's architecture and parameters.

◆ **Black-box attacks** – The attacker has no access to the model but tricks it by observing its outputs.

💡 **Example**: A hacker could repeatedly test images on Google's AI to find small changes that fool it without knowing how the model works internally.

3. How Adversarial Attacks Work

Adversarial attacks are generated using mathematical techniques that take advantage of how neural networks process data.

3.1 Fast Gradient Sign Method (FGSM)

📌 **How it works**: Adds small noise in the direction that maximizes model error.

📌 **Effect**: A slight perturbation makes the AI confidently misclassify an object.

📌 **Example**: A dog image could be slightly modified so the AI sees it as a cat.

💡 **Real-world use**: Attackers have used FGSM to fool AI malware detection systems into classifying malicious files as safe.

3.2 Projected Gradient Descent (PGD)

📌 **How it works**: Repeatedly applies small adversarial changes while ensuring the image still looks natural.

📌 **Effect**: More effective than FGSM and used to attack deep networks.

📌 **Example**: Can make medical AI misdiagnose diseases by modifying patient scans.

💡 **Real-world use**: PGD-based attacks have tricked AI-based medical imaging systems into missing tumors in CT scans.

4. Real-World Consequences of Adversarial Attacks

Adversarial attacks are not just theoretical—they have serious implications for AI safety.

4.1 Security and Facial Recognition

● Attackers can trick AI-powered surveillance to misidentify people.
● Criminals could bypass face recognition systems using adversarial tricks.

💡 **Example**: In 2020, researchers showed how carefully designed glasses could let one person bypass facial recognition as someone else.

4.2 Self-Driving Cars

● AI in autonomous vehicles relies on image recognition for road safety.
● Adversarial attacks could make a car misinterpret traffic signs, leading to accidents.

💡 **Example**: By placing black tape on a stop sign, researchers made a Tesla misread it as a speed limit sign.

4.3 Medical AI and Healthcare Risks

● Adversarial attacks can fool AI into misdiagnosing diseases, leading to life-threatening consequences.
● Hackers could alter patient scans to make it seem like a tumor is missing.

💡 **Example**: Researchers successfully used adversarial perturbations to make a medical AI misdiagnose benign cases as malignant tumors.

5. How to Defend Against Adversarial Attacks

AI researchers are actively working on ways to make models more robust against adversarial attacks. Some of the most effective defenses include:

5.1 Adversarial Training

✓ Train AI models using adversarially modified images, so they learn to recognize and ignore adversarial noise.

💡 **Example**: Google's AI team has used adversarial training to make image classifiers more resilient.

5.2 Defensive Distillation

✓ AI models are trained to ignore small changes in images, making attacks less effective.
✓ Slows down attack efficiency by reducing sensitivity to small noise.

💡 **Example**: A distillation-based defense reduced misclassification rates by 50% in adversarial attack scenarios.

5.3 Model Verification and Robust AI Architectures

✓ AI models should be tested for adversarial weaknesses before deployment.
✓ AI developers should apply certifiable defenses to prevent attacks.

💡 **Example**: Facebook AI now includes adversarial robustness checks in its deep learning systems.

6. Conclusion: The Ongoing Battle Between AI and Attackers

Adversarial attacks reveal a fundamental weakness in AI vision systems—deep learning models can be easily fooled with tiny changes. As AI becomes more embedded in security, healthcare, and autonomous systems, protecting models from attacks is critical.

♦ AI researchers must build more resilient models.
♦ Governments and industries must enforce security standards for AI-powered applications.
♦ Ethical hackers and cybersecurity experts will continue testing and defending AI systems against threats.

📌 **Final Thought**: The fight between attackers and AI defenses is ongoing—but understanding adversarial attacks is the first step toward creating safer AI. 🚀

15.4 Towards Fair and Responsible AI in Computer Vision

As artificial intelligence (AI) becomes increasingly integrated into critical applications such as facial recognition, autonomous vehicles, healthcare, and surveillance, the ethical implications of computer vision systems cannot be ignored. AI models often inherit biases from their training data, leading to unfair treatment of certain groups, security risks, and unintended societal consequences. Building fair and responsible AI in computer vision is crucial to ensuring that these technologies benefit everyone equitably and ethically.

In this chapter, we will explore:

✓☐ The ethical concerns of AI in computer vision
✓☐ How bias emerges in AI models and its real-world impact
✓☐ Steps towards building fair and transparent AI systems
✓☐ The role of regulation, explainability, and human oversight

1. The Ethical Concerns of AI in Computer Vision

Computer vision has the potential to revolutionize many industries, but without proper oversight, it can reinforce discrimination, threaten privacy, and create dangerous security risks. Some of the key ethical concerns include:

1.1 Bias in AI and Unfair Treatment

📌 Many computer vision models perform worse on certain racial, gender, or age groups due to biased training data.
📌 Inaccurate facial recognition has led to wrongful arrests, hiring discrimination, and biased policing.

💡 **Example**: A study found that AI-powered facial recognition misidentified Black and Asian individuals up to 100 times more often than white individuals.

1.2 Privacy and Surveillance Issues

✦ AI-powered mass surveillance raises serious concerns about personal privacy and human rights.

✦ Unauthorized facial recognition is used for tracking people without their consent, leading to ethical dilemmas.

💡 **Example**: Some governments use AI-powered surveillance to monitor citizens, raising concerns about human rights violations.

1.3 Deepfakes and Misinformation

✦ Generative AI tools can create highly realistic deepfake videos, spreading false information and identity fraud.

✦ Fake AI-generated images and videos are being used for political manipulation, scams, and cybercrime.

💡 **Example**: Deepfake videos of political figures have been used to spread fake news and misinformation, threatening democracy.

1.4 Security Risks in AI-Powered Systems

✦ AI models can be fooled by adversarial attacks, leading to security vulnerabilities.

✦ A self-driving car could misinterpret a stop sign due to maliciously altered input data, posing safety threats.

💡 **Example**: Researchers have demonstrated that placing small stickers on road signs can trick AI-powered self-driving cars into misreading traffic signs.

2. How Bias Emerges in AI Models

AI models do not create bias on their own—they learn bias from the data they are trained on. Bias can emerge in various ways, including:

2.1 Data Bias: Poorly Collected Training Data

✦ AI models reflect the demographics of their training data. If a dataset is skewed towards certain races, genders, or environments, the model will perform poorly on underrepresented groups.

💡 **Example**: An AI trained mostly on Western faces may fail to recognize individuals from other ethnic backgrounds.

2.2 Labeling Bias: Human Prejudice in Annotation

📌 Training data is labeled by humans, and their own biases can influence how data is categorized.
📌 If a dataset of job applications associates men with leadership roles, an AI model may favor male candidates.

💡 **Example**: AI hiring tools have been found to favor male applicants over female applicants due to historical hiring biases in tech.

2.3 Algorithmic Bias: Unequal Model Learning

📌 Some models overfit to certain demographic patterns, leading to systematic discrimination.
📌 Even if data is diverse, the way the AI processes patterns can lead to biased predictions.

💡 **Example**: AI crime prediction models have been found to disproportionately target certain racial groups due to biased training.

2.4 Deployment Bias: Mismatch Between Training and Real-World Use

📌 AI models trained in controlled environments may fail when applied in diverse, real-world conditions.
📌 AI used in hospitals, law enforcement, or hiring should be tested for fairness before deployment.

💡 **Example**: A medical AI trained on data from one country may fail when used in another region with different patient demographics.

3. Steps Towards Fair and Responsible AI in Computer Vision

To create ethical and fair AI systems, developers and organizations must take active measures to reduce bias and improve transparency.

3.1 Collecting Diverse and Representative Datasets

✓□ AI models should be trained on diverse datasets that reflect real-world populations.
✓□ Data collection should avoid underrepresentation of any group to prevent biased learning.

💡 **Example**: Researchers are working on balanced datasets that include diverse age groups, races, and backgrounds.

3.2 Bias Auditing and Fairness Testing

✓□ AI models should undergo fairness tests to check for bias before deployment.
✓□ Organizations should publish AI fairness reports to ensure transparency.

💡 **Example**: Google and IBM have developed fairness testing frameworks to evaluate AI discrimination risks.

3.3 Explainable AI (XAI): Making AI Decisions Transparent

✓□ AI decisions should be interpretable, so users understand why a model made a specific prediction.
✓□ Explainable AI (XAI) tools help detect bias and errors in model predictions.

💡 **Example**: Explainable AI methods can show which facial features an AI model uses to recognize a person, helping identify bias.

3.4 Ethical AI Governance and Regulations

✓□ Governments and AI researchers must create guidelines and laws to ensure ethical AI use.
✓□ Companies deploying AI should follow ethical AI standards to prevent misuse.

💡 **Example**: The EU AI Act is one of the first legal frameworks regulating AI fairness and transparency.

3.5 Human Oversight in AI Decision-Making

✓□ AI should assist, not replace, human decision-making in sensitive areas like healthcare, hiring, and law enforcement.

✓☐ A "human-in-the-loop" approach ensures that AI predictions are reviewed by experts.

💡 **Example**: AI-powered medical diagnosis tools should be used alongside human doctors, not replace them entirely.

4. The Future of Fair and Responsible AI

The path to ethical and fair computer vision is ongoing. AI developers, governments, and users must work together to:

✓☐ Reduce bias in AI systems by improving datasets and fairness testing.
✓☐ Ensure transparency by making AI decisions explainable and interpretable.
✓☐ Follow ethical AI regulations to prevent misuse and protect human rights.
✓☐ Encourage human oversight in AI decision-making processes.

📌 **Final Thought**: AI has the power to transform society for the better—but only if it is developed responsibly, fairly, and ethically. The future of AI depends on building systems that respect human rights, protect privacy, and create equal opportunities for all. 🚀

16. The Future of Computer Vision

Computer vision is evolving rapidly, with breakthroughs in AI pushing the boundaries of what machines can see and understand. This chapter explores emerging trends and future directions, including self-supervised learning, neuromorphic vision, edge AI, 3D vision advancements, and AI-driven creativity. You'll learn how innovations like real-time vision processing, quantum computing for AI, and human-AI collaboration are shaping the next generation of intelligent vision systems. We'll also discuss the role of AI ethics, regulation, and societal impact in guiding responsible development. By the end of this chapter, you'll have a forward-looking perspective on how computer vision will continue to transform industries and everyday life.

16.1 Emerging Trends: Self-Supervised and Few-Shot Learning

Traditional computer vision models rely heavily on large-scale labeled datasets for training, but labeling data is time-consuming, expensive, and sometimes impractical. As AI research advances, self-supervised learning (SSL) and few-shot learning (FSL) have emerged as revolutionary approaches to overcoming these limitations. These methods reduce dependence on labeled data and enable AI models to learn more efficiently—sometimes with just a few examples.

In this chapter, we will explore:

✓☐ What self-supervised learning (SSL) is and how it works
✓☐ The concept of few-shot learning (FSL) and its real-world applications
✓☐ How these approaches are transforming computer vision
✓☐ Future trends and their potential impact on AI

1. What is Self-Supervised Learning (SSL)?

1.1 The Challenge of Labeled Data in AI

Most deep learning models rely on supervised learning, where AI learns from massive datasets with labeled images. However, labeling millions of images is:

📌 **Expensive** – Requires human effort and expertise.

📌 **Time-Consuming** – Manually labeling complex datasets takes months or years.

📌 **Unscalable** – Some real-world tasks (e.g., medical imaging) lack enough labeled data.

1.2 How Self-Supervised Learning Works

Self-supervised learning (SSL) is a method where AI learns without labeled data by using patterns and structures in unlabeled images.

◆ The model generates its own supervision signal by creating pretext tasks—small challenges it must solve before learning the actual task.

◆ Instead of human-labeled datasets, SSL uses data itself as the teacher.

💡 **Example**: A model can be trained to predict missing parts of an image, which helps it understand object structures without labels.

1.3 Key Techniques in Self-Supervised Learning

📌 **Contrastive Learning** – The model learns by distinguishing similar vs. different images.

📌 **Pretext Tasks** – AI solves puzzles like predicting image rotations, missing pixels, or colorization.

📌 **Transformers for Vision (ViTs)** – Used in models like DINO and MAE for SSL-based representation learning.

💡 **Example**: SimCLR and MoCo, two popular SSL models, outperform supervised models on many computer vision tasks without labeled data.

2. What is Few-Shot Learning (FSL)?

2.1 The Need for Learning with Few Examples

Humans can recognize a new object after seeing it just once or twice—but deep learning models require thousands of labeled images. Few-shot learning (FSL) aims to bridge this gap by training AI to generalize from just a handful of examples.

2.2 How Few-Shot Learning Works

◆ Instead of learning from millions of labeled images, FSL extracts knowledge from prior experiences and applies it to new tasks.

◆ Uses meta-learning ("learning to learn"), where the model learns how to learn efficiently from small amounts of data.

💡 **Example**: A few-shot learning model trained on many types of animal species can recognize a new, unseen species with just 5-10 examples.

2.3 Types of Few-Shot Learning

✓☐ **One-Shot Learning** – Learning from just one labeled example.

✓☐ **Few-Shot Learning** – Learning from a handful of examples (5-10 images per class).

✓☐ **Zero-Shot Learning** – AI makes predictions without any labeled examples, using prior knowledge.

💡 **Example**: OpenAI's CLIP can recognize new images without being explicitly trained on them, thanks to zero-shot learning.

3. Real-World Applications of SSL and FSL in Computer Vision

◆ **Medical Imaging** – AI models trained with few labeled scans can detect diseases faster.

◆ **Autonomous Vehicles** – SSL helps self-driving cars learn road patterns without requiring manually labeled images.

◆ **Robotics** – Robots can recognize and manipulate objects with fewer training examples.

◆ **Facial Recognition** – Few-shot learning improves security systems by allowing AI to recognize new faces with limited data.

◆ **Satellite Image Analysis** – SSL helps process vast amounts of unlabeled satellite images for environmental monitoring.

4. The Future of Computer Vision with SSL and FSL

✗ **Better AI Generalization** – AI will require less labeled data and still perform well.

✗ **More Efficient Learning** – Models will learn from real-world interactions rather than static datasets.

✗ **Wider AI Accessibility** – Developing countries and smaller organizations can use AI without massive labeled datasets.

🚀 **Advancements in AI Hardware** – Edge devices will leverage self-supervised and few-shot models to run efficiently with minimal data.

📌 **Final Thought**: The shift towards self-supervised and few-shot learning is transforming how AI learns and adapts, making computer vision more efficient, scalable, and closer to human-like intelligence. 🚀

16.2 Quantum Computing and Its Potential for Vision Tasks

Quantum computing is one of the most exciting frontiers in artificial intelligence and computer vision. Unlike classical computers, which process data using binary bits (0s and 1s), quantum computers leverage qubits, allowing them to perform complex calculations at exponentially faster speeds. While quantum computing is still in its early stages, researchers are exploring its potential to revolutionize image processing, pattern recognition, and deep learning models for vision tasks.

In this chapter, we will explore:

✓☐ What quantum computing is and how it differs from classical computing
✓☐ Quantum algorithms and their potential impact on vision tasks
✓☐ Challenges and current limitations of quantum computing in AI
✓☐ Future possibilities for integrating quantum computing with computer vision

1. What is Quantum Computing?

1.1 Classical vs. Quantum Computing

Feature	Classical Computing	Quantum Computing
Processing Unit	Uses bits (0 or 1)	Uses qubits (0, 1, or both simultaneously)
Computational Speed	Solves problems sequentially	Solves problems in parallel
Scalability	Struggles with large data	Efficient in handling vast computations
Key Strength	Great for traditional tasks	Ideal for complex simulations & optimizations

💡 **Example**: A classical computer checks one password at a time, while a quantum computer tests multiple passwords simultaneously, making it exponentially faster.

1.2 How Quantum Computing Works

◆ **Superposition** – A qubit can be 0, 1, or both at the same time, allowing quantum computers to explore multiple solutions at once.

◆ **Entanglement** – Qubits can be interconnected, meaning changing one qubit instantly affects others, leading to faster computations.

◆ **Quantum Parallelism** – Quantum systems can process many possibilities in parallel, making them ideal for complex AI tasks.

💡 **Example**: A quantum-enhanced AI model can analyze thousands of medical images at once, improving disease detection efficiency.

2. Quantum Algorithms for Computer Vision

Quantum computing could significantly improve image processing, feature extraction, and deep learning. Here are some promising quantum algorithms:

2.1 Quantum Fourier Transform (QFT) for Image Processing

📌 The Fourier Transform is widely used in vision tasks like image filtering, compression, and edge detection.

📌 Quantum Fourier Transform (QFT) performs these operations exponentially faster than classical methods.

💡 **Example**: QFT can enhance MRI images for faster and more accurate medical diagnosis.

2.2 Quantum Machine Learning for Image Recognition

📌 Quantum computers can speed up training deep learning models, reducing computation time from weeks to hours.

📌 Quantum Neural Networks (QNNs) aim to outperform classical CNNs in tasks like image classification and object detection.

💡 **Example**: Quantum-enhanced AI could help autonomous vehicles recognize objects faster and more accurately, improving safety.

2.3 Quantum Edge Detection and Pattern Recognition

📌 Edge detection is a key step in vision tasks, such as detecting objects, medical imaging, and autonomous navigation.

📌 Quantum computing can perform matrix operations efficiently, making edge detection faster and more precise.

💡 **Example**: Quantum-based edge detection could be used in satellite imagery to track climate change patterns with higher accuracy.

2.4 Quantum Optimization for Deep Learning Models

📌 Training AI models requires optimizing millions of parameters, which is computationally expensive.

📌 Quantum algorithms like Quantum Approximate Optimization Algorithm (QAOA) can speed up deep learning training.

💡 **Example**: AI models for facial recognition could be trained in minutes instead of weeks, making security systems more efficient.

3. Challenges and Limitations of Quantum Computing in Vision Tasks

3.1 Hardware Limitations

📌 Quantum computers require extremely low temperatures (-273°C) to function, making them costly and difficult to maintain.

📌 Current quantum processors lack enough stable qubits to handle large-scale vision tasks.

💡 **Current Status**: Companies like IBM, Google, and D-Wave are working on improving quantum processors, but practical applications are still years away.

3.2 Quantum Noise and Stability Issues

📌 Qubits are highly sensitive to their environment, leading to errors in calculations.

📌 Quantum error correction techniques are needed to improve reliability.

💡 **Potential Solution**: Researchers are exploring fault-tolerant quantum computing to overcome these errors.

3.3 Integration with Classical AI Systems

📌 Current AI models are built for classical hardware, meaning quantum AI must be integrated with existing frameworks.

📌 Quantum AI frameworks like Pennylane and TensorFlow Quantum are being developed for this purpose.

💡 **Example**: Hybrid AI models combining classical CNNs and Quantum Neural Networks (QNNs) could lead to breakthroughs in vision tasks.

4. The Future of Quantum Computing in Computer Vision

🚀 **Faster AI Model Training** – Deep learning models could be trained 100x faster with quantum computing.

🚀 **Revolutionizing Image Processing** – Quantum techniques could enable real-time high-resolution image enhancements.

🚀 **Advancements in Medical Imaging** – Quantum AI could analyze complex medical images more accurately, improving early disease detection.

🚀 **More Efficient AI for Autonomous Systems** – Quantum-powered AI could enhance vision-based decision-making in self-driving cars and drones.

📌 **Final Thought**: While quantum computing is still in its early stages, it has the potential to revolutionize computer vision, unlocking faster, more efficient AI models that were previously impossible. The future of AI will likely be a hybrid of classical and quantum computing, leading to breakthroughs in machine perception, medical imaging, security, and beyond. 🚀

16.3 The Role of AI Vision in Future Smart Cities

As cities continue to grow and evolve, artificial intelligence (AI) and computer vision are becoming essential in building smarter, safer, and more efficient urban environments. AI-powered vision systems can analyze real-time data from surveillance cameras, traffic sensors, drones, and IoT devices to optimize urban planning, improve security, and enhance daily life for citizens. From intelligent traffic management to AI-driven waste disposal, computer vision is revolutionizing how cities function.

In this chapter, we will explore:

✓☐ How AI vision is transforming smart cities

✓☐ Applications in traffic management, security, waste management, and energy efficiency

✓☐ Challenges in implementation, including privacy concerns

✓☐ Future trends in AI-driven urban development

1. AI Vision for Smart Traffic and Transportation

1.1 Intelligent Traffic Management Systems

📌 AI-powered cameras analyze real-time traffic flow, adjusting traffic signals dynamically to reduce congestion.

📌 Computer vision detects accidents and roadblocks, alerting authorities in real-time.

📌 AI can predict peak traffic hours and recommend alternative routes for drivers.

💡 **Example**: Cities like Singapore and Barcelona use AI traffic control systems that reduce congestion by up to 25%.

1.2 AI-Powered Public Transport Optimization

📌 AI vision monitors buses, trains, and subways, ensuring efficient scheduling and preventing overcrowding.

📌 Smart cameras detect maintenance issues in vehicles before they cause breakdowns.

📌 AI-powered pedestrian detection enhances safety at crosswalks and bus stops.

💡 **Example**: London's Transport for London (TfL) uses AI vision to analyze passenger density and improve train schedules.

1.3 AI in Autonomous Vehicles and Smart Parking

📌 Self-driving cars rely on computer vision for object detection, lane tracking, and pedestrian safety.

📌 Smart parking systems use AI to detect empty spots, reducing time spent searching for parking.

📌 AI-driven toll booths and automated license plate recognition reduce congestion at highways.

Example: San Francisco's AI-based parking system reduces traffic congestion by 30% by guiding drivers to available spots.

2. AI Vision for Urban Security and Surveillance

2.1 AI-Powered Surveillance Cameras

✦ AI vision detects suspicious activities, abandoned objects, and unauthorized intrusions in public areas.
✦ Smart cameras use facial recognition to identify missing persons or criminals.
✦ AI enhances crowd monitoring, improving safety at large events.

Example: Dubai's AI surveillance system has reduced crime rates by 35% in monitored areas.

2.2 AI for Emergency Response

✦ AI can detect fires, floods, or natural disasters through vision-based sensors.
✦ AI-powered drones provide real-time aerial surveillance during emergencies.
✦ Smart cities use AI to prioritize emergency services, sending help where it's needed most.

Example: AI-driven disaster response systems in Japan use real-time video analysis to guide earthquake and tsunami evacuations.

2.3 Facial Recognition and Privacy Concerns

✦ AI vision enables automated identification for law enforcement, but raises ethical concerns.
✦ Many countries are debating regulations on facial recognition to prevent misuse.
✦ Future systems may integrate privacy-focused AI, which ensures security without storing personal data.

Example: The European Union's AI Act restricts real-time facial recognition in public spaces for privacy protection.

3. AI Vision in Waste Management and Environmental Monitoring

3.1 Smart Waste Management with AI

📌 AI cameras monitor trash levels in public bins, optimizing garbage collection schedules.

📌 AI vision in waste sorting facilities improves recycling efficiency by recognizing materials.

📌 Drones and satellites track illegal dumping in cities and rural areas.

💡 **Example**: Seoul's AI waste management system reduced collection costs by 20% by using real-time monitoring.

3.2 AI for Air and Water Quality Monitoring

📌 AI vision systems analyze satellite images to detect pollution sources.

📌 Smart cameras monitor factory emissions, ensuring compliance with environmental laws.

📌 AI-powered river and ocean monitoring detects plastic waste and oil spills.

💡 **Example**: China uses AI-powered drones to track air pollution levels in major cities and enforce clean air regulations.

4. AI Vision for Smart Energy and Infrastructure

4.1 AI in Energy Efficiency and Smart Grids

📌 AI vision optimizes street lighting, adjusting brightness based on pedestrian and vehicle activity.

📌 AI-driven solar panel monitoring ensures maximum efficiency in renewable energy systems.

📌 Smart grids use AI to predict power demand, preventing energy shortages.

💡 **Example**: Amsterdam's smart grid system has improved energy efficiency by 40%, reducing carbon emissions.

4.2 AI for Building Maintenance and Infrastructure Monitoring

📌 AI-powered drones inspect bridges, roads, and buildings for cracks and structural damage.

📌 AI cameras analyze traffic patterns to detect roads needing repairs.

📌 AI detects gas leaks, water pipe leaks, and electrical failures, improving city maintenance.

💡 **Example**: New York City's AI-based infrastructure monitoring has prevented major pipeline failures, saving millions in repair costs.

5. Challenges and Future of AI Vision in Smart Cities

5.1 Key Challenges

✖ **Privacy Concerns** – AI-driven surveillance raises ethical issues about mass data collection.

✖ **High Implementation Costs** – Building AI-powered infrastructure requires significant investment.

✖ **Cybersecurity Risks** – AI systems must be protected against hacking and data breaches.

✖ **Bias in AI Models** – Computer vision models need to be fair and unbiased to avoid discrimination.

💡 **Possible Solutions:**

✓ Implementing privacy-focused AI (e.g., encryption and anonymization).

✓ Developing affordable AI solutions for developing countries.

✓ Strengthening AI ethics regulations for fair and responsible use.

6. The Future of AI Vision in Smart Cities

🔋 **AI-Powered Smart Homes** – AI vision will enable fully automated homes that adjust lighting, temperature, and security.

🔋 **Self-Healing Infrastructure** – AI will detect and repair infrastructure issues before they become serious problems.

🔋 **AI in Disaster Prevention** – AI vision will predict earthquakes, floods, and wildfires, improving disaster preparedness.

🔋 **5G & AI Integration** – Faster data transfer will make AI vision systems more responsive and real-time.

🔋 **AI-Driven Citizen Engagement** – Smart cities will use AI to improve public services based on real-time citizen feedback.

📌 **Final Thought**: AI vision is reshaping the future of urban life, making cities safer, greener, and more efficient. While challenges remain, responsible AI deployment will unlock a new era of intelligent urban living, where technology enhances both security and sustainability. 🚀

16.4 Next-Generation Applications: Holograms, Robotics, and Beyond

The future of computer vision is rapidly evolving beyond traditional applications, pushing into next-generation technologies such as holography, robotics, and immersive AI-driven experiences. These advancements will redefine human-machine interaction, enabling real-time holographic communication, AI-powered robotic assistants, and ultra-intelligent vision systems capable of understanding the world with near-human perception.

This chapter explores the cutting-edge innovations shaping the next decade, including:

✓☐ Holographic displays and augmented reality (AR) advancements
✓☐ AI-powered robots and their role in daily life and industries
✓☐ Computer vision in brain-computer interfaces (BCIs) and human augmentation
✓☐ The convergence of AI vision with quantum computing and bio-inspired technologies

1. Holographic Displays and Immersive AI

1.1 AI-Driven Holograms: The Future of Communication

📌 AI vision is enabling real-time 3D holographic projections, making video calls and virtual meetings more immersive.
📌 Holograms can replicate human gestures and expressions, creating lifelike virtual assistants.
📌 AI-enhanced medical holography allows doctors to visualize organs in 3D for surgery planning.

💡 **Example**: Microsoft's HoloLens 2 is already being used for remote collaboration and surgery visualization.

1.2 Holography in Retail and Marketing

✦ AI-powered holographic displays allow customers to try on clothes virtually or interact with digital products.

✦ Brands are using AI-driven holograms for interactive advertising, enhancing consumer engagement.

✦ AI holograms can translate languages in real-time, enabling seamless global communication.

💡 **Example**: AI-powered holographic fashion shows allow designers to showcase digital models wearing virtual clothing.

1.3 AI in Augmented and Mixed Reality (AR/MR)

✦ AI-enhanced AR glasses provide real-time object recognition for navigation and accessibility.

✦ Mixed reality (MR) blends holograms with real-world environments, revolutionizing gaming, education, and training.

✦ AI-powered AR assistants can guide technicians in complex repairs by overlaying instructions onto real objects.

💡 **Example**: Apple's Vision Pro uses AI vision to create a fully immersive computing environment.

2. AI-Powered Robotics: The Next Leap

2.1 Humanoid Robots with AI Vision

✦ AI-powered robots can now understand and interpret human emotions, making interactions more natural.

✦ Advanced vision systems enable robots to perform delicate tasks, such as surgery or elderly care.

✦ AI-driven robots are being used in warehouses, restaurants, and customer service for automation.

💡 **Example**: Tesla's Optimus robot is designed to perform human-like tasks using AI vision and robotics.

2.2 AI Vision in Autonomous Robots for Industry

📌 AI-powered robotic arms in factories use computer vision for quality control and assembly line tasks.

📌 AI drones with real-time vision are being deployed for disaster response, agriculture, and security.

📌 AI robots are assisting in nuclear plants, deep-sea exploration, and space missions.

💡 **Example**: Boston Dynamics' robotic dogs use AI vision for rescue missions and hazardous environment monitoring.

2.3 AI and Robotics in Healthcare

📌 AI-powered robotic surgeons can perform precision surgeries with extreme accuracy.

📌 AI-driven prosthetics and exoskeletons provide mobility to disabled individuals.

📌 AI-powered robotic nurses assist in hospitals by delivering medications and monitoring patients.

💡 **Example**: The Da Vinci Surgical Robot uses AI vision to assist doctors in minimally invasive surgeries.

3. AI Vision in Brain-Computer Interfaces (BCIs) and Human Augmentation

3.1 AI Vision for Brain-Machine Interaction

📌 AI vision is helping develop brain-computer interfaces (BCIs), allowing paralyzed individuals to control devices with their thoughts.

📌 AI-enhanced neural implants can help restore vision to the blind by translating images into neural signals.

📌 Future AI-BCI systems could allow direct brain-to-brain communication, transforming human interaction.

💡 **Example**: Neuralink is developing AI-powered BCIs that could enable thought-controlled computing.

3.2 AI-Powered Superhuman Vision

📌 AI-assisted bionic eyes can restore vision for the blind, detecting objects in real time.

📌 AI-driven contact lenses with built-in AR displays may replace smartphones in the future.

📌 AI-enhanced vision implants could give night vision or zoom capabilities to humans.

💡 **Example**: Mojo Vision's AI-powered smart contact lenses provide real-time augmented information directly in a user's vision.

4. The Convergence of AI Vision with Quantum Computing

4.1 How Quantum Computing Enhances AI Vision

📌 Quantum computing can process image data exponentially faster than classical computers.
📌 AI models for image recognition and medical imaging will become more precise and efficient.
📌 Quantum AI vision could enable real-time AI-assisted decision-making at an unprecedented scale.

💡 **Example**: Google's Quantum AI Lab is exploring how quantum computing can improve image processing.

4.2 AI Vision in Space Exploration and Extraterrestrial Discovery

📌 AI-powered vision systems help analyze images from Mars rovers and space telescopes.
📌 AI in astronomy is being used to detect exoplanets and classify galaxies from telescope data.
📌 AI vision will enable future robots to navigate alien planets autonomously.

💡 **Example**: NASA's Perseverance Rover uses AI vision to identify rocks, soil, and potential signs of life on Mars.

5. The Ethical and Societal Implications of Next-Gen AI Vision

5.1 Ethical Considerations in AI Vision and Robotics

✖ AI-powered deepfake holograms could be misused for fraud and misinformation.

✖ AI-powered humanoid robots may lead to job displacement in various industries.

✖ AI vision in surveillance drones could raise concerns over privacy and human rights.

💡 **Solution**: Developing ethical AI policies and transparent governance for next-gen AI vision applications.

6. Future Predictions: The Next 20 Years of AI Vision

🚀 Holographic AI assistants will become a normal part of daily life, replacing screens and touch interfaces.

🚀 AI-powered humanoid robots will work alongside humans in homes, offices, and public spaces.

🚀 AI-driven superhuman vision implants will enhance human capabilities beyond natural biology.

🚀 Quantum-powered AI vision systems will unlock new frontiers in medicine, space exploration, and climate science.

🚀 Brain-computer interfaces with AI vision will allow direct thought-to-image communication, revolutionizing human creativity.

📌 **Final Thought**: AI vision is not just about recognizing images—it is shaping a new era of human experience, where digital and physical realities merge seamlessly. From holograms to humanoid robots, the future of computer vision will be defined by limitless possibilities. 🚀

Computer vision is at the heart of the AI revolution, enabling machines to interpret and understand the world through images and videos. From self-driving cars and medical imaging to facial recognition and augmented reality, the power of AI-driven vision systems is shaping the future. But how do these systems work? How can you build one from scratch?

In **Computer Vision: Teaching AI to See the World**, the ninth book in the *AI from Scratch series*, you'll embark on a step-by-step journey to mastering computer vision. This book bridges the gap between fundamental theory and hands-on practice, equipping you with the skills to develop cutting-edge vision applications using Python, OpenCV, TensorFlow, and PyTorch.

Inside, you'll explore:

✅ **The Foundations of Computer Vision** – Learn about image processing, edge detection, and feature extraction.

✅ **Classical Techniques** – Master traditional object detection and recognition methods like HOG, SIFT, and Viola-Jones.

✅ **Deep Learning for Vision** – Build powerful models with Convolutional Neural Networks (CNNs), YOLO, and U-Net.

✅ **Generative AI & Vision Transformers** – Discover GANs for image synthesis and ViTs for state-of-the-art AI vision.

✅ **Real-World Applications** – Implement vision-based security, healthcare, and autonomous systems.

✅ **Future Trends & Ethical AI** – Understand AI bias, privacy concerns, and the next breakthroughs in computer vision.

Whether you're an AI enthusiast, developer, researcher, or student, this book provides an accessible yet comprehensive guide to mastering computer vision. Packed with real-world projects, coding exercises, and expert insights, it will empower you to build intelligent vision systems from scratch.

🔍 *Ready to teach AI how to see? Take the first step into the world of computer vision today!* 🚀

Dear Reader,

Thank you for embarking on this journey into the fascinating world of computer vision with me. Writing Computer Vision: Teaching AI to See the World has been an incredible experience, and knowing that you've chosen this book as part of your learning path means the world to me.

Artificial intelligence and computer vision are transforming the way we interact with technology, and I hope this book has provided you with the knowledge, confidence, and inspiration to create something truly impactful. Whether you're just beginning or are already deep into AI development, your curiosity and dedication to learning are what drive innovation in this field.

I am deeply grateful for your time, effort, and trust in this book. If even a small part of what you've learned here helps you build something meaningful, solve a real-world problem, or spark a new idea, then this book has fulfilled its purpose.

A special thank you to my readers who have followed the *AI from Scratch series*—I appreciate your continued support and passion for mastering artificial intelligence. Your feedback, questions, and insights inspire me to keep writing and sharing knowledge.

If you found this book helpful, I'd love to hear your thoughts. Your reviews, discussions, and shared experiences help make this community stronger and guide future learners along their own AI journey.

Once again, thank you. Keep learning, keep building, and never stop exploring the endless possibilities of AI.

With gratitude,

Gilbert Gutiérrez